Louis McRed

Thrown Among Strangers

John Henry Newman in Ireland

'No one knows but myself the desolateness in leaving Birmingham, and being thrown among strangers — I trust it will be taken as my penance, and be of eternal good to me.'

— J. H. Newman to Edward Caswall,
Limerick, 25 February 1854

VERITAS

First published 1990 by
Veritas Publications
7-8 Lower Abbey Street
Dublin 1

ISBN 1 85390 180 6

The author and publishers are very grateful to the Oratory, Birmingham, for their kind permission to reproduce extracts from the letters and diaries of John Henry Newman.

The cover illustration is a detail of a bird's-eye view of the city of Dublin, first published by the *Illustrated London News* in 1846.

Cover design by Philip Melly
Typesetting by Printset & Design Ltd, Dublin
Printed in the Republic of Ireland by Mount Salus Press Ltd

For Maeve

Contents

Foreword

The life of John Henry Newman, as Anthony Cockshut has written in *Truth to Life* (1974), was one 'which combined in an extraordinary degree the passionate and the uneventful'. For his own person Newman was a man in whom intense shyness was combined with great personal charm, and a vivid memory with 'the sense of a bond, physical almost in its intensity, with any place in which significant experience had come to him'. Ireland indeed brought him significant experience, though not always in the way he had hoped or imagined when first called upon to undertake the work of founding and developing a Catholic University, which for him, if not for his Irish partners, was envisaged as being the intellectual home of English-speaking Catholics. Here in Ireland he encountered men of passion in the highest ranks of the Irish Church and experienced agonies of frustration at the obstacles and delays placed in his path, often expressed in the form of gross discourtesy so alien to his nature and understanding. Yet a bond was formed from the beginning between himself and the Irish people, with the land which he so poignantly described as a country in which an English Catholic 'is in the midst of those who will not despise him for his faith's sake'.

Newman in Ireland and Newman's Ireland is powerfully conveyed to the reader by Louis McRedmond's own acute sense of place. His historical imagination appears schooled and shaped by the maxim of the great scholar of Victorian Britain, G.M. Young: Read until you can hear them talk. His account catches his subject's exquisite self-deprecation and -irony. It is fluent, clear and critical in its insights into the minds and motives of the protagonists, especially those at whose hands Newman suffered—and to the way in which the thinking of these men was historically conditioned. The author engages his reader from the outset in a dialogue and sustains the relationship to the end. The reader closes the book with a sense of familiarity with complex issues and complex personalities, but also with the generality of Irish society of the day—from archbishops to Dublin charladies, from the mixed audiences of the Dublin Discourses to the parish priests of rural Ireland, plying him in their hospitable way with the underdone mutton so inappropriate to his delicate digestion.

The 'Irish episode' in Newman's career has always been recognised for its intrinsic importance by Newman scholars, as has the early history of the Catholic University for the development of education in our own country. But rarely have both been made so accessible, their interaction been treated with such critical yet intuitive understanding as in Thrown Among Strangers.

Eda Sagarra
3 April 1990

Preface

The facts set down in this book have been culled from original sources by other hands than mine. I gave myself the easier task of sifting through printed works of genuine scholarship to isolate those elements of national, foreign, social and ecclesiastical information which together explain why Newman's 'campaign in Ireland' took the course it did. The synthesis, if not its components, may in some degree be new and thought-provoking. Such is my hope and my main justification for writing.

If I might risk a generalisation, most lives of Newman leave the impression that his involvement with the Catholic University was an aberration, an unhappy interlude and time which could have been better spent. Newman's own fragments of reminiscence suggest that he felt this himself. It therefore remains a credible judgement, but it has had the unfortunate consequence of causing biographers to skip lightly over the Irish experiment so that a very considerable achievement tends to be written off as failure. It can readily be forgotten that University College, Dublin, the largest university institution on the island today, stands in lineal succession to Newman's foundation and perhaps closely represents what the Catholic University would have become through the logic of circumstances even if its beginnings had been more auspicious and successful: by which I mean to say that neither the model of Louvain nor the concept of an international university drawing its student body from the English-speaking countries of the world had much hope of taking root in nineteenth-century Ireland with its radically different and desperate needs.

If some writers — mainly English — have thus been inclined to play down what Newman accomplished in Dublin as a noteworthy episode in his long life, many others — mainly Irish — have relegated it to the background of more dramatic and seemingly more momentous happenings. Newman's University scarcely looms at all in the Irish political history of the period. It rates little notice by comparison with the event which was its *fons et origo*, the repudiation of the Queen's Colleges by the Catholic bishops and, at the instigation of some among the bishops, by the Pope. Even in church history it takes a lowly second place to the Romanisation of Irish Catholicism through the single-minded determination of Archbishop Cullen and the spectacular growth in the power of the Catholic Church as a quasi-political social institution.

Finally, with one or two notable exceptions those who have chosen to analyse Newman's work in Ireland have been more concerned with the relationship between his ideas and the evolution of Irish education than with the burdensome pressures under which he had to struggle in order to make any progress of measurable significance. Accordingly, they have paid little attention to what was taking place during those years in Birmingham and Rome, in Tuam and in the London Oratory: matters which in themselves were often unconnected with the University project but which undoubtedly impeded it or influenced its course. The same might be said in a broader sense of those who have analysed the theories of education found in the discourses and lectures from which Newman fashioned *The Idea of a University*.

I merely record these various approaches. All are valid, given the objectives of the individual authors. I presume to add my contribution with its own objective, namely to show Newman in the context of people, places and developments which bore upon his Irish enterprise. We know more today than ever before under each of these headings, thanks to the ongoing archival researches of a score of distinguished historians. We can therefore see more clearly the combination of factors producing the successive turns in the story. That story, in short, is ripe for updating.

I offer no overall conclusions, preferring that the reader should form an independent judgment from the evidence. At the same time, I make no effort to conceal my assessment of persons, their behaviour and the goals they set themselves. A judicious impartiality may be preferable in an author. I cannot say. But it would unquestionably be artificial. An author enters into his story and would be less than human if he did not respond to the lively, opinionated, determined characters whom he encounters on the way — and there can be few stories in which the characters display as much self-assurance and determination as those who people the story of Newman in Ireland. Rightly or wrongly, I have responded by commenting on them as they reveal their nature by word or action.

From these comments some of my own attitudes will become clear. It will be evident, for example, that I feel little rapport with the bullying tactics of Archbishop MacHale but think the principles which he propounded were worthy of a respect that cannot be granted to the views and machinations of Archbishop Cullen. The problems caused by the mutual antipathy of these Irish prelates makes it impossible to withhold sympathy from the very English Newman, caught between them through no fault of his own but ever courteous to the agents of his frustration. His immense intellectual capacity, his prophetic insight and his exquisitely crafted writing style can, of course, only be admired with awe. None the less, I cannot avoid the impression that his genius flourished in spite of, rather than because of, the knowledge which he brought to the task in hand.

It can indeed be staggering to discover how much Newman did *not* know within the fields of his closest concern: he was thoroughly at home with the Church of the Fathers but had a surprisingly limited acquaintance with the Reformation; he could not read German, which isolated him from much that was going on in philosophy and theology; the medieval concept of the university and its curious survival in the dessicated Oxbridge of his prime provided the basis on which he constructed his Irish experiment — devising improvements and adapting to local conditions, certainly, but drawing no lessons from contemporary Germany, France (particularly interesting just then) or the burgeoning foundations in America. The narrow ground on which he took his stand prevented him even from perceiving the extent of his own influence. At the very time when he thought that nobody but Catholics were interested in his thoughts on university education, the Baptist president of the newly-established University of Rochester in upstate New York was quoting at length, in public and with approval from the Dublin Discourses.

Because of these deficiencies we do not have to fall in unquestioningly behind his theorising, however brilliant, as some of his hagiographers would have us do. Perhaps presumptuously, but in the hope of stimulating objective reflection, I have indicated at various points where I feel his reasoning begs more questions than it solves: I stress, for example, the difficulty of reconciling the Dublin Discourses with his view in later years on the propriety of Catholics studying at Oxford. It seems relevant also to note that universities quite simply did not develop anywhere since his time in the way he thought they could and should. Most of them have become inter-denominational or non-denominational, and few voices are raised in objection to that. Specifically Catholic universities nearly all function under clerical control, which Newman dreaded. Any who challenge this must explain how it was possible for so many theologians to be removed from academic office in recent years when their theologising offended Church officialdom.

Broadly speaking, then, Newman's *Idea* has attracted no comprehensive endorsement. It may surely then be wondered whether he started off from indisputably correct assumptions. I refer to his ready concurrence in the proposition that the Queen's Colleges were unacceptable and that a Catholic university could alone meet the needs of Irish Catholics ... and Catholics of any nationality. If this book has a hero, it is neither Newman nor any of those with whom he had to deal but Daniel Murray, the wise and percipient predecessor of Cullen as Archbishop of Dublin. Murray had to suffer the taunts of men who dubbed him Gallican for no better reason than that he presumed to know Ireland more intimately than Italian or Italianate ecclesiastics. He was accused of being a lackey of the British administration for no better reason than that he preferred to take a measure of relief for his underprivileged people from the source which could deliver it than to postpone every advance until he was given all that he sought.

In this spirit, he favoured acceptance of the Queen's Colleges, and who is to say that in time these institutions would not have become as fully reconcilable with Catholic principle as the national schools? Let me hasten to record that I do not offer the national schools as a desirable model, but only as proof that a British concession could be built upon to the advantage of those who would ideally have liked to be given more. Cullen's intransigence left two generations of Irish Catholics without access to the full university facilities that Murray's adaptability would have obtained for them. And in this conflict of attitudes, Newman provided intellectual backing of the highest order for the less worthy and less worthwhile option.

None of this is to dispute the greater part of Newman's brilliant analysis of higher education and its function in society. Neither is it to devalue what he managed to set in motion despite so many obstacles nor the commitment which he brought to a project designed in the first place — whatever its ultimate purpose — to lift Irish Catholicism out of its provincial and subordinate status on to an upland where it could be a light to the world. To treat

Newman in an adult manner by seeing his fallibility as well as his greatness of heart, his breadth of vision and his sanctity is surely to bring him into the realm of rational discussion which he would be the first to consider appropriate.

In compiling the story I have drawn on many printed sources, to all the authors of which I am indebted. Some, however, must be specially mentioned. *Newman's University: Idea and Reality* by the late Father Fergal McGrath, SJ, retains undiminished its authority as the definitive account of the travail through which the University was established, its fortunes during Newman's Rectorship and the educational values which he aspired to inculcate. Incredibly, after forty years and the appearance of numerous other studies of Newman under every conceivable aspect, the only error detectable in Father McGrath's book is — typically — one rooted in charity: he could not believe that Cullen would have obstructed Newman's appointment as a bishop in 1854. Sadly, it has since been made clear beyond doubt that this is precisely what happened.

Professor Emmet Larkin's richly documented narrative, *The Making of the Roman Catholic Church in Ireland, 1850-1860*, describes in graphic detail the struggle for domination between Cullen and MacHale in Ireland and in Rome, together with an analysis of secular politics as these affected the attitudes of churchmen. Without the assistance of this superb work of archival research my story would be left with many gaps. A valuable source of supplementary documentation has been the relevant volumes of Father Peadar Mac Suibhne's *Paul Cullen and his Contemporaries*, while on Newman's personal life, and in particular his relationship with the members of the Birmingham and London Oratories, I have been entirely happy to be guided by Miss Meriol Trevor's two volumes of biography, *The Pillar of the Cloud* and *Light in Winter*, undeterred by the pedants who criticise Miss Trevor for daring to make profundity readable. I much regret that Father Ian Ker's new biography of Newman, which has been so well received, appeared too late for me to take it into account. Finally, it goes without saying, or rather it *must* be said, that everybody working in Newman studies today and for the future can only be immensely grateful to the late Father Charles Stephen Dessain of the Birmingham Oratory and his collaborators for their prodigious and many-volumed compilation of *The Letters and Diaries of John Henry Newman*, in which we meet the man and his mind with more immediacy than anywhere else.

The staffs of the Central Catholic Library and the Dublin Public Libraries in Dundrum, Rathmines and Ballyroan were unfailingly helpful in meeting the demands I made of them. My son David and his wife Penny presented me with the first (1852/53) edition of the *Dublin Discourses* which I used throughout in preference to the amended version incorporated in the *Idea*. Denton Print of Dundrum cheerfully and efficiently met my repeated requests, always at short notice, for photocopies and Fiona Biggs supervised the whole project for Veritas with impressive competence.

Prologue

They said it was the worst winter in forty years. Snow and a hard frost marked the first days of 1854 and strong winds kept blowing even when the weather improved for a week towards the end of January. John Henry Newman, Doctor of Divinity by courtesy of Pope Pius IX and Superior of the Oratorian Fathers in Birmingham, always found such conditions trying for he was prone to head-colds and had a horror of damp and draughts. It made matters no better that the Oratory was short of money or that the Oratorians were going through a crisis of uncertainty over their calling.

The Oratory of Saint Philip Neri was an unusual religious congregation. Its members were (as they still are) secular priests who took no vows of poverty or obedience and retained their own property, but who lived together in community with the purpose, in particular, of providing a service to the people of large cities. Each house, or Oratory, of the congregation was autonomous and the common Rule could be adapted to local circumstances with the approval of the Holy See. This structure seemed especially suited to the young Anglican clergymen who looked on Newman as their mentor and followed him into the Roman Catholic Church. A number of them had already been living with him in community at Littlemore and membership of the Oratory merely ordered more precisely, within their new allegiance, the life of prayer and ministry to which they were accustomed. Once established in Birmingham, the Oratory attracted further converts.

A problem arose, however, regarding the work to be undertaken by the Oratory. Some Oratorians found their fulfilment, with Newman's approval, in meeting the pastoral needs of the thousands of destitute families, many of them Irish, who were crowding into the soulless back-to-back streets and new slums beneath the smokestacks and factory walls of Victorian Birmingham. Others believed an ascetic, almost monastic, spirituality would be closer to their vocation: it should, they felt, manifest itself in lofty preaching, attract thoughtful Protestants and produce an endless stream of conversions to Catholicism — an approach exemplified in Frederick Wilfrid Faber, Superior of the London Oratory which had been founded from Birmingham. Faber had been a devotee of the elderly Wordsworth, was himself among the last of the Lake District poets and, from being a fawned-upon vicar, eventually became a fawned-upon Catholic preacher. His syrupy hymns and gaudy Italian devotions may, like his earlier sentimental poetry, be little to the modern taste but they had their own appeal for more than one of the High Anglican, High Tory, idealistic young men who came over to Rome through the Oxford Movement. That worried Newman, who consistently rated the intellect above the emotions and detected theological deviation in the more-Roman-than-the-Romans fervour of the converts in Faber's circle of influence.

The well-being of the Birmingham community dominated Newman's many concerns. When, as now happened, the Oratorians were troubled in themselves, he became anxious for them and impatient of demands on his time or his less than robust health by persons who failed to appreciate the pressures under which he lived. Before Christmas he had complained to a friend: '... they say "Oh, Dr Newman writes so easily, it gives him no trouble ... he can sit up and write a sermon for next morning" ... I am tried day and night by earnest requests, that I should come only here or only there; and though I do refuse, yet people think me ungracious and unaccommodating ... I cannot bear this gadding to and fro. It is against the habit of my life, and against our Rule.'[1] Perhaps it was the weather, perhaps the discomfort of a stuffed nose and sore throat, but most likely it was the tension in the Oratory which determined him to bring to a head what he considered the indecision of the Irish bishops over the project for a Catholic University, of which he had agreed to be Rector three years previously and had already been given the holding-title of President.

The Pope had asked the bishops to establish the University because the Queen's Colleges, recently opened by the government in Belfast, Cork and Galway, were judged obnoxious for Catholics: they were interdenominational, excluded the teaching of religion and were staffed by state-appointed professors. 'The Godless Colleges', their opponents dubbed them. Whether a Catholic University without government approval would prove feasible remained to be seen. It had become, at any rate, the major demand on Newman's time, the major occasion for his gadding to and fro, the major cause of gnawing frustration. He had had to travel to Ireland for discussions which bore no tangible fruit and had had to hold himself available for months on end lest a summons should come from the bishops. The Archbishop of Tuam, in ongoing disagreement with the Archbishop of Dublin, treated Newman as something of a whipping-boy. The Archbishop of Dublin, who had brought Newman to Ireland in the first place, was reluctant to allow him the freedom of action proper to a Rector, fearing an outcry if an Englishman were given too much of a say in Irish affairs. Premises for the University were acquired by Cullen without consulting him and he got nowhere with his repeated request to be allowed nominate his Vice-Rector. It was troublesome, distressing, disruptive of Oratory business. He had so much else to do.

To describe the situation as Newman saw it does not, of course, exhaust the perspectives from which it can be understood. It would be wrong, for example, to suppose — as so many commentators did at the time and so many biographers have done since — that every bishop belonged either to the school of thought represented by Archbishop Paul Cullen of Dublin or that of Archbishop John MacHale of Tuam. A ghostly figure presided over many of the discussions in which the English churchman found himself involved that February. ... Meanwhile, encouraged by Frederick Lucas, Editor of the *Tablet* (then published in Dublin), and emboldened by a letter from Cardinal Wiseman of Westminster which informed him that he could expect soon to be a bishop himself, Newman decided to call upon as many of the Irish prelates as he could and persuade them either to invite him to proceed with setting up the University or accept his resignation. 'I am going to tell them', he wrote, 'that they must take me or give me up.'[2] And so, with the weather worsening, he set off.

It took him twelve hours to reach Dublin, which hardly represented the best performance possible by train across the newly-opened Menai Railway Bridge ('the Menai pea-shooter', as his future Professor of Fine Arts colourfully described the tubular structure[3]) or on the ferry-boats of the Dublin Steam Packet Company, then rated the fastest in the world. But the wind seems not to have abated for he said it was 'a very stiff passage' and he suffered from what he called 'the pain of *not* being sick ... a compulsive compression of the stomach, a sense of burning there, a bad taste in the mouth, and a difficulty in breathing.'[4] By the following day, he had still not got over it. It was an omen of problems to come. The room which he had reserved as his Irish *pied-à-terre* in the school run by the Rev. Dr James Quinn at 16

Harcourt Street had been given over to billiards and such of his property as had not disappeared had been removed to the room above, where he proceeded to take up residence despite the draught coming in 'at top, bottom and side of the door'.[5] It took him several days to settle in and even then he was so cold that he could hardly write. To counter the freezing conditions, he foolishly allowed himself to be persuaded by a Sackville Street shop-assistant into buying a plaid cloak on the assurance that it was a clerical garment, which it certainly was not, and to assuage his hunger he dined one night in a hotel which charged him the outrageous sum of four shillings for a glass of porter and 'a small steak, so small that I ate it to the bone'.[6]

These happenings, it should be said, were reported by Newman not at all by way of grumbling but as a wry joke of fate against himself, intended to provoke chuckles when read aloud at recreation back in Birmingham. He drew on his Irish misfortunes as a lighthearted but clever means of uniting his community around a common interest, lowering the tension among them and maintaining an illusion of his own presence. He addressed his letters to different members of the community, too, so that all could feel involved and remembered. His mid-winter tour of Ireland was in truth no joke, but he saw the hilarious side of it and turned it to a paternal purpose. It calls constantly for a wrench of the imagination to realise that the Newman of this Pickwickian adventure was the famous preacher of the University Sermons in Oxford, the author of Tract 90 and the future cardinal.

The frustrations mounted. It was 'very blowy and blustery'.[7] His Dublin publisher was sick. His personal friends were away. The wife of one of them he found in bad humour and she neglected to give him the high tea for which he had politely prepared himself by eating early rather than dining in the evening at Dr Quinn's. The Archbishop was away. The Jesuit provincial, Father John Curtis, told him that 'the class of youths *did not exist* in Ireland, who would come to the University', that evening classes of the kind offered by London University would never succeed in Dublin and that he should go to Dr Cullen and advise him 'Don't attempt the University — give up the idea.'[8] Whether he put this view to Dr Cullen, Newman does not relate, although he notes that when the Archbishop returned the following week he dined with him twice, notwithstanding the persistence of 'a *bad* cold'.[9]

In fact Newman by now was showing an English resilience in

the face of obstacles which contrasted with Irish pessimism. He put tentative proposals to several people who might join the University staff, thoroughly surveyed 86 St Stephen's Green, which was to house the University, and wrote back to England for information about climatic conditions in the United States as he was contemplating a tour of 'the *principal* Catholic cities from New York to New Orleans'[10] to drum up support for the University and to lure American students to enrol. Support nearer home had yet to be pursued, however, and that meant undertaking the journey which he had carefully mapped out with the aid of his Bradshaw; an appropriate guide, for this famous railway timetable had a religious connotation, having been produced by a civic-minded Quaker, not as a commercial enterprise but as a service to the traveller perplexed by the ever-growing number of lines and connections of which he could avail himself.

'It blows a tempest, and rains furiously', wrote Newman the day before he left Dublin.[11] It was snowing as he departed for Kilkenny to meet the Bishop of Ossory, which explains why he wrapped himself in his plaid cloak. That in turn explains why the cabman at Kilkenny station brought him to the Church of Ireland bishop's palace, for who had ever heard of a Catholic priest so colourfully accoutred? Dr Edward Walsh, the Catholic bishop, enjoyed the story when the confusion had been resolved, probably not least because his Protestant counterpart had been a doughty critic of the Tractarians in the past and had accused Newman of 'the dishonest casuistry to which the Jesuits have given a name'![12] To the visitor's alarm, Bishop Walsh then brought him 'along planks and up corkscrews'[13] to the top of the unfinished St Mary's Cathedral, by which he was much impressed, and then sat him down to dinner — kindly serving him the outer cut of the mutton roast, for Newman had an aversion to the rare meat presented *saignant* after the French manner — Newman called it 'raw' or 'underdone' — which so often confronted him on Irish clerical tables. (He never suspected that the meat might have been in his honour. Some of the clergy in the southern counties had little taste for it. Describing the Maynooth of a decade later, Father Peadar Ó Laoghaire admitted that 'the best mutton that human being ever ate' was served there, but 'we were not reared on that food. We were not accustomed to it. It did not agree with us.'[14] Oatmeal bread, eggs, milk and potatoes were their preferred diet.)

From Kilkenny to Carlow, from Carlow to Waterford, Newman continued on what he called his 'circuit', being warmly received by the bishops in both places and by the staffs of their diocesan colleges. His only difficulty was that, his fame having gone ahead of him, he was expected to address gatherings of priests and — in the Ursuline Convent of Waterford — a hall full of schoolgirls. Invitations to speak impromptu always left him groping for words and being fatigued made the task no easier. In the convent he took refuge in requesting the Reverend Mother to grant the girls a holiday: his request was refused! A bigger rebuff awaited him in Cork. Bishop William Delany called to see him at the Vincentian house where he was staying. 'He cautiously came with his Vicar General', Newman recalled later, 'he wished to show his respect, he said, to my *character*. Directly I got so far as to say that I wished the advice of the Bishops, he rose and went away.'[15] Newman's immediate reaction was sharper: 'the Bishop of Cork was cold and courteous — stiff and donnish — and I should never get on with him, I am sure. He is the only Irish Bishop I have met unlike an Irishman; I think I had rather be pawed by the lion.'[16] The lion was the 'Lion of St Jarlath's' or 'of the West', the formidable Archbishop MacHale of Tuam.

The episode was revealing, for Delany had been appointed bishop in 1847 through the influence of Dr Cullen, then Rector of the Irish College in Rome, who thought him less likely to collaborate with the British authorities than the expected appointee, Father Theobald Mathew, the temperance promoter, who had too many Protestant friends for Cullen's liking. But Delany had been parish priest of Bandon, a better place to take the measure of Irish Protestants than Rome — or Tuam, for that matter — and he knew a bird in the hand when he saw one. He had a 'Godless College' in his diocese — Queen's College, Cork — which he thought a valuable asset for Catholics and he held determinedly to this view, Tuam, Dublin and Rome notwithstanding. Significantly, Bishop O'Donnell of Galway and Bishop Denvir of Down and Connor, whose dioceses also harboured Queen's Colleges, shared the same opinion of the government institutions.

All three had strongly supported Cullen's predecessor, Archbishop Daniel Murray of Dublin, when he pleaded that the Queen's Colleges be accepted as a practical means of access to university education for Catholics. Murray spoke from long experience of dealing with the British administration and gradually securing improvement after improvement in the circumstances of his co-religionists. He thought the Catholic University was an illusory ideal, not worth pursuing when opportunities of true value were at hand for the taking. Many in the episcopal body agreed with him, even if they now felt hampered in expressing their views, given the stance of the Holy See. The caution and abrupt exit of the Bishop of Cork can be readily understood and what Newman took for coldness may have been no more than self-protective reticence on the part of an Irish prelate before a visitor *of* whom he knew but whom personally he did *not* know.

At the human level Irish warmth soon reasserted itself. In Thurles Newman discovered Archbishop Slattery to be 'a most pleasing, taking man — mild, gentle, tender and broken.'[17] Broken? He does not explain. But nobody could mistake his rapport with Bishop Ryan of Limerick. 'He is a man I like very much — a down-right, honest, bluff person — very hearty and very positive — arguing and laying down the law, and abusing his young priests who take his kicks and stick out against him. He is the cleverest bishop I have met, and certainly to me the kindest.'[18] No reticence here! Yet neither was there much encouragement. Dr Ryan, like Murray in the past, could simply not believe in the viability of a university institution lacking state support. He allowed Newman to enter his name on the University Books (in effect, to make him a patron) on the firm understanding 'that he should not be supposed to prophesy anything but failure'.[19] The failure, he hastened to say, would not be Newman's fault. It would be in the nature of the enterprise.

Newman's competence to sort out the complexity of Irish attitudes came under pressure in Limerick not only from his host's ebullience but also from his own prime anxiety, distress among the Birmingham Oratorians. For this fresh upset Newman was himself responsible, or perhaps it should be blamed on the distractions and frustrations of trying to do business in Ireland. As part of his plan for keeping in close touch with the Oratory he had asked in a letter from Dublin that information be sent to him about internal community matters. He expressed himself with untypical lack of clarity and replies from his colleagues now voiced pain at what they thought was a requirement to spy on one another. This was unnerving. Newman rushed placatory explanations into the post and then reviewed his position. He rejoiced at the heart-warming welcome he received in so many parts of the South of Ireland and from so many bishops, but beyond the chance this gave him to outline his thoughts on the University it could not be said that he had noticeably advanced the project: the bishops he had met gave it only a limited priority at best, and some did not favour it at all. The Oratory was in trouble. His cough and cold were still plaguing him. It was raining. And the next stage of his circuit would take him to Galway *en route* for Tuam, there to beard the Lion in his den. He would have to travel by coach, for he had reached the end of the railway line. It was all too much. He boarded the train for Dublin instead ... not without yet another bizarre surprise, for somebody committed a schoolgirl laden with bandboxes to his care on the journey.

That Newman's good nature responded to the bonhomie of his hosts cannot be doubted. At the same time he had to conceal the increasing abrasion which Irish hospitality worked upon his somewhat fastidious tastes and very English reserve. He unburdened himself to a London Oratorian, telling him about 'the little annoyances of strange houses, of being in the hands of others who do not know what hurts one', not to mention the recurrent irritation of draughts, 'raw mutton that would turn a Tartar's stomach' and demands for speeches after dinner.[20] The cumulative effect was wearing him down and he permitted himself a short cry of anguish in a letter to his own Oratory: 'No one knows but myself the desolateness I sustain in leaving Birmingham, and being thrown among strangers — I trust it will be taken as my penance, and be of eternal good to me.'[21] It was an older British reaction to immersion in the company of the Irish than Newman realised. 'It is not practical for me to consider leaving them and going to Britain', Saint Patrick had written 1,400 years earlier. 'How dearly would I love to go ... God knows how I yearned for it, but I am tied by the Spirit.'[22]

Back in the capital, Newman's resilience revived and he made contact with an old friend, Dr Charles William Russell, Vice-President of the national seminary at Maynooth. Despite his friendship, Russell looked 'despondently . . . on the prospects for the University'.[23] The refrain was becoming familiar and was not modified by comments from lay quarters that 'there was simply no demand for it'. Newman began to detect the ghostly presence, as he confessed when looking back to that time in later years: 'Dr Murray I never saw, and now he was gone; but he still spoke in such men as these.' It was not for a moment that they would obstruct the wishes of the Holy See, but they were not convinced that the Pope was well advised and in consequence 'they had an omen of failure, dampening all their endeavours'.[24] Post-famine conditions sustained their despondency. Newman cited emigration and the 'ruin of families' among the factors which, together with a want of determination 'induced by centuries of oppression created the general belief that Ireland could not provide enough students to fill a Catholic University'.[25]

It was easy to appreciate why many should have thought it wiser to let Catholics use the institutions of more modest ambition provided at government expense, if they could afford to do so, rather than undertake a costly exercise themselves which seemed destined for failure. There were also those who felt a lingering discomfort over what might be regarded as Catholic inconsistency in spurning the government which had conceded their long-standing demand for equal — not exclusive — opportunities with Protestants in higher education. And apart from all of these, the Lion of the West was growling his distinctive nationalism against the government and his distinctive norms of episcopal authority against Dr Cullen .... Small wonder if Newman asked himself why he had abandoned his community and the tasks awaiting him in England for a country which put him to so much inconvenience, embroiled him in quarrels not of his making, involved him in ludicrous trivialities and showed little desire for his services. Small wonder if a hint of suspicion invaded his thoughts. 'If this use of me was what called me to Ireland, viz. to be flung at the head of the advocates of the Queen's Colleges, and not to introduce a positive policy, this might be a great object, but a very different one from that which filled my own mind.'[26]

Newman's vision of what the University might be, and should be, differed radically from the more limited understanding widespread in Ireland: he did not, as it happened, think of it as an Irish institution at all, or at least not solely Irish. His vision of education differed also from the pragmatic expectations of a people and a local Church seeking to lift themselves from destitution and subjection. But for all that, Newman had to work in a specific place, at a specific time, with specific people and under specific conditions. Place, time, people and conditions, in turn, belonged together to a moment in history. They subsisted in a context. It was the Age of Revolution, political and industrial. It was the Age of Reform, social and intellectual. Cries for liberty filled the air. So did counter-cries for order.

Newman more than most sought to speak to the age, to enter into dialogue with it. And he made it his own in another sense by using its facilities to the full. He took railways for granted, oblivious of the novelty they still were for many around him. The temporary station outside Waterford had been open for less than a year when he arrived there on his 'circuit' of Ireland; that in Kilkenny was only three years in operation, that in Limerick five. Without steamships he could not have maintained the appearance of bilocation in Dublin and Birmingham, which can make even the modern reader tired to contemplate, so much dashing over and back was involved. More distant journeys were possible, too: a tour of America, as we saw, could be considered and a visit to Rome at the end of 1855 was remarkable in Newman's account, not for the speed of travel most of the way, but for the absence of railways when he reached the Papal States. Steam power, it might be added, sped the post as well as passengers and Newman took every advantage of this development to keep closely in touch with Birmingham.

Rapid transport typified the scientific and engineering genius of the nineteenth century which stimulated the idea that progress need know no bounds, a theory sitting uneasily with traditional religious belief in humankind's dependence on God. A watering-down of religion, its abandonment in some places and the growth of indifferentism — the suggestion that one religion was as good, or as limited, as another — showed itself elsewhere. Some churchmen reacted by setting their faces against progress. Newman thought otherwise, not arguing like the indifferentists for a reconciliation of religion with science, but insisting that religion and science could not contradict one another for the sufficient reason that truth could not contradict truth. Promotion of this reality, which would establish how religion was as relevant in the Victorian era as in any that went before, ranked high among Newman's objectives in wishing to see the Catholic University brought into being. Knowledge of God belonged in the same firmament as all other knowledge and if it were not treated with the same respect and presented with the same sophistication it would fall behind the other sciences in the estimate of the world. To divert young Catholics from setting off on this road of indifferentism leading to unbelief, to enable them to recognise the limits in the sphere of influence proper to each of the sciences while at the same time ensuring that their minds matured through the acquisition of knowledge — such were Newman's aims for his University.

What had such elevated reasoning to do with a plaid cloak and the Bishop of Ossory's scaffolding, with the bandbox girl and the school hall in Waterford? The winter journey served at least to reveal a gulf of disagreement between Newman and much of the Irish Church leadership as real as the division between their Graces of Dublin and Tuam, although based on different considerations and politely phrased. It showed the lengths to which Newman was prepared to go in coping with the problem, the strain it caused him and his difficulty in giving it all his attention when concern for the Oratory, his first responsibility, kept intruding. His use of the railway system to tackle as much business as he could in as short a time as possible vividly bespoke his modernity, and the gentle self-mockery with which he described the mishaps that befell him underscored his attractive human qualities. These manifold factors threw light on the story of the University to that point, and they presaged what was to come.

1

A tale of three cities

The circumstances which brought Newman to Ireland so often in the 1850s arose from a convergence of events which had their origin in places geographically and temperamentally far apart: Rome, Dublin, Oxford. Perhaps a market-town should be added to these famous cities, even if it seems incongruous to name in the same breath 'the old town of Tuam ... a dirty and ruinous-looking place', where the recently-erected Catholic cathedral was 'sadly out of harmony with the dull and dingy habitations' upon which it looked down.[1] That was how Tuam struck a visitor on the eve of the Great Hunger. It must have been more dilapidated still when famine had come and lingered and at last subsided. The misery to which the west of Ireland had already been reduced, and into which it was now further sinking, played its part in the drama of the Catholic University by steeling the will, self-reliance, sense of grievance and quirky suspicion of everything and everyone east of the Shannon which characterised John MacHale throughout his long episcopate. But first to Rome ...

The Rome in which Paul Cullen lived from 1821 until 1850 was quaintly romantic, soporific except on a day of religious ceremonial or in a jubilee year ... or a year of revolution. The Pope ruled there in a double sense. He was sovereign of the Papal States, the least efficiently administered principality in the Italian peninsula. He was Supreme Pontiff of the Roman Catholic Church. The contrast between the two aspects of the Papacy smacked of an improbability more appropriate to Italian opera than to the science of government. The Supreme Pontiff acquired more power, more authority, more respect and a more elevated position in the world-wide Church with every year that passed. His little princedom remained extraordinarily backward in the amenities of the nineteenth century. Travellers decried the deplorable roads, the highwaymen, the lack of railways, the towns where no writ seemed to run. Until the 1840s a layman could hold no office of consequence in the civil service.

The city of Rome itself had contracted to a fraction of its size in imperial times. There were farms and pastures within the Aurelian Wall and cattle grazed in the Forum — or, rather, on top of it, for its monuments lay half buried in the silt of centuries. Poets, painters, antiquarians and many persons of private means and discernment from northern Europe surrendered to its lotus-lure: tea-rooms and Weinstuben flourished in the neighbourhood of the Piazza di Spagna and a competence to converse in French was an asset in polite society. But no lampstandards lit the dung-strewn streets after dark and the energies of papal administration seemed confined to refurbishing the churches, propping up the Colosseum and draining the Pontine Marshes. The Pontine Marshes were actually undrainable. Several of the Caesars had tried in classical times and Mussolini would be found at it in the 1920s. It was altogether typical of Papal officialdom to make a virtue of the impossible and to neglect the improvements that would have been of real public benefit.

The cult of the past so imbued the Roman system, and indeed the Roman people, that it became almost a philosophy of government. For Italian patriots looking forward to the modernisation and unification of their country, and for bourgeois liberals in Italy and all the countries to the North, it was an offence to history that the progress represented by the Industrial Revolution and the freedoms proclaimed as the Rights of Man should be denied in the city which had given the world the very concept of the republic. It would be futile to attempt a justification of the *system* of autocracy in the Papal States right up to the fall of Rome in 1870, apart from the interlude of Pius IX's short-lived reforms and the even shorter-lived Roman Republic of 1848-49. What has to be said, however, against stereotyped history still being written is that the papal *regime* was a lot gentler than its harsh laws would imply. There might be a ghetto but there were no pogroms of the kind known in Russia and Poland. Convicts might be sent to the galleys, but there were no galleys and they were soon released: this was at a time when children could be hanged in England for theft. Conspirators against the state indeed suffered the death penalty, as everywhere in Europe, but nobody was held to account for using the safety-valve of Pasquino, the stump of a statue to which anybody was permitted to attach a derogatory comment about the authorities — even to imply, as was implied of Paul Cullen's patron, Leo XII, that the Pope was a Mahommedan because he tried to curtail excessive drinking! As a civil government, the Papacy was illiberal and inefficient. It was in no real sense tyrannical.

While the Papal States languished in sleepy anarchy, the

ecclesiastical office of the Pope grew steadily in stature. This was simultaneously obscured and acknowledged by the anti-clerical mood of the nineteenth century. Only an office of the highest significance could have evoked the fanatical vituperation of religious fundamentalists in England, of French radicals and German nationalists, as well as Italian irredentists chanting their slogan 'Rome or Death'. In so far as the impression hardened of the Pope as a tottering Anti-Christ, an ogre on his last legs, it grossly misrepresented the truth of a new-style papacy in the making. Ultramontanism was on the ascendant. By and large, even respected historians today remember this movement only as a massive campaign of loyalty to the Pope, a defensive reaction by Catholics against the anticlerical onslaughts of the day; they stress, too, how it was characterised by a rigid, conservative and inflexible theology, comforting for those who looked 'beyond the mountains' to Rome as the sure guiding light in the gathering gloom. Certainly, the rally around the Pope took place and rigid theology secured a dominant status in the mind of the Church. But ultramontanism, in its nineteenth-century manifestation, had started with an altogether different emphasis. Its primary *aim* initially had been to *free* the Church to *live in freedom* rather than in thraldom to transitory political systems.

The progenitors of the movement were progressive and forward-looking Catholics who wished to see acknowledged in the post-Napoleonic era the harmony which they believed to exist between God and freedom, between the Church and the Revolution. That is to say, they were precisely those Catholics who in the familiar version of the story were the opponents and victims of the ultramontanes. The true conservatives did not at first look beyond the mountains. They sought to revert to Gallicanism or Josephism, the eighteenth-century principle of a national Church linked to Rome in faith but dependent on the monarch for episcopal nominations, financial support, protection and prestige. Liberal Catholics saw a double hazard in this. The Church could have no vigorous or independent life as a department of state. It ran the risk of having no life at all when the revolution broke out, for it would have drawn on itself quite unnecessarily the wrath of those who set out to demolish the monarchy. Accordingly, while Church conservatives favoured the old-style alliance of Throne and Altar, their liberal fellow-Catholics argued for total separation of Church from state and they looked to Rome as the centre of strength, authority and unity for believers who conceded no function to civic governments in what pertained to religion. Rome and only Rome, as these liberals saw it, should nominate bishops (normally on the advice of the diocese), promulgate decrees, provide for the Church's welfare.

The 1820s were not the 1960s. Not even the most prophetic at the earlier date envisaged the ideal of a vibrant local Church that would grow from the thinking of the Second Vatican Council. At the earlier date, the liberal objective was simply to ensure that the Church, as a divine institution, should be kept free from intrusion upon its affairs by a predatory state. It may be noted that this was the point of departure for Newman and the Tractarians from the Erastian mainstream in the Church of England (when parliament presumed to suppress a number of dioceses — ironically, in Ireland), as it was later to be the issue on which the future Cardinal Manning and others went over to Rome (when the Privy Council overruled an Anglican bishop's decision on a question related to doctrine). In a further refinement of the argument, there were those like Daniel Murray, Archbishop of Dublin from 1823 to 1852, for whom collaboration with the state could be the route to freedom for an oppressed Church. If the state conceded a facility of benefit to Catholics (e.g. state-supported schools provided on a nation-wide scale which an unendowed Church could not possibly match), Murray was quite prepared to accept it as a step forward. To Paul Cullen, any collaboration smacked of contamination and every step taken with state involvement was a step backwards. Although he could sometimes relax his resistance a little if he found the reality less harmful than he feared (as in the case of schools), he never abandoned the classic ultramontane attitude and had no sympathy with the mounting doubts among liberal Catholics over the danger to legitimate freedom of thought and action posed within the Church by the ever-growing control exercised by the Roman authorities.

Be that as it may, all the great liberal Catholic names were Rome-looking at the outset: Lacordaire and Montalembert, Doellinger and Ketteler, Rosmini and Ventura, Dupanloup and Acton. When Lamennais was rebuffed by Gregory XVI the anticlericals rejoiced over what they saw correctly as rejection of a papalist by the Pope. When Lacordaire, wearing his Dominican habit, took his seat in the parliament of the Second French Republic, he proclaimed not the subjection of Church to state but the independence of the Church which enabled him to act as a citizen rather than as a civil servant. Daniel O'Connell, who can fairly be described as the first Christian Democrat, began his career by resisting a proposal that the government should pay the salaries of Irish priests and he died while travelling on pilgrimage to Rome. As the liberal tempo, whether Catholic or anticlerical, quickened the Church disentangled itself — or was forcibly disentangled — from the old-type association with the state in country after country. Rhinelanders resisting Prussianisation, French publicists concerned at the materialist values of Louis-Philippe's monarchy, newly-emancipated Irish Catholics seeking to stand on their own feet ... all pegged their hopes and their standards to the Roman flagstaff. The personal authority of the Pope grew by leaps and bounds until by mid-century his office dominated the life of the Church as it had not done since the High Middle Ages.

Sadly and incredibly, none of the holders of the papal office correctly identified the source of its new prestige. They sensed the power and wielded it but wielded it *against* the liberal forces which gave it its impetus. They condemned the French and the Poles, urged obedience to the most tyrannical sovereigns — and stood stoutly in the path of the Risorgimento, the campaign for the unification of Italy. Here, of course, lay the root of the problem. The popes, as Italian princes, faced a strident nationalism posited on the revolutionary ideals of democracy and liberty. Liberalism as they saw it on their own doorstep was anti-papal, obsessed with seizing the Pope's dominions, not to be trusted and meriting no collaboration. Reacting as local participants in the story, these popes rejected the Risorgimento. In rejecting it, they rejected also the high-flown liberal theorising employed to justify it. In rejecting the whole complex of liberalism, they invoked the majestic authority of their newly-strengthened ecclesiastical office. In this way, the pressure of local politics on a minor Italian government helped to generate a titanic struggle between the world forces of religion and liberalism.

It is easy in summarising to be simplistic. Because of the importance to Newman of distinguishing between the true and false in liberal values, and because Cullen's fear of liberalism explains some of the positions he adopted which exacerbated the antipathy of MacHale, it needs to be said that there were elements in European liberal philosophy and in the actions it inspired which justified Church caution without reference to Italian politics. The French Revolution of 1789 had led to theories of state supremacy and to the establishment of a state Church, not to mention the arrest of successive popes and the decapitation of bishops and priests. In so far as the revolutionaries were merely anticlerical, opposed to a clergy-dominated institution, modern thinking on the nature of the Church would suggest that perceptive Catholics might have sought dialogue with them. In so far as the Revolution presumed to usurp the function of the Church, persecute its ministers and substitute its own theorising for the faith derived from Revelation, Catholics had no choice but to spurn it.

In Rome, only the errors of liberalism were noted. This meant, unhappily, that the Church had to wait until the second half of the twentieth century before giving official recognition to the truths embodied in the great revolutionary document, the Declaration of the Rights of Man. It also meant that many of those Catholics who had winnowed the liberal theories and found much good in them were treated as suspect, rebuked, silenced and, in a few cases, notably Lamennais and Doellinger, driven into revolt against the Church they loved: thus was ultramontanism purged of its progressive content and the hope of reconciliation with the new age undermined. Rome took no account of the better-grounded liberalism evolved in America, scientific advance was thought a hazard to faith and new philosophies — economic, political, social — took shape without an input from the Church which had once been the custodian of civilisation. When Nicholas Wiseman wrote learned analyses of Church history, Anglicans marvelled for they had come to believe that scholarship was beyond the competence of papists. The *Times* reflected the same assumption in its first reaction to the proposal that a Catholic University be set up in Ireland: 'The Romish priesthood' could not educate because, among various deficiencies, it lacked the necessary learning.[2] To supply this want in the Catholicism of the day was Newman's special ambition and was his primary motive in agreeing to participate in the University project.

As Rector of the Irish College in Rome for nearly twenty years, Paul Cullen held a not insignificant position in the upper echelons of Church administration. While the British government had informal but close relations with the Holy See, the permanent tension between a Protestant administration and its Catholic subjects in a country where they formed the majority of the population required Rome to have an alternative source of advice on Irish affairs to the lobbying of English diplomats ... and of English Catholics, whose interests and attitudes often differed sharply from those of the Irish. Cullen, therefore, as the senior and official Irish presence in Rome (since the Irish bishops appointed the College Rector) enjoyed ready access to the popes under whom he served. His status also grew over the years because so many of the bishops in Ireland individually employed him as their Roman agent: that is to say, he conducted business for them with the Holy See, conveyed their views to the Curia and reported back not only the outcome of their representations but the general news from Rome and the Roman view of world events.

The Roman view was Cullen's personal view and he did not have to await the establishment of a Republic in the city in 1848, during which he gave sanctuary in the Irish College to more than one official on the new authorities' 'wanted' list, before developing his lifelong revulsion towards liberalism in all its forms. He summarised his opinions in a sentence which he wrote into the statement published by the Irish hierarchy in 1850 after the Synod of Thurles. Liberalism, according to that document, was 'no longer a single heresy, or an eccentric fanaticism, the denial of some revealed truth, or the excesses of some extravagant error, but a comprehensive, all-pervading, well-digested system of unbelief, suited to every capacity and reaching every intellect, that corrupts and desolates the moral world.'[3] This was the developed ultramontane position and it left little room for the Catholic liberals who saw the possibilities of dialogue rather than confrontation with the mood of the century. O'Connellite pre-Famine Ireland had been the mentor of Europe in liberal Catholicism, as so many of its continental advocates acknowledged. It was unlikely that internal confrontation could be avoided in the Irish Church when Cullen returned to his homeland in 1850 as Archbishop of Armagh and Apostolic Delegate. The confrontation came over one aspect of what he judged to be liberal infiltration of sound Catholic values: mixed, or interdenominational, education. Like Pius IX, he believed that 'to the Church and its Apostles, its divine Founder has committed the great right and duty of teaching'.[4] His Roman suavity of manner long concealed how comprehensively he interpreted this view and applied it to every aspect of study, to every learning activity. In Ireland, when the occasion arose, he would make his position clear. Meanwhile, in Dublin ...

*   *   *

When Daniel Murray was consecrated Archbishop of Dublin in 1823 the city had three Roman Catholic places of worship which, because of their design and solidity of structure, could be properly called churches. A Metropolitan Church (later the Pro-Cathedral) was nearing completion. The teeming Catholic population of the capital, about 165,000 out of 200,000 inhabitants, had otherwise to make do with mean, irregularly built Mass-houses, often hidden from the public view down lanes and alleyways — reminders of the Catholics' second-class citizenship and of the furtive expression of religious belief which had been as much as they could risk under the disabilities of penal legislation only recently repealed. By the date of the Archbishop's death in 1852 every parish in the city, and many in the suburban and rural parts of the diocese as well, had its permanent purpose-built church, small or substantial as parochial needs dictated, often aesthetically pleasing and sometimes (St Paul's, St Audoen's, the Metropolitan Church) a building of high architectural quality in a city of fine buildings.

These churches bore physical witness to the regeneration of Catholic life achieved in the early to middle decades of the nineteenth century. Although Archbishop Murray was among the outstanding — as he was certainly the most saintly — of the leaders of the Catholic community in this period, it would be wrong to suppose that the awakening resulted from clerical prompting and direction. The Catholic people as a whole, laity and clergy, had walked out of the shadows and laid claim to their rightful place in their own country. Daniel O'Connell showed them what could be brought about by political action. When a popular movement, acting politically, wrested Catholic Emancipation in 1829 from a government reluctant to grant it, Catholic morale soared to unprecedented heights and pressure was initiated on a succession of questions, each representing a grievance which Catholics wanted remedied: tithes (a tax levied for the support of the Anglican Church of Ireland), primary schooling, financial support for Maynooth, bequests for religious purposes, access to university education.

The British authorities responded politically to political campaigning. While refusing to budge on the major Irish demand — repeal of the Act of Union binding Britain and Ireland together in a United Kingdom under not only the one sovereign but the one parliament — the government in London sought to conciliate

Irish opinion by proposing remedies for the specifically Catholic grievances as they arose. It would make an offer, which would normally be resisted from the Irish side as inadequate. Consultations would take place with Irish parliamentarians and perhaps with churchmen. A new offer would be put. This in turn would be argued over until a formula emerged which proved acceptable to the Irish Catholic interest concerned, not because it was judged the perfect solution but because it was the best solution attainable and represented a very real advance on the circumstances which it replaced. Thus, after much discussion and negotiation the government established 'national schools' in which Catholic and Protestant children were taught together, free from interference with their respective religions and with Catholic representation on the Board set up to administer the system. Archbishop Murray approved and some years later vigorously defended his decision, referring to 'the difficulty we have had in procuring the present system, the utter hopelessness of obtaining aid from Parliament for anything better, the dangers of allowing the education funds to go back to the exclusive management of Protestants, the experience which the Catholics have had of the beneficial effects of the system ...'.[5] This was the use of O'Connellite political method and reasoning: aim high, mount as much pressure as you can, settle when you are satisfied that the government has gone as far as it will go and that the proposal involves a tangible improvement. In this way, the position of Catholics in Ireland grew better by leaps and bounds during the years before the Famine.

The initiative in demanding reform was as likely to be undertaken by Catholic laity as by Church leaders (in the matter of tithes, for example) and a certain symbolism could be seen in the fact that the foundation-stone of St James's Church in Dublin was laid, not by the Archbishop, but by Daniel O'Connell. Irish Catholics, their poverty notwithstanding, had become a self-confident body, sure of what they wanted and sure of how to go about getting it. Indeed, their poverty also was beginning to erode with the emergence of a successful middle class, concentrated in the towns and especially in Dublin. In evidence to a House of Commons committee in 1825 O'Connell estimated that over half of the commercial activity of the city was conducted by Catholics, and four years later the French political theorist, Gustave de Beaumont, calculated that as much as nine-tenths of the funds in the Bank of Ireland belonged to Catholics.[6] The masses in town and country, of course, remained irredeemably destitute but gave their mite as cheerfully as the rich left legacies or made large donations to the common causes of Emancipation, Repeal ... or the construction of churches. The churches were not, as pious fable would have it, 'built on the pennies of the poor' for few of them would have been completed without the aid of those legacies and large donations, but the pennies of the poor were never missing from the building fund. All gave willingly since all felt themselves part of the resurgence. The Irish majority were not to experience again so exhilarating a sense of liberation as they enjoyed in the twenty years from 1825 to 1845. The Famine put an end to it. But not the Famine alone.

Paul Cullen, observing from afar, rejoiced at the growing strength of Irish Catholicism and therefore supported O'Connell as the inspirational leader of the revival. Whether he really understood the principles on which O'Connell was acting can only be doubted. O'Connell believed in religious freedom in the same sense as the American political theorists of the day and, indeed, as the far-distant Second Vatican Council. 'The right of every man to freedom of conscience, he said, was 'equally the right of a Protestant in Italy or Spain as of a Catholic in Ireland'.[7] In one respect at least he outflanked the Americans, proclaiming 'may my tongue cleave to my mouth if for Ireland, even for Ireland, I forget the poor negro one hour!'[8] In short, he argued for the rights of *persons*, not of *Catholics*, but Cullen and many others (not least in England) saw only that Catholics were the beneficiaries of O'Connell's political activity and that was enough to please or worry them, depending on their viewpoint. It pleased Cullen who, by his own ultramontane standards should have been worried by the enormous respect of liberal Catholics, especially in France, for the achievements and implications of O'Connellism. He would certainly have been distressed had he heard Lacordaire's summary of the message to be drawn from O'Connell by the Church: 'In denying the rights of man, we deny the rights of God ... the rights of God and human rights form a unity ... liberty is a work of virtue, a holy work and therefore a work of the spirit.'[9] The Church was not to make such thoughts its own until 1963, when Pope John XXIII published *Pacem in Terris*.

Much else should, logically, have upset Paul Cullen. It should have given him pause for thought that the liberal Catholic, Father Antonio Rosmini, whose appointment as papal prime minister

22

Roman demonstrators demanded in 1848, was an admirer of O'Connell. It should have troubled him to know that O'Connell told the utilitarian philosopher, Jeremy Bentham, in 1829 that 'I avowed myself on the hustings this day to be a "Benthamite" ... our sect *will* prosper.'[10] In other words, O'Connell was an adult and prophetic Christian, who could think for himself and, while profoundly respecting the place of the papal office in his religion, saw no reason to align his politics with papal emphases. Had he done so he could have claimed few of the rights he sought for the Irish since so many of them were denied by Rome, either in principle or in the governmental practices of the Papal States. He was, quite simply, a liberal Catholic who believed in the rights of the people and, in particular, the people's right to pursue redress by effective political means. Because he was an activist rather than a theorist, a popular orator rather than an academic analyst and, above all, because the fruit of his labour was so largely the betterment of Irish Catholics and of the Catholic Church in Ireland, neither Rome nor Cullen found occasion to object as they objected to liberal Catholics elsewhere.

The independent spirit of the Irish Church, typified in the determination of bishops like Murray to insist on knowledge and experience of the Irish situation as better guides than ultramontane theory in dealing with the government, reflected O'Connellite self-reliance and self-confidence. It would be difficult to prove that the first was inspired by the second. It is certainly true that each strengthened the other and contributed to the assurance which was such a mark of Irish Catholicism as it emerged from the shadows. It should not be wondered at, for Catholics were citizens also and the same instinct moved them in whichever capacity they acted. And so it was entirely natural that, if they were politically certain they had negotiated the best deal to be had on an educational issue, they were willing to endorse it from the religious perspective also. Optimism was very much part of the mood. They registered the advantage actually gained, not the theoretical hazard created. Pessimism, by contrast, marked the Roman mood. There absolute values prevailed so that arrangements anywhere arrived at between Church and state which gave the Church less than what Rome deemed ideally desirable were frowned upon as dangerous to faith. Advantage would not be admitted if disadvantage could still be perceived. This was especially so when the state retained powers of control in matters which Rome believed to belong as of right to the

Church. Whatever the objective arguments which might be made in support of this attitude, it was unrealistic to hold to it unbendingly in Irish circumstances where every concession extracted from the British authorities amounted to a major achievement and every conciliatory proposal they put forward needed to be considered seriously even if its defects had then to be pointed out.

Two factors encouraged Rome, or more precisely encouraged Cullen in Rome, during these years to hold to unyielding positions, especially on matters related to education where the government (if only because the taxpayers' money was involved) insisted on reserving to itself a degree of control. O'Connell tended to criticise government proposals when they were first put forward, not only because of their inherent inadequacy but as a tactical move to secure favourable amendments. Noting the Irish leader's opposition to government policy while failing to detect or anticipate a political ploy, Cullen felt encouraged in advising the Holy See of the iniquity of what was proposed and in urging the bishops at home to stand fast against an unacceptable measure. The Irish bishops became adept at this negotiating procedure also and more than once Cullen found himself embarrassingly abandoned at the heel of the hunt when a question was settled to general satisfaction after the political or consultative manoeuvring had gained its objective. Among the bishops, however, general satisfaction was rarely total. In whatever involved resistance to a British government initiative or government control of even the slightest kind in matters concerning the Church, Cullen could invariably rely on the Archbishop of Tuam, John MacHale, to reject the proposal and to continue rejecting it long after others had agreed to a settlement.

*　　*　　*

Seen from Rome, MacHale's position for long seemed to match Cullen's on every question that arose. Like Cullen, the Lion of the West doubted the good intentions of an English Protestant government, feared for the faith of Catholic children subjected to a school system under state control, disliked any hint of compromise on the Catholic side of a public argument and harboured a strong conviction regarding the authority of bishops ... at least, the cynic might say, the authority of those bishops who agreed with him! What Cullen failed to appreciate for many years was that, in spite of superficial appearances, MacHale was not at all ultramontane in the Roman sense. His intransigence arose from his nationalism, itself a compound of resentment over the maladministration so noticeable in the west of the country, anger at the proselytism conducted with more brashness than Christian charity by certain Protestant evangelicals, and a narrowness of view attributable to the fact that he was the first Irish bishop of post-penal times to have been educated solely in Ireland. In non-essentials he submitted to Roman direction only in so far as it enabled him to outface British politicians or fellow-bishops like Murray, whom he considered far too temporising for their own or the Church's good. Despite an embarrassing experience on the charitable bequests issue, when Roman officialdom began to doubt the Irish Rector's discretion because of an extreme stance into which he had allowed himself to be led by MacHale, Cullen came to see the vast chasm separating him from the Archbishop of Tuam only after his return to Ireland in 1850.

Cullen's last four years in Rome were turbulent, first with news of the terrible famine devastating Ireland, then with the agitation which led to the Roman Republic, the exile of Pope Pius IX and the besieging of the city — ironically by the army of the Second French Republic, a regime in which liberal Catholics took a prominent part and which through their influence came to the Pope's assistance in his hour of need. These events kept Cullen busy. He worked strenuously to raise funds for the relief of Irish famine victims and he organised the protection of various papal personnel and premises during the Republic and the siege. The post from Ireland was scarcely more tranquil. It brought news not only of the Famine and of the 1848 Rising but of the Queen's Colleges. The last were a very typical English response to an Irish demand. Irish Catholics, now insistent on attaining full equality with their fellow-citizens, wanted equal access to university education. Trinity College, the only constituent and functioning institution within the University of Dublin, was also the only institution of university status in Ireland. It had been founded by Queen Elizabeth I specifically as a Protestant university for the promotion of the established Church (the Anglican Church of Ireland) and was, indeed, the place where aspirants to holy orders were trained for the Anglican ministry. Although Catholics had been admitted as students, together with Nonconformist Protestants, since 1794 they could not hold scholarships or fellowships. They were effectively barred from participation in running the affairs of the University and having a voice in the appointment of professors and lecturers. This was scarcely unreasonable, given the purpose for which Trinity had been established, but it underscored the discrimination which Catholics wanted redressed.

After what can only be described as very careful consideration by the Prime Minister, Sir Robert Peel, but having foolishly omitted to discuss the plan first with the Archbishops and leaders of Irish Catholic opinion (it was apparently thought sufficient to seek advice from lesser public figures), the British government announced plans in 1845 for 'Queen's Colleges' in Belfast, Cork and either Limerick or Galway (Galway was eventually chosen). These colleges would provide university education in the arts and sciences for students of any religious persuasion and would involve no disabilities on the grounds of religion. Government funding would be generous but would not be available to endow the teaching of religion — i.e. to support either religious instruction or a chair of theology — and the government would retain the right to approve the appointment of college officers and academic staff.

Reaction followed along the now predictable lines. Said Archbishop Murray: 'The new colleges would seem to be not what we would wish if we had the power to do better, but at least a step in advance in our favour.'[11] O'Connell rejected the proposal, making it clear that he did so on a pluralist principle: 'While I ask education for the Catholics, I freely and gladly concede it to the Protestants and Dissenters.'[12] He encouraged the bishops to hold out for better terms which, in his political judgement, could be had from Peel's pliant administration and there is evidence to suggest, as one would expect, that he was ready to settle for 'mixed education' if government control were whittled down. MacHale set his face against interdenominational teaching and government control alike and Cullen, in Rome, as ever recoiled from the nightmare of a Protestant virus infecting the education of Catholic students, whether through their neighbours on the classroom benches, their lecturers, government nominees on the controlling body ... or Catholic bishops putting their trust too innocently in Dublin Castle rather than being guided by Roman norms. The bishops united briefly on the wording of a compromise memorandum to government asking for a number of amendments but soon Rome was being asked to adjudicate between the conflicting views. Letters, spokesmen, British government emissaries and the formidable Archbishop of Tuam himself arrived there to urge one or other case regarding the colleges.

Twice Rome issued Rescripts warning against the 'grave danger to the Catholic Faith'[13] represented by the colleges, even after a number of concessions had been promised by government. The Rescripts recommended that a Catholic University be established on the model of the recently revived University of Louvain in Belgium. These documents may have been inspired by Cullen's influence, or Pius IX's anxiety to keep education within Church control, or possibly anti-British sentiments in the Curia, or even the persuasive powers of MacHale who warned the Pope in Homeric language to beware of the English bearing gifts. The origin of the documents did not matter for they left loopholes enough for the argument to continue. Rome might caution and Tuam roar, but Dublin held fast to the opinion that the Queen's Colleges would serve Irish Catholics well ... at least as well as the National Schools which even Cullen had come to admit were of considerable benefit and functioned for all practical purposes as Catholic establishments in which the wishes of the Church prevailed and the hand of government was rarely evident. Half the bishops of Ireland favoured the Dublin view. The others backed Tuam.

Cullen visited Ireland to advise himself on famine conditions at first hand. To his distress over the appalling condition of the people and the division between the bishops was added confirmation of other phenomena in Ireland which had been worrying him for some time. Priests were adopting an active role in politics, using their pulpits to inculcate the nationalist attitudes associated with the Archbishop of Tuam.

Even worse, to Cullen's Roman perception, liberal opinions were finding more explicit expression than formerly in the speeches and journalism of the new ginger group within the O'Connellite political party, known as Young Ireland. Cullen jumped to the conclusion that this was the Irish version of Young Italy, the Mazzinian and largely anti-clerical revolutionary party causing so much trouble in the Papal States. Although there would in fact be contact later between the two movements, the liberalism of Young Ireland was little different from that of

O'Connell apart from its refusal to condemn the use of force in the national cause — the question on which O'Connell had repeatedly criticised them in the two years before his death in 1847. They were also less inclined than the old leader to engage in political tactics: their outspoken comments on events of the day, as well as on recent and ancient history, lacked subtlety, however noble their assertion of Irish grievance. They certainly gave ground to suspicious minds to see in them the ominous tendencies of continental liberalism. Although not at all anti-clerical, they had Protestants among their leadership, which was scarcely calculated to endear them to the Rector of the Irish College. He was not surprised to be told by conservative clergy that the Young Irelanders were 'latitudinarian', while their approval of the Queen's Colleges can have been no more than he expected of them.

It was one more among the bewildering contradictions in the volatile Irish situation that Young Ireland should have been found on the same side of the university debate as Archbishop Murray, who was the least revolutionary-minded man in the country. Their reasons, of course, differed. Young Ireland liked mixed education as a liberal principle; Murray accepted it *faute de mieux*. It still led to the same kind of confusion as arose from Cullen's apparent alignment with MacHale when in fact radically different motives inspired them. Then there was the curious similarity between criticism of Peel by his opponents in parliament and criticism of Murray and his supporters by Rome: in both cases, failure to consult on the colleges question was denounced. But in the Prime Minister's case it meant failure to consult the Catholics, in Murray's case, failure to consult the Holy See. There is no evidence, incidentally, that Cullen ever heard of Young England. This would surely have puzzled him since it was a *Tory* ginger group which for a time numbered the future Father Faber in its ranks! Such overlapping in the use of words and concepts should not be dismissed as mere curiosities. They *could* obscure reality for the disparate participants in complex events.

Oddest of all, perhaps, was the origin of the slogan which O'Connell, MacHale, Cullen and so many others made their own in speaking of the new institutions — 'the Godless Colleges'. It derived from a strong condemnation of the government proposal from a *Protestant* point of view by Sir Robert Inglis, Member of Parliament for Oxford University, who denounced it as 'a gigantic scheme of godless education'.[14] By a further coincidence, Inglis happened to be an anti-Catholic Low Church Anglican for whom the young John Henry Newman had campaigned when he offered himself for election by the University in 1829 as an opponent of Catholic Emancipation. Inglis won the election and ousted the sitting Member, Sir Robert Peel. Newman had disapproved, not of Emancipation, but of state interference with the University which he thought was being brought to bear through influential lobbying on behalf of the measure. Newman's attitude infuriated his patron, Dr Richard Whately, Principal of Alban Hall and a former Fellow of Oriel, who protested at Newman's encouragement of intolerance. Whately was now Church of Ireland Archbishop of Dublin. No doubt he thought often of Oxford, as Newman did in Birmingham.

*   *   *

If Newman took railways for granted, this reflected their presence everywhere as a typical feature — perhaps *the* typical feature — of Victorian life. As early as 1830 a Minister of the Crown was run over and killed by a steam locomotive. In 1845 passenger trains were so familiar that an epitaph in Ely Cathedral could be composed on the analogy of a railway line:

> The line to heaven by Christ was made
> With heavenly truth the rails were laid,
> From Earth to Heaven the line extends
> To Life Eternal where it ends.[15]

Not only do casual references to railways spatter Newman's correspondence — meeting his brother Frank on the line from Cheltenham, noting a comment made by his publisher on the train to Kingstown, observing the spires of Oxford 'as they are seen from the railway'[16] — but he used the symbol of the age with equal casualness to give a homely context to some of his arguments, 'Wonder is not religion', he wrote in a letter to the *Times*, 'or we should be worshipping our railroads.'[17] In his Dublin Discourses he spoke of the ill-informed opinions heard 'in every railway carriage'.[18]

Steam had its victims also. Steam depended on coal, coal fuelled the furnaces to smelt the iron to make the engines; there were many kinds of engine and engines had many uses. Their consequences included mass production, whence came the factories and slag-heaps, the overcrowded little houses, the child-workers and their grimy exploited parents. It was the world of Mr Gradgrind and the Industrial Revolution. To minister in this world would be the pastoral commitment of the Birmingham Oratory. Yet, although he took full advantage of technological innovation and was to commit himself to helping its victims as well as to rectifying the philosophical superficialities it engendered, Newman's ideas had not begun in contemplation of the scientific revolution taking place around him.

He came to prominence in Oxford as a young Anglican priest, a graduate of Trinity College and Fellow of Oriel, who took the faith of his Church very seriously and found it affronted in the compromising attitudes of many senior clergy. As preacher in the University Church of Saint Mary the Virgin, he developed a riveting style of quiet intensity which soon had the thoughtful and the curious crowding in for his four o'clock Sunday sermons. He spoke only of religious subjects, not of the controversies over the nature of the Church which engaged so much of his attention otherwise. He reminded them that all they knew of God, and the destiny to which they were called, came to them from Revelation, the Revelation which culminated in Jesus. Their religion was therefore God-made, not man-made. Christians who accepted it and lived by it admitted the Holy Spirit into their souls and this *in-dwelling* of the Spirit established the relationship with the Triune God which lay at the heart of the Church of Christ. It was a theme to which Newman would return again and again, for it led on to observations concerning the superiority of conscience (the voice of God) over reason (the voice of man), the deficiencies of 'private judgment' in matters on which God had provided a sure and certain guide, the absurdity of indifferentism which held contradictory beliefs to be each as worthy as the other.

Above all, it led Newman to question tendencies within his own Church. He greatly admired, for example, the Evangelical — 'low church' or Methodist — tradition because of the stress it put on revealed religion, on the Bible, the salvation purchased by Christ and personal conversion. But he found it fell short of the collective concept of Church. When articles of faith and the celebration of sacraments were played down, it seemed to him that religion became a matter of emotion and emotion was an uncertain yardstick in a world where people might easily suppose that they could reason their way to the truth. Newman feared that, instead of the truth, this could produce preening self-righteousness or the rejection of any belief that could not be sustained by logical proof: both, certainly, were attitudes characteristic of Victorian England and they coincided with an Evangelical revival, although others would have been slower than the young Oxford don to argue *post hoc, propter hoc.*

Be that as it may, he held ever more firmly to his understanding of Church as the Christ-given dispenser of sacrament — that is, the means by which Christ chose to remain with his people and to unite them through the Spirit with his Father. Faith therefore was not only from God but was , as it were, God-organised within the community of the 'people of God' (a now-familiar phrase which Newman liked to use). What was of faith was to be learned from the Church, which had long ago assembled its beliefs in the creeds and dogmas extracted from Divine Revelation. It followed that external interference with the Church could not be tolerated. In particular, it was not for the state to regulate the life of the Church and still less to regulate its doctrines. This put Newman on a collision course with many in the mainstream of the Church of England, the Church established by law in the Elizabethan settlement of Protestant-Catholic and Church-state controversy, a settlement considered reasonable, reverential and conducive to the good of the realm by generations of English Christians. Newman was not alone in deploring the intrusion of the state in the affairs of the Church and his name became associated with those of Keble and Pusey as a champion of the independence which they all held to be the Church's entitlement ... *God's* entitlement.

The outcome of the argument was the Oxford Movement, whose members were often called the Tractarians from the Tracts or monographs on theological subjects which they published to advance their cause. Because they went far beyond the Evangelical emphasis on religion as personal experience, because they placed only a limited value on 'private judgment', because they attached such importance to creed and dogma, and because they disapproved of the role exercised by government and parliament in regulating Church matters such as the boundaries of dioceses, the appointment of bishops and even the definition of belief, the Tractarians soon acquired the reputation of leaning towards Rome: a reputation which, in the England of their day and class earned them the kind of opprobrium directed a century later at persons suspected of fellow-travelling tendencies towards communism. Newman lost good friends as a result, friends who had helped shape his ideas as well as promote his rising star in Oxford. Dr Whately had made him Vice-Principal of Alban Hall, a minor Oxford 'house', equivalent to a college and since merged with a larger neighbour, and had fixed in his mind the impropriety of allowing politicians of all beliefs and none to have a say in running the Church. From Edward Hawkins, Provost of Oriel (elected over the head of Keble through Newman's influence with the younger Fellows), he learned to respect tradition, the instrument used by the Church to explain the message of the Bible. Both, with others he admired, were to be among Newman's most relentless critics.

The problem, as they saw it in their kinder moments (when not accusing Newman of lust for power or forming a clique), was that he refused to be satisfied with the plain meaning of an argument and had to trace it back through all its implications. It was not enough to agree that non-Anglican members of parliament should have no voice in the affairs of the established Church. Newman had to work his way through Revelation and the writings of the early Christian Fathers to demonstrate how the deposit of faith had been entrusted to the Church alone and that the Church *therefore* should be free from outside control, which implied that it should be treated neither as the creature nor the client of parliament. This was going too far for Whately, who saw no harm in a reasonable working relationship between Church and state (summed up in the idea of an established or state Church) which would make for order in society; the Church's job was to maintain decent standards rather than preach doctrine. Tradition for Newman had not merely to be acknowledged but had also to be identified. He asked himself how the Church's traditional teaching had emerged and by whom it had been stated. Such questioning and the immense scholarly research involved in seeking the answers proved to be Newman's path to Rome, which certainly had not been the direction in which Hawkins had intended to point him with the commonsense observation that the Bible needed to be interpreted if we were to arrive at a full appeciation of its riches and meaning.

It would probably be fair to say that, despite his innately English qualities of reserve, understatement and gentle self-mockery, Newman was quite unEnglish in his inclination to track down the ultimate reality behind every serious statement to which he committed himself and in the intensity of conviction which he so often voiced. To English ears this could sound extreme, even fanatical. It is unfashionable but salutary today to note the impressions of those who respected Newman without admiring him uncritically. Mark Pattison, an Oriel contemporary and a Tractarian for a time, deplored in retrospect that Newman had belonged to a coterie of 'narrow and desperate devotees of the clerical interest', while his Movement had 'desolated Oxford life, and suspended for an indefinite period, all science, humane letters, and the first strivings of intellectual freedom which had moved in the bosom of Oriel'.[19] He had been unable to read German and 'all the grand development of human reason, from Aristotle down to Hegel, was a sealed book to him'.[20]

Edward Whately, son of the Archbishop, recalled Newman's sermons in Saint Mary's. 'His countenance ... was calm, placid, and intellectual, and rather ascetic in its expression. But the calmness was of a peculiar sort, the calmness of suppression, the calmness of an earnest and inquiring mind, a mind which underneath that quiet exterior nourished a spirit seething with restless and agitating thoughts'.[21] In the pulpit 'there was something not only impressive but awe-striking in the perfect stillness of his body (a stillness which might be felt), and his calm, unimpassioned voice, which seemed to cut the very air with its sweet and clear tones', but 'the matter of his discourses was little calculated to communicate peace to those who heard them, and certainly did not proceed from one who was himself at rest ...'[22] A hundred years later the Professor of Modern History at Oxford could find 'something feverish, a touch of absurdity' in the anxiety of the Tractarians, who 'knew little of the world to which their teaching was addressed'.[23] That teaching 'appeared to be an unnecessary assertion of clerical authority' and was 'set out in words which offended every section of church opinion'.[24]

Against such judgements, contemporary and subsequent, can of course be set the multifarious testimony of those who were moved, inspired, persuaded by Newman's eloquence and the vision of the Oxford Movement to change their lifestyles or beliefs. The numbers who followed him to Rome speak for themselves. It remains important to savour the distaste which Newman could, and still can, arouse across a segment of fair-minded English opinion. It was a Frenchman who said 'surtout, pas de zèle', but it is the English who have most consistently held back from excessive enthusiasm in the world of ideas or ideology, from pressing arguments beyond the point of reasonably wide acceptance. They will tell you that for centuries this kept the country at peace and spared it the bitter internecine conflicts of peoples elsewhere more passionately wedded to a creed, a political system or a social doctrine. Hence the ingrained suspicion of what is deemed narrow-minded because it excludes other viewpoints or fanatical because it is urged with an intense conviction of its importance. Newman accordingly found himself at odds not only with those who disputed his opinions but also with many who found his approach to be alien, out of step with the mood of the country ... and the age.

The age of science, progress, steam, made for a tolerance of new and different ideas since nobody could tell what exciting fresh discovery lay around the corner that would require a revision of old assumptions. This reinforced the natural English tendency to steer clear of attitudes vehemently advocated. Particularly disliked, as tyrannical and obscurantist, was any attitude which challenged the liberal values of the scientific age. It heightened the popular abhorrence for the Church of Rome since Rome had refused to fall in with current intellectual fashion, to pay obeisance to, or even show respect for, technological innovation. No railways in the Papal States! But Newman was unable to temporise. The truth as he perceived it had to be followed wherever it led. Inexorably it led him towards Rome. The deeper he delved into the history of the early Church, and of the controversies surrounding the Arian and Donatist heresies, the more he saw the vaunted *via media* of the Church of England — the national doctrine of a tolerant and wide-embracing middle ground — as compromise with untruth corresponding to the compromises by which leading minds of the early Church had sought to placate the heretics. Twice what he called a ghost came to haunt him out of the ancient and forgotten story, the vision of Rome standing its ground against compromising the truth, as he believed it to be standing now.

In 1845 he became a Roman Catholic, as also did a number of the young Anglicans who had for years been following his lead within the Oxford Movement and more recently living with him as a quasi-monastic community at Littlemore near Oxford. Despite their companionship, it was a lonely step for Newman, since it meant parting company with the mainstream of English intellectual life, the finest and some of the holiest minds of the English Church, the normal instincts of the English people and the optimistic temper of Victorian England. It pained him deeply to be thus separated from his roots and he had tried in some desperation to avoid the decision: as when, in the famous Tract 90, he attempted to prove the catholicity of the Church of England in a thesis more extreme than the Anglican bishops could accept, and when, later, he pointed to what he argued were corruptions which Rome had allowed to accrue in its faith and practice. None of this could prevail in the end against the weight of evidence which for him was irresistibly persuasive but if we would understand him, and especially understand the frustrations yet to come (not least in Ireland), we must never forget the isolation which was the first consequence of conversion and was to remain with him for many years.

The culture of his upbringing and his prime imbued him too deeply for him ever to be totally at home in the company of 'born Catholics', while his age (he was now in his mid-forties) inhibited him from indulging in the 'born again' ecstacies of the younger converts like Faber and Ward, whose Catholicism was more heady, romantic and medieval than Catholics who had grown up in the Church could always stomach. In 1845 he had known few Catholics at all and none intimately. With the exceptions of Nicholas Wiseman, soon to be Cardinal of Westminster, and Charles William Russell of Maynooth, no Catholic had contributed to the profound research and meditation through which he arrived at his decision to convert. Essentially, he thought and prayed his way into the Catholic Church. He had not been drawn to it by anything he perceived in the behaviour or pronouncements of the general body of Catholics in England. Perhaps most trying for Newman was the absence from nineteenth-century English Catholicism of any strong theological tradition, or indeed any intellectual tradition at all. To a greater degree than he acknowledged, he was a scholar with nobody to talk to.

Perhaps it was this many-faceted isolation which impelled him to construct a home as personally congenial as he could contrive. It made the establishment of the Birmingham Oratory attractive, since he could retain a modicum (and he needed little) of personal possessions. He could assemble a community of companions to whom he felt attuned ... and, indeed, nudge away those whom he found overpowering (the London Oratory was to be the result). But it also cocooned him more than somewhat from his new community of faith, for the Fathers of the Oratory were all converts like himself, apart from the grandly named John Stanislas Woulfe Flanagan — an Irish 'cradle-Catholic' destined to leave Birmingham in the 1860s and become Dean of Limerick as well as parish priest of Adare — whose presence was hardly enough to prevent the Oratory from being Littlemore under a new allegiance. By the same instinct, when the Catholic University was set up in Dublin Newman looked for a house to share with English students and staff, insulating himself again from the world in which he had chosen to work. So far from disparaging his desire to live among those with whom he felt rapport, we should sympathise with the wider loneliness to which it pointed and which it helped to mitigate. None the less, it meant that Newman in the Catholic Church and Newman in Catholic Ireland always stood a little apart from the other protagonists in a common enterprise. And that did not always make for mutual understanding.

A problem of comprehension which would dog his heels for many years after he had been ordained a Catholic priest and had founded his Oratory concerned his stance vis-à-vis the liberal mind of the nineteenth century. As an Anglican he had firmly and repeatedly denounced that liberalism which he defined as 'the anti-dogmatic principle'.[25] No truths were held in this theory — or, rather, this attitude of mind — to be final and absolute, since all or any might be overturned by some new concept. The truths of Revelation accordingly were thrown open to human questioning. For Newman that was blasphemy to be resisted and rejected whenever it was put forward or when further theories, such as the need for scientific proof of anything asserted as fact, were built upon the liberal principle. Revelation was neither to be proved nor disproved. It was simply to be accepted. To nineteenth-century listeners, including many Anglican and Protestant listeners, his statement of faith was deplorably rigid, anachronistic, reactionary. Newman was judged to be an illiberal conservative of the deepest dye. Yet within a few years of his conversion to Catholicism many Catholics, ranging from officials in the Roman Curia to a number of English converts, were to look on him as a dangerous liberal cuckoo who had taken up residence in the Catholic nest. Newman himself found this reversal of his image difficult to understand since his views on Revelation, faith, Church and other essentials had undergone little or no change.

The trouble lay not so much in the differences of emphasis between nineteenth century Protestantism and Catholicism as in the finely-honed precision of Newman's thinking. When he saw

Revelation as the word of God, neither to be added to nor cut down and certainly not to be judged, he meant exactly that ... and no more than that. Specifically, he did not mean that the Bible was to be understood literally (he had no difficulty, for example, in accepting the archetypical nineteenth-century theory of evolution) nor did he mean that the Church, as custodian of God's revealed religion, could not vary the words it used and the concepts it invoked according as the historical context altered. What was *revealed* could not be *changed*, or accepted provisionally, to fit in with the temper of an age but each age had its own needs, as also did each person, and so different aspects of unchangeable Revelation had to be stressed to serve different wants of the human condition. As Newman put it in one of his Oxford sermons, 'The most winning property of our Saviour's mercy ... is its dependence on time and place, person and circumstance; in other words its tender discrimination. It regards and consults for each individual as he comes before it.'[26]

And more than that. The *meaning* of a revealed truth might have to be elucidated. The Church might have to contemplate, discuss and pronounce. As it did this through history, doctrine *developed*, flowering out to a broader and deeper meaning than had first been apparent. Newman saw it therefore as natural that the Church of his day had a larger body of teaching to propose than the early Church and that the meaning of what it taught had been more extensively elaborated. For Newman, the Church lived in history and grew with it, ever faithful to the original message it had been given to transmit but ever ready to meditate and mediate that message in the light of changing circumstances — and not hesitating, if appropriate, to absorb ideas wherever they had arisen if they illuminated the truth: Newman was always willing to admit that aspects of the truth might be more clearly appreciated and expressed outside the Church than within it: he would speak in Dublin, for example, of the possibility that Protestants might instruct Catholics in the correct principles of education. *Possession* of the truth did not guarantee automatic *perception* of it and a Church living in history could learn from the historical circumstances in which it lived.

Here was effected a junction between Newman and the liberal Catholics of Europe. Just as much as Newman, they rejected those liberal attitudes which implied indifferentism: the theory that one religion was as good as another, that the only knowable truth was provable truth, that man was sufficient to himself. Rosmini distinguished sharply between political liberalism, which he favoured, and the superficial approach in religion which tried to replace Revelation with subjective reasoning. Montalembert insisted that 'the more one is a democrat the more it is necessary to be Christian because the fervent and practical cult of God made man is the indispensable counter-weight of that perpetual tendency of democracy to establish the cult of man believing himself God.'[27] But these Catholics stood for *liberty*, freedom from coercion in matters of conscientious belief, seeing it as a right pertaining to man because of his God-given personal dignity. They took the concept from the revolutions in America and France but underscored its conformity with Revelation. As Montalembert said of Lacordaire's approach to contemporary ideas, 'he never pretended to discover new truths, he never sacrificed an old truth, but he took hold of these ideas and made them Christian, in order to reconcile the aspirations of the day with the Gospel.'[28]

The distillation of truth by the liberal Catholics from the amalgam of truth and falsehood in the world evolving around them so attracted Newman that he went out of his way to explain a problem which he had with the word 'liberal' itself. '. . . such great Catholics and distinguished writers as Count Montalembert and Father Lacordaire use the word in a favourable sense, and claim to be Liberals themselves', he wrote. 'I do not believe it is possible for me to differ in any important matter from two men whom I so highly admire. In their general line of thought and conduct I enthusiastically concur. ... If I hesitate to adopt their language about Liberalism, I impute the necessity of such hesitation to some difference between us in the use of words or in the circumstances of country.'[29]

Elsewhere he suggested that the only real difference between Lacordaire and himself was that they had different inheritances from history to interpret, the recent history of France being quite different from the recent history of England. That remark in turn brings us almost full circle to the relevance or otherwise of Newman's thought to the Railway Age. It was in fact highly *contemporary* thought at all times, in the sense that it was a commentary upon contemporary attitudes. It belonged to another era only in the sense that Newman drew his lessons from eternal verities which he judged true for every age and he illustrated them from a fourth-century debate if that happened to make the point most effectively.

Embattled Rome looked with great suspicion on all that

smacked of contemporaneity, seeing the falsehood in it rather than the truth, and on all that it judged to be tainted with liberal values, whether these were anti-clerical, indifferentist or actually directed towards the good of the Church. Lacordaire struck a totally Newmanesque note when he said 'Nothing is new, but as the point of view is different things can be seen from another angle.'[30] When Montalembert saw advantage in the liberal doctrine of 'a free Church in a free State',[31] he sought what Newman had asserted on behalf of the Church of England and would defend for the Church of Rome. Rome, sadly, could not in those days accommodate new angles and it distinguished freedom for itself in a Protestant state from the refusal of a Catholic state to enter into alliance with the Church. Thus the Church which welcomed Newman into its fold as the champion of tradition, of permanent attitudes unchanged and unchanging, became unsure and wary of him as it discovered his commitment to the development of doctrine and, later, to the role of the laity in promoting such development. In Dublin he would much rely on all this to elaborate his theory of knowledge — *liberal* knowledge — as its own end and to press his insistent pleas for lay involvement in the affairs of the University. But, in 1850, these matters lay in the future.

One matter lay in the past and should be noted as a gloss on Newman's openness to the age. 'I had an unspeakable aversion to the policy and acts of Mr O'Connell', he confessed later, 'because, as I thought, he associated himself with men of all religions and no religion against the Anglican Church, and advanced Catholicism by violence and intrigue.'[32] Newman had no knowledge of Ireland during O'Connell's lifetime. His antipathy reflected the general but mistaken assessment by the English ruling class of speeches made in unavoidably demagogic terms to 'a roaring multitude of disinherited peasants, met on some windy hill' — to borrow Tom Kettle's graphic phrase on the means by which O'Connell 'shouted slaves into the status of manhood'.[33] O'Connell, of course, eschewed violence. The only time when it might have been said that he acted against the Anglican Church was when he sought the abolition of tithes, and that was a question of equity, not of preference for one religion over another. If he 'intrigued' and associated with people whose opinions Newman rejected, this was no more than to say he was a politician who made legitimate use of the parliamentary system to advance his cause in an unsympathetic forum. That cause, foreshadowing our modern concept of human rights and the freedom of the citizen, was prophetic and seen to be so by the liberal Catholics of Europe, whom Newman so admired. In the end, O'Connell's sin was probably his regard for Bentham, whose utilitarian philosophy Newman detested. The Irish Liberator saw the good in it without permitting it to dilute his own principles, religious or political. In that, he revealed a broader mind and more balanced judgment than the distinguished Fellow of Oriel and Vicar of Saint Mary's.

2

'A few lectures on education'

Paul Cullen was in a hurry. The divisions among the Irish bishops scandalised him. The persistence of Archbishop Murray and his friends in continuing to support the Queen's Colleges when Rome had expressed such grave doubts about them shocked him deeply. He determined to restore peace to the hierarchy and to inculcate a due submissiveness towards the Supreme Pontiff with the least delay. He came equipped not only with his Primatial office as Archbishop of Armagh but also as Apostolic Delegate, representing the authority of the Holy See and empowered to summon a National Synod at which the matters in contention could — theoretically — be resolved. Archbishop MacHale, the Lion of the West, rejoiced, believing he had acquired a powerful ally against the compromising stance of those churchmen who did not share his own suspicions of the British administration. Cullen drew no comfort from his initial meetings with Murray: the old man told him plainly that he favoured the Colleges and could not change his opinion. When he sent copies of a letter from the Cardinal Prefect of Propaganda to the Bishops of Cork and Galway banning the clergy, and discouraging the laity, from involvement with the Queen's Colleges in any capacity, Bishop Delany of Cork said he would obey but that he thought the letter 'most imprudent'.[1] Bishop O'Donnell of Galway acknowledged receiving the letter but said he would withhold his comment until the proposed Synod had assembled in Thurles. These and other reactions to Cullen's first moves confirmed him in his belief that the Irish Church had fallen into morose and incorrigible rebellion.

The judgement was excessive. A hint of paranoia comes through the Apostolic Delegate's private correspondence during those early months in Ireland between May and August 1850. The only way to deal with the Bishops of Cork and Galway would be 'to remove one of these Bishops and put an administrator in his place', wrote Cullen, adding 'one such step would re-establish things as they ought to be'.[2] He warned his successor as Rector of the Irish College that a representative of the Bishop of Galway might turn up in Rome and that the Secretary of Propaganda should be alerted to give him 'the reception he deserves'.[3] The

41

behaviour of these bishops left him in little doubt that there was not 'the least wish to obey the Pope's orders in these quarters'.[4] When the Synod met in August, Cullen got his way but only by a narrow margin. Propositions warning clergy and laity against the Colleges were carried by majorities of only fifteen or sixteen to thirteen or twelve. Cullen rushed his thoughts on to paper (in Italian): 'The Holy See must vindicate her authority, otherwise the faith is lost in Ireland.'[5] *The faith is lost?* All that Archbishop Murray had said in the Synod was that he did not wish to prevent young people from attending institutions which he considered good and useful, and that he believed the Pope did not understand the nature of the Colleges ... which was likely enough, since the Pope (for whom, read the Prefect of Propaganda) had been advised on the matter over the years by Dr Cullen, who lacked the day-to-day experience of coping with the problems of the post-penal Church which the Archbishop of Dublin had been handling for more than quarter of a century.

Cullen showed no capacity at the Synod or during its aftermath to *listen* to the case being made on the other side of the argument and supported by nearly half the Irish episcopate. The Roman Rescripts and the letter from Propaganda had been posited on the assumption that the Queen's Colleges constituted a hazard to the faith and morals of those who might frequent them. The Murrayites thought the hypothesis was unproven and unlikely to be true — a view which they were surely obliged, if they held it, to enunciate in the interest of Irish Catholics now being offered the opportunity of university education. They were in a better position than Cullen, with his arguments evolved in abstraction from the Irish reality, to put forward a practical opinion. The Rescripts were admonishments, inviting further comment, rather than directives closing discussion, and a letter from the prefect of a Roman Congregation scarcely carried the binding force of a papal decree. The provisional and limited nature of these documents is evident from the Roman refusal for months to reject the British government's plea, made through its unofficial diplomatic agents, that approval for the Synod decision on the Colleges should be withheld. For Cullen to make the issue a question of loyalty to the Holy See, and even a question of *faith*, and not at all to allow for reasonable discussion of pastoral needs, revealed the ultramontane mentality at its most obsessional.

This is not to say that there were no good arguments against the Colleges or that on balance Archbishop Murray had the better case. It is not to say that Cullen misrepresented the belief towards which the Holy See inclined. It simply shows that Cullen's style of leadership was regrettably dictatorial in a way which did offence to the authority of his brother bishops and the dignity of the Irish Church. More regrettably still, it did offence to justice since Cullen made free with words like 'Gallican' and 'Jansenist' to condemn his opponents.[6] Neither term was appropriate when speaking of Daniel Murray, who entered into no alliance of Throne and Altar and betrayed no hint of spiritual pride. He merely worked with difficulty within the political system of the day to achieve as much betterment as he could for the Catholics of Dublin and Ireland. For this he and his supporters were described by Cullen as 'Castle bishops'[7] (meaning that they were subservient to the British administration based in Dublin Castle) and their efforts after Thurles to explain both to Irish opinion and to the Roman Curia the situation as they saw it evoked a tirade from the Apostolic Delegate: 'They are determined not to yield an inch to the Synod of Thurles, nor to the Pope himself.... Is it not an awful thing to have the education of the Irish clergy depending on those men? They will make all Ireland Jansenistical in a dozen years. There is no way of removing them.'[8] As for the Archbishop of Dublin, he 'is so bound up with the Government that he will never oppose any project that emanates from that Government.'[9] Cullen delved deep for evidence. As late as 1852, he pointed to the report of what Murray and Bishop James Doyle of Kildare (long famous as 'JKL') had told the House of Commons commission which O'Connell had addressed in 1825: 'I never saw such a quantity of Gallicanism put together. It is astonishing that any Church could exist in which such doctrines are held. I dare say a great deal of our misfortunes have arisen from acting on and holding such doctrines.'[10] He directed the Vice-Rector of the Irish College to pass on 'a few abstracts from this examination'[11] to the Secretary of Propaganda.

Cullen's enormous influence at Rome, corroboration of which can be read in the hostile reports of British agents in Italy during the early 1850s, meant that his apoplectic comments prevailed over the attempts to defend themselves by Irish churchmen who had borne the heat of the day. His proposed remedy for the situation was adopted. It relied on *force majeure* instead of dialogue and persuasion. With no great subtlety he informed Cardinal Fransoni, Prefect of Propaganda, that 'The Archbishop of Dublin is already more than eighty-three years of age. The Bishop of Killaloe, who was the most furious defender of the Colleges, has dropsy, and it is believed that he will hardly survive Christmas. The Bishop of Dromore is totally deaf and is not fit to govern his diocese. The Bishops of Down and Connor and of Kerry are both very ill.'[12] So to an obvious suggestion: 'If the Sacred Congregation will take great care in the choice of new Bishops, within three years, the condition of things will be totally changed in Ireland.'[13] So it would happen, although more slowly and less smoothly than Cullen envisaged. The Murray tradition ran deeper and was held with more conscientious conviction than Cullen allowed for. John MacHale was observing events from his western fastness, happy to let the Apostolic Delegate make the running against those who would put too much trust in the English bearing gifts, but less sure as time went by about the dominance of Paul Cullen who seemed determined to make the bishops interpreters of Rome to Ireland rather than of Ireland to Rome — and inclined to present his own whims as the mind of the Holy Father, which it was treason to challenge.

Denigration of Cullen has become something of a stereotype in Irish historiography during the past thirty years and it would be refreshing to have a more sympathetic appraisal, based perhaps on his reform of inefficient administration and on the scholarship sustaining his theological opinions, however rigidly he held to them: in this he emerged the more balanced by contrast with Manning, as his willingness to vouch for Newman's orthodoxy at a critical moment would show as well as his stance on infallibility at Vatican I. Unfortunately, he stands so often condemned out of his own mouth, most of all by his wilful determination to crush the self-confident Irish Church of the earlier nineteenth century in favour of an alien model, that it is difficult to warm to him or to enthuse about his motives. His secretive nature makes his methods no more attractive: he rarely explained himself in public and it is only the availability of much of his correspondence today which enables judgements to be made about events which in the past engendered more puzzlement than understanding. His dedication to the good of the Church as he understood it need not be doubted. But MacHale, for all his obstructiveness, had a clear and consistent sense of a wrong direction taken. Newman came in time to understand that fruitful liaison was impossible with a man of narrow preconceptions who was slow to trust others, unwilling to confide, reluctant to delegate authority and absorbed in his own role as redefiner of Irish Catholicism. The University's fortunes would revolve around these tensions.

* * *

In 1847 Newman and his fellow-convert, Ambrose St John, went to Rome where they attended the College of Propaganda prior to their ordination as Roman Catholic priests. There can have been little enough in the way of theology for Newman to learn there, given not only his scholarly attainments but also his tortuously theological growth into Catholicism, but immersion in the manners and ethos of their new confession was clearly desirable and there is some evidence that the Englishmen attended lectures on Hebrew and Scripture given by Dr Cullen, then still Rector of the Irish College. Newman himself, however, would later recall that their first contact arose in Rome when he translated some of his own works into Latin and Cullen acted as official censor of the exercise. They seem to have impressed one another and Cullen must have been talking around about his famous acquaintance for as early as May 1847 Father Rosmini knew they had been in contact with one another and in a letter to Cullen he asked him to 'present my respects to Mr Newman'.[14] When Newman had returned to England and established the Birmingham Oratory, he needed help in Rome regarding a series of 'Lives of the Saints' which Faber was translating from Italian. He wrote to Cullen, who replied that he would 'always feel happy to execute any commission you may charge me with',[15] and this in spite of the many other matters occupying the Irish Rector's attention at a time when Rome was in the hands of the revolutionaries.

By 1850 Cullen was back in Ireland. Within two months he was writing to Newman again, inviting him to preach at the consecration of a new church in Killeavy, County Armagh. Newman was unable to come but it cannot be doubted that the rapport formed between the two in Rome survived. The next year Newman dedicated his lectures on the *Present Position of Catholics in England* to 'The Most Reverend Paul, Lord Archbishop of Armagh and Primate of All Ireland', referring *inter alia* to 'the honour of associating my name with that of your Grace, whose kindness I had already experienced so abundantly when I was at Rome in 1847.[16] These were the lectures in which Newman exposed the dissolute character of the former friar, Giacinto Achilli, who had become a Protestant and was giving anti-Catholic talks at various venues in England. A prosecution for criminal libel was brought against Newman, which could have resulted in a prison sentence. It was to cause him much worry over the greater part of two years. Cullen wrote to say that Irish Catholics would help him to pay any expenses that might be incurred. 'About the dedication of the book', he added, 'the very fact of your being prosecuted for exposing an imposter and telling the truth would make me more ready to accept the dedication.'[17]

By now the University project was under way. The passing references to a Catholic University in the Roman Rescripts against the Queen's Colleges had not at first received more than polite acknowledgment in Ireland. Ironically, in view of later events, the first positive step was taken by the bishops of the western province, meeting in Tuam. Led by Archbishop MacHale, they announced in 1849 their 'full concurrence'[18] with the Pope's proposal that a Catholic University should be established. They promised to raise subscriptions and engage the interest of people who would be in a position to help. A year later, at the beginning of 1850, a committee was formed to promote the University and raise money, pending the more detailed decisions which were expected from a forthcoming National Synod (which in the event became the Synod of Thurles). This shadowy preparatory group attracted criticism from Cullen who, even before he left Rome for Ireland, wrote to MacHale: 'I fear however that the committee now acting will do no good ... it may be discredited unless some of the first men in Ireland, lay and clerical, be induced to give their names ...'.[19] At Thurles a new committee was substituted which went far towards meeting Cullen's requirements. Its members were the four archbishops together with an additional bishop from each province as well as a priest and layman nominated by each of the episcopal members.

Although the laymen appointed to the University Committee tended to be landed gentry rather than the popular leaders whom the people preferred to follow after the exciting decades of O'Connell's political movement, they did include Charles Bianconi, the pioneer of road transport in Ireland, and Myles O'Reilly, a prominent propagandist for educational reform (who ten years later would command the papal garrison at Spoleto against the Garibaldian army). The acceptance of membership by

Archbishop Murray was considered to be a triumph of diplomacy on the part of Cullen since, quite apart from his views on the Queen's Colleges, the aged prelate had forcibly indicated his belief that a Catholic University was impracticable, if only because money on the scale needed to support it could not be found in the impoverished country. It may be assumed that Murray in fact joined the Committee as the best means of keeping himself informed about its activities. This he did through his nominee, William Meyler, dean and vicar-general of Dublin, since after the early meetings he no longer attended in person. He continued in his resistance, however, refusing to contribute to the project and disowning responsibility for a collection got up in his diocese. This drove Cullen to further indignant protests in his letters to Rome: 'There is a real conspiracy to render Protestant or unbelieving the education of the Catholic youth, and what is deplorable is that Catholic Bishops are among those who promote the views of our enemies. They are encouraging atheistic schools, and are themselves opposing an institution truly Catholic.'[20] He was a little calmer when he wrote to MacHale: 'Have you seen Dr Murray's letter of yesterday about the collection for the university? It is really provoking. However it is better to let him go on quietly to the end of his career which cannot now be far off.'[21] The thought may have been spurred by the death of the Bishop of Killaloe, 'the fiercest defender of the Queen's Colleges', according to Cullen, who hoped that 'God has forgiven him. His death is not a great loss to our Church.'[22] Soon Cullen was at work to ensure the appointment of a safe successor. The reconstitution of the little diocese of Ross enabled him also to strengthen the hierarchy in his favour.

Meanwhile, he had been persuaded that the prestige of the proposed University would be enhanced by associating it with the most famous name of all among English-speaking Catholics. It was apparently the convert lawyer and member of parliament, James Robert Hope (later Hope-Scott, after his wife had inherited the novelist's family home), who told Cullen, 'First get Newman.'[23] The advice was reinforced by Robert Whitty, a young priest from County Wexford who had been working among the emigrants in England and had spent some time at the Birmingham Oratory (he considered founding a second Oratory in London's East End, to the horror of Faber who advised Newman 'Don't go and take any more Irish, Padre ... abstain from Irishmen for ye rest of your life'[24]) before eventually joining the

Jesuits. What Whitty had in mind was that Cullen should invite Newman to Ireland for consultations on how to go about setting up the University, a subject on which the former Oxford don might be expected to have useful comments to offer. Whitty also recommended, after talking with Frederick Lucas, Editor of the *Tablet*, that Newman might be commissioned to deliver a course of lectures on the subject of education. Cullen lost no time in acting on these suggestions. On 15 April 1851 he wrote to Newman telling him that a successful collection had been undertaken 'for the purpose of establishing a Catholic university in Ireland'. His advice on the selection of 'a fit and proper superior' for the institution would be much valued, as well as any thoughts he might have about the appointment of a vice-president and professors. Should Newman be coming to Dublin, it would be 'most useful' if he could attend a meeting of the Committee. The letter ended with a by-the-way afterthought, 'Indeed if you could spare time to give us a few lectures on education you would be rendering good service to religion in Ireland.'[25] Rarely can a great work of literature and philosophy have been set in motion with so light an impetus!

Newman did not rush to commit himself. The request had come at a busy and anxious time. 'No Popery' agitation had been bubbling in England since the previous autumn following the re-establishment of the Catholic hierarchy. Newman was involved on the one hand in receiving new converts into the Church — including all the Anglican clergy of a Leeds parish in April — while fending off the worst kind of anti-Catholic bigotry on the other. For the latter purpose he was preparing his lectures on 'The Present Position of Catholics', to be delivered weekly from June to September. He was supervising the construction of the Oratory's new house in the Edgbaston district of Birmingham and, of course, was all the time instructing, confessing and tending to the wants of the Birmingham poor. Neither travelling to Ireland nor composing yet another lecture series were attractive proposals. The chore of composition was always a burden to Newman. The previous year, when preparing some talks at the request of Cardinal Wiseman, he groaned to one correspondent 'I am writing them intellectually against the grain more than I ever recollect doing anything',[26] and he remarked to another, 'I cannot convey the misery it is to me.'[27] And about the time he heard from Cullen he was appealing to a friend, 'Let no one suppose that my books do not cost me labour — they are as severe a trial as hedging or ditching.'[28] He also felt an obligation in conscience to avoid undue distraction from his responsibilities as paterfamilias of his community and the duties binding on him under the Rule of his Congregation — which did not envisage constant travel or the administration of institutions in no way associated with the Oratory. Yet he could not but be interested in the news from Ireland and Whitty confessed in old age that he had rightly calculated 'the weight of a Bishop's word'[29] with Newman.

So it happened that in July the Irish Primate twice visited the Oratory in Birmingham, first en route to a meeting in London where he was to discuss the University project with Hope and other prominent English Catholics (including the recently converted Henry Manning), and on the way home to persuade Newman to be Rector of the Catholic University, as the London meeting had agreed he should be. Newman wriggled. The post seemed to be incompatible with his Oratorian vocation. Perhaps he could be Prefect of Studies, 'a temporary office' and purely functional without the symbolic implications of the Rectorship, which would be 'almost identified with the University itself'?[30]

He sought time to look for his friends' advice. Hope and the Oratorians urged him to accept the offer: the success of the University depended on the status of the people associated with it; it *needed* Newman. The pressure must have become intense for the day after Cullen's second visit Newman wrote to the widow of an Oxford acquaintance: 'I am quite overpowered with work. Here is the Catholic University which, of all things, I wish to help ... I physically cannot, till these lectures are done.'[31] He could not hurry the lectures, he said, explaining with another of his railway metaphors, 'it would be like attempting to run 50 miles an hour on the narrow gauge'.[32]

Within a week Cullen was writing again, promising to send 'the observations on our university which I mentioned'[33] and enclosing a gift of money to be used for the Oratory in any way Newman wished. Before the month was out the University Committee had addressed an appeal to the clergy and laity of England, pointing out what would certainly have enthused Newman and was to be a major factor in his understanding of the project in the future: 'The university is destined for the benefit not merely of the Catholics of Ireland but those of the empire.'[34] Cullen must have stressed the point on his first visit to Birmingham if we are to make sense of Newman's note at the time, 'there is no doubt [the

Primate] feels Dublin to be the place; and it is now only a few hours from England, from London'[35] — like so much else, the character of the Catholic University would be shaped by the Age of Steam. In August Dr Patrick Leahy, President of the diocesan college in Thurles, arrived with Myles O'Reilly in Birmingham on behalf of the Committee to discuss with Newman how best to organise the establishment of the University: all three had been appointed as a sub-committee to report on what should be done and were empowered to consult a number of authorities, among them Manning, Doellinger in Munich and the Rector Magnificus of Louvain. Whether Newman knew in advance how far he was being drawn into the activities of the Committee is unclear (Cullen did not mention it in a letter asking him 'to devote a little time'[36] to the two-man delegation) but he now began to yield to the importuning and arranged to travel to Ireland.

As companions he brought with him Stuart Bathurst, a sickly young Oratorian who, he hoped, might benefit from a holiday, and Thomas William Allies, an Oxford convert who was to make several appearances in the story of the Catholic University. After a rough passage, during which a bottle of medicine spilt in his suitcase 'making everything very sticky',[37] Newman arrived in Thurles on 1 October to stay with Dr Leahy. O'Reilly joined them and the trio set about drafting their report. Then Newman went on to Drogheda to discuss the draft with Cullen (Drogheda being at that time the residence of the Archbishop of Armagh), paid courtesy calls to Maynooth and All Hallows — the Dublin college where priests were trained for pastoral work in England and other foreign countries — and met Lucas, the editor of the *Tablet*, with his assistant, Robert Ornsby, before returning to Birmingham on 8 October. Only the railway, we may surmise, made it possible to fit so much into a hectic week.

The result was a report giving the first clear picture of the Catholic University as it might be: its curriculum, its teaching methods, its institutional structure. This was badly needed. The concept of a Catholic University had arrived in Ireland unheralded, unasked for and virtually unexplained in the papal rescripts on the Queen's Colleges. Until then Catholics had sought equal treatment with Protestants in the matter of university education. This at first meant access to Trinity College. When that was conceded, equality came to mean freedom from a system too closely associated with the established Church. The argument then turned on the adequacy of the colleges offered by the government, the extent to which the Catholic authorities might have a voice in the appointment of professors and, of course, the place of religion in the curriculum. When Rome recommended that the bishops should establish a Catholic University nobody quite knew what it meant. The example of Louvain, quoted by Rome, was remote from Irish circumstances, actual or potential. Although only recently reconstituted, Louvain had an ancient tradition, altogether lacking in Ireland, and buildings ready for it to occupy as soon as it had been re-established. Although administered under the authority of the Belgian bishops, it was knit into the state's higher education system (students sat for state as well as university examinations) and, most importantly, it could confer degrees. The prerequisite for such a happy arrangement in Ireland was precisely what had made it possible in Belgium: a successful nationalist revolution with religious freedom written large on its manifesto! This reality of the Belgian situation must have escaped the notice of Archbishop Cullen or he would surely have been a little more cautious in adopting the Roman predilection for Louvain.

Future events would show that Cullen himself had difficulty in imagining a university as anything other than the papal institutions which he knew in Rome ... universities in the content of their teaching but major seminaries in their administration and discipline. In fairness, it should be said that he seems to have sensed his lack of experience. He looked to his advisers, Newman especially, to define what a university should do and how it should go about its business. He limited his own public pronouncements to comments negative or hortatory — negative in rejecting the Queen's Colleges root and branch, hortatory in proclaiming the need to protect Catholic youth from the indifferentist ideas in circulation and to equip them to combat these ideas wherever they might meet them. In a letter to a town councillor of Drogheda who had sought his guidance, Cullen explained why he thought that only a Catholic education would produce such stalwart defenders of the faith. 'There is indeed a sort of knowledge not encouraged by our Church, a knowledge without religion…. The effects of knowledge of this kind can be easily traced in the history of Europe during the past eighty years. Its fruits have been sedition, rebellion, immorality, impiety or at least an indifference to every sort of religion.'[38]

The accent of the Roman ultramontane is easily detected in the *post hoc, propter hoc* reasoning, and not least in the illustration he went on to give of what he meant by 'the effects of knowledge of this kind': within the previous twenty years, he said, 'the occupier of the throne of France and his ministers became its patronisers in their university system and though that system was altogether under their control, yet they fell victims to the wicked spirit which their favoured godless education called into existence and nurtured.'[39] In other words, Louis-Philippe was overthrown in a revolution engendered by men educated in his 'godless' system. It was a strangely blinkered assessment on several levels. Under the Restoration Bourbons, the University (there was in fact only one institution, to which all French secular colleges were affiliated) had close links with the Church. This did little for the faith of its students: in an 1827 debate the motion 'That God Exists' was approved by a majority of only a single vote. As for Louis-Philippe's ministers, the most famous of them was the Protestant Guizot who was strongly of the conviction that education should be based on religion. And if it was the graduates of the godless University who overthrew the king, it was the Republic which they established that sent an army to Italy to restore Rome to the Pope and the Pope to Rome ... as Cullen saw at first hand. It was also, incidentally, the same Republic which restored Church representation on the governing body of the University and facilitated access to degrees by students attending Church-controlled colleges.

Once again, let the atmosphere of the 1850s be recalled. The siege mentality of Rome had hardened not out of bigotry but under the ceaseless barrage of insults directed against traditional religion in general, and the Roman Church in particular, by the devotees of deified reason, science, democracy and nationalism, in country after country. Painfully in our ecumenical times, it must be recalled that Evangelical Protestantism in its various manifestations from fundamentalist sects to a major segment of the Anglican Church coasted easily on this wave, as Newman had foreseen would happen when religion became more an emotional instinct than commitment to articles of faith, assembled in a creed and understood through the collective wisdom of believers guided by the authority of the Church. It was the heyday of Maria Monk, of whom Newman made much fun in his lectures on the 'Present Position' but whose fictional tribulations at the hands of sadistic and superstitious Roman clerics were widely thought typical. This prejudice infiltrated British politics, where it took a virulent form during the 'No Popery' agitation following

the restoration of the Catholic hierarchy in England and Wales
— a development which coincided with the aftermath of the
Synod of Thurles and the first public moves to promote the
Catholic University. The same mentality had been evident in
Ireland in the evangelising efforts of Protestant sects (naturally
described as proselytising on the Catholic side) in the years just
before and during the Famine.

Paul Cullen saw Europe and Ireland all of a piece, all threatened
by the evil of infidelity unchained to which the Church of Christ
could yield no jot of its belief or its authority. Hence his lack of
interest in the details of current affairs in liberal France, his
conviction of his own righteousness so that an Irish bishop who
had opposed him was assumed to stand in need of God's
forgiveness, and his reluctance to relinquish control (even to
fellow-bishops, let alone to Dr Newman or to the laity) of
whatever pertained to the good of the Church. He was an
embattled pastor, commissioned as Apostolic Delegate to rally
the Irish Church to the vanguard of the Church Universal in its
travail. Given the attitudes shaped by his long residence in Rome,
nothing he found in Ireland was, humanly speaking, likely to alter
his outlook. Historical hindsight should not deny him the right
to be understood. Neither, though, should the narrowness of his
vision, his inclination to be ruled by his preconceptions and his
suspicious nature be forgotten. In the long run, they hindered
Newman greatly. But at first they seemed to sustain certain basic
norms to which Newman attached much importance.

Newman in fact brought preconceptions of his own to Ireland
and some of these were more narrowly based than Cullen's for
they grew out of the incestuous controversies of mid-nineteenth-
century Oxford, a smaller, more inturned and frenetically
disputatious city than Rome. The knowledge that Whately was
in Dublin — in propria persona, as Newman put it[40] — revived the
memory of battles in Oxford over the independence of the Church
and the place of religion in higher education. As a young don
he had looked with disfavour on any attempt to dilute the intimate
relationship between the ancient university and the Church of
England. His motive was not bigotry but that same abhorrence
of indifferentism which he would show as a Catholic: a university,
dedicated to truth could not accept the proposition that one
religion was as good as another. Nor was his position political.
He had strong pastoral instincts. On his ordination as an Anglican
deacon, he wrote 'I have the responsibility of souls on me to the

end of my days.'[41] He insisted that a tutor should be concerned
for his pupils' religious formation and should make them aware
of the religious dimension in what they learned and how they
lived. Broad churchmen like Whately saw only a kind of
reactionary medievalism in this and assumed it to be a clever ruse
to create the nucleus of a party through which Newman and his
friends might advance their ambitions. Friendships became
strained and mutual antagonism evolved which would eventually
be subsumed in the tension churned up by the Oxford Movement.

With a sense of *déjà vu*, Newman detected the selfsame
arguments at stake in the Irish situation, with the Queen's
Colleges and their apologists in the role of the Broad Church
modernisers and the Catholic University embodying the concept
of religious-based education. It elated him, for he felt that he had
now acquired a powerful ally. 'The battle there will be what it
was in Oxford twenty years ago', he wrote after his first visit to
Ireland, and 'while I found my tools breaking under me in
Oxford, for Protestantism is not susceptible of so high a temper,
I am renewing the struggle in Dublin with the Catholic Church
to support me. It is very wonderful ....'[42] It was also slightly
ludicrous to suppose any analogy between the pragmatic policies
of Archbishop Murray, struggling to improve the opportunities
open to his people, and Senior Common Room theorising by
privileged academics which went almost unnoticed in the world
outside. The one feature in Ireland which corresponded to the
Oxford story was the proposal by the State yet again to make
dispositions regarding the Church — Newman's old *bête noire* —
and the most radically different feature was the independent
stance of Archbishop Cullen — and, indeed, of the Pope himself
— which effectively endorsed Newman's strongly-held beliefs.
Small wonder that he faced the renewed fight with enthusiasm.

The report on organisation drafted by the sub-committee while
Newman was in Ireland brought together elements from the
Oxford system, from Louvain and from Newman's own priorities.
The document amounted to an embryonic constitution for the
University and a key clause read: 'As all academic instruction
must be in harmony with the Principles of the Catholic Religion,
the Professors will be bound, not only not to teach anything
contrary to religion, but to take advantage of the occasion the
subjects they treat of may offer, to point out that Religion is the
basis of Science, and to inculcate the love of Religion and its
duties.'[43] Here at a stroke was the Oxford argument resolved in

54

Newman's favour. From Louvain, where a model familiar in European universities since the Middle Ages had been recreated, came the broad division of the curriculum: a general faculty of arts which all students would enter, together with higher faculties of law, medicine and theology to which those who wished might proceed if they did not want to persevere in senior arts grades. In Dublin, arts would cover 'letters' and 'science', the first embracing classical and modern languages, history, archaeology and English literature; 'science' would include philosophy in its various branches, natural philosophy (i.e. physics), chemistry, mathematics, geology and other subjects as the opportunity might arise to incorporate them. There would also be a school of engineering within the faculty of arts. It was envisaged that the University could be inaugurated on the basis of this arts faculty, with the higher faculties being added later.

For its day, and certainly by comparison with Oxford and Cambridge, the range of subjects to be offered was remarkably wide and, although the inculcation of knowledge as its own end (as Newman would soon be defining it) clearly took pride of place in the scheme, the provision of practical learning directed towards functional ends was not omitted. If the plan could be carried out, it would produce a university conforming to the traditional pattern of faculties, specifically Catholic in its ethos and incorporating those areas of knowledge most relevant to the contemporary world of scientific progress. Teaching would be consigned to professors (an important distinction would later be made between professors and lecturers), with a tutorial system (as at Oxford) to ensure individual attention for the students, and the whole would be under the direction of a rector to be nominated by the Catholic hierarchy. Deans of faculties, deans of discipline, a Rectorial Council and an Academic Senate were provided for to discharge specific functions. The University would be residential and the sub-committee recommended that scholarships be made available so that 'meritorious' children of poor families might have the opportunity to attend.

The Committee adopted the Report on 12 November 1851, and resolved to invite Dr Newman to accept the Presidency (in effect, the Rectorship) of the University. The bishop-members, on behalf of the hierarchy who had the right of appointment, passed a similar resolution. Cullen, as chairman of the Committee, wrote to Newman, offering a salary of £400 a year and a residence, and added that 'No other appointment was made; as the selection of other persons is to be made with the concurrence or on the recommendation of the President.'[44] Newman hastened to accept. It seemed to be the sole item of good news in a winter of anxiety. By coincidence, bouts of illness had smitten several of the Oratorians simultaneously so that Newman, already fatigued by the exertions of the summer and the journey to Ireland, had to undertake more parish work and more time in the confessional. By the end of October he was attending a London specialist himself and after Christmas he had to turn to the problems of the London Oratory which was simmering on the edge of revolt over the eccentricities of Father Faber.

Meanwhile, Achilli had launched the prosecution proceedings against Newman for criminal libel on 5 November. Newman's legal advisers could offer him little hope since neither Cardinal Wiseman nor the authorities in Rome, from whom he had sought documents that would help his case, had exerted themselves. On the 21st came the preliminary hearing, when the case was sent for trial. A lawyer friend told Newman that he would get a year in prison. Friends had now to be dispatched to the continent in search of witnesses who would testify to the dissolute life led by Achilli: a fact essential to Newman's defence. The superhuman effort required to process intellectual work with the worry of the pending trial ever-present can be imagined, and a year would pass before the burden was lifted from him. Ireland was to make major demands on Newman in that harrowing twelve months, although it must also be said that few aspects of the Achilli affair brought him such consolation as the subscriptions to the fund set up for his defence which poured in from Irish sources, and not least from the Irish poor. In this Archbishop Cullen was a prime mover ... and a true friend.

Cullen now faced the difficulty of proceeding with the University in the face of Murray's opposition. This was a practical matter, since everybody was agreed the the new institution would have to be sited in Dublin. How was this to be done without the active approval of the city's archbishop? For the moment progress was delayed. The dilemma disappeared with the death of Murray on 24 February 1852, and the transfer of Cullen from Armagh to succeed him two months later. This transpired not to be quite the dramatic reversal of fortune which the supporters of the University or the more ultramontane among the Irish clergy may have expected. Murray had represented a widely-shared attitude in the country which would survive him for years to come and

MacHale, for quite other reasons, was beginning to doubt that he had much in common with the Apostolic Delegate. In the short term, however, Cullen found his path much smoother and saw at least one of his cherished hopes come to fruition. Despite his many troubles and commitments, Newman had found time to block out his line of argument for the 'few lectures on education' which he had been asked to give and, with his trial put off until June, he set out for Dublin on 7 May.

He knew clearly enough what was expected of him. Cullen had spelt it out in a letter the previous September. 'What we want in Ireland', he wrote, 'is to persuade the people that education should be religious. The whole tendency of our new systems is to make it believed that education may be so conducted as to have nothing at all to do with religion. Moral philosophy, law, history are proposed to be taught in this way. The project is in itself absurd and impossible, but it is necessary to instruct us a little upon the matter. To do so however I suppose the whole question of education should be reviewed.' He then suggested some of the subjects which might be dealt with: 'the advantages of educating the people and the sort of education they ought to receive; mixed education; examination of the education given to Catholics in Trinity College and its effects; education in the Queen's Colleges, or education without any religion; the sort of education which Catholics ought to seek for.'[45] Apart from *naming* TCD and the Queen's Colleges as little as possible (no doubt a judicious decision), Newman was to follow this brief very closely indeed. His major emphases would be on the place of religion in education and the value of education in its own right. He would consider these questions in the context of universities of various kinds and of various theories concerning what could or should be taught. While he prepared the ground with great care, seeking advice on Irish attitudes from English friends living in the country so that he might temper his approach to the likely mood of his audience, and while he drew richly on the opinions he had formed long before in Oxford, the parameters of his Dublin Discourses were those drafted in broad outline by Archbishop Cullen. Cullen did more than commission the 'few lectures'. He was also progenitor of their content.

Hearing that it would be better not to give the impression that the University might be dominated by Englishmen, Newman decided against staying with his friend, the convert clergyman Henry Wilberforce, who was living in Kingstown, and he took

57

lodgings instead in Dorset Street, stipulating only that he should have 'a low iron bed with a single hard mattress' which he could make himself.[46] As a final check he discussed his theme in detail with the future Bishop of Kerry, Dr David Moriarty, then President of All Hallows, and on Monday afternoon, 10 May, went down to the Assembly Rooms of the Rotunda Hospital to deliver the first of his *Discourses on the Scope and Nature of University Education*, which were destined to secure a permanent place in English literature — after much editing — under the title *The Idea of a University*. Awaiting him in the small room beneath what is now the Gate Theatre were some 400 people — 'all the intellect, almost, of Dublin', according to James Duffy, his publisher, '... thirteen Trinity Fellows etc., eight Jesuits, a great many clergy, and the most intense attention.'[47] What he had to say was very well received and not least by the champions of the Queen's Colleges, whom he calculated would have to be led along by courteous argument. He continued his *tour de force* for four Mondays more, with the same success, until he had to return to England. The remaining lectures were published, but not delivered, at intervals over the following months.

*   *   *

Newman himself believed that his argument in the Discourses could only be understood as a unified concept. You could not accept it in part and reject the rest. To appreciate his case, therefore, we have to survey the whole of it rather than examine any one Discourse in detail. This is best done by reading the collected lectures *as published at the time* rather than the refined and revised version, *The Idea of a University*, which appeared after he had severed his connection with the University and with Ireland. Even then we cannot be absolutely certain that we have before us the exact phrasing of the five lectures delivered in the Rotunda: Newman was forever honing his language and altering galley proofs, and we have his own word for it that the printer in Dublin — whose intelligence he much admired — was also capable of substituting what he thought was a better word for that in the manuscript! What we can be sure of is that the *argument* has not been changed. The following account, therefore, is based on the edition of the Discourses published by James Duffy in Dublin in 1852 together with the lively preface incorporated by

Newman to explain the need for reasoned thought on the subject in an age of rampant woolly-headedness.

He disclaimed a denominational attitude. The principles in question were to be arrived at 'by mere experience of life'.[48] They might be 'held by Protestants as well as by Catholics',[49] they might be taught *by* Protestants *to* Catholics and might 'sometimes or somewhere [be] understood outside the Church more accurately than within her fold.'[50] It was a matter of clear thinking, but clear thinking was not the most obvious characteristic of the day. 'What is more common', he asked, 'than the sight of grown men talking on political or moral or religious subjects' in an 'offhand, idle way?'[51] They frequently contradicted themselves in successive sentences. They found no difficulty in forming opinions on the most complex subjects. He was referring, he said, 'to what meets us in every railway carriage, in every coffee-room or *table-d'hôte,* in every mixed company.'[52] This assertiveness had become a social necessity. 'It is almost thought a disgrace not to have a view at a moment's notice on any question from the Personal Advent to the Cholera or Mesmerism.'[53] He had little doubt what drove these know-alls on and kept them spouting away. 'It was owing in great measure to the necessities of periodical literature.'[54] Newman had taken fair measure of what we call the media. 'Every quarter of a year, every month, every day there must be a supply for the gratification of the public of new and luminous theories on the subjects of religion, foreign politics, home politics, civil economy, finance.... The journalist lies under the stern obligation of extemporising his lucid views, leading ideas and nutshell truths for the breakfast table.'[55]

Newman, as it happened, was not unsympathetic towards much of the popular literature of his day. He conceded the value of the encyclopaedias and books of general knowledge promoted by the Mechanics Institutes and similar bodies set up to benefit the working class. What troubled him was the extent to which people who should have known better were falling in with the Babel of instant opinion-making regardless of their competence, or lack of it, to comment at all. He saw this as a kind of addiction, a vice of the age: 'the multitude of offhand sayings, flippant judgments and shallow generalisations' arose from 'the irritation which suspense occasions' so that the mind was 'forced on to pronounce without sufficient data for pronouncing'.[56] People were unhappy unless they had a viewpoint and when they could not achieve a true one they made do with 'an illusion'.[57] Worst of all was the usurpation involved: 'the Authority, which in former times was lodged in the Universities, now resides in very great measure in that literary world, as it is called.... This is not satisfactory if, as no one can deny, its teaching be so offhand, so ambitious, so changeable.'[58] From here Newman began his advocacy and at the end of the Discourses, after many pages of tautly-reasoned analysis, he returned to the hazard of valuing too highly what had little enough intrinsic worth. He did so in a passionate plea against the censorship of literature which the pious might demand for the protection of students. This, in Newman's view, would leave the student at the mercy of the world's 'newspapers, its reviews, its magazines, its novels, its controversial pamphlets ... its platform speeches, its songs, its drama, its theatre'.[59] The censor, allegedly so concerned for the student, would 'have succeeded but in this — in making the world [the student's] University'.[60]

For Newman, therefore, the mind and the intellect as well as the learning which nourished them were too important, too *sacred*, to be confused with fashionable theorising or to be reduced to conformity with popular standards. Against such superficiality he contrasted knowledge as he understood it: 'something which sees more than the senses convey; which reasons upon what it sees and while it sees; which invests it with an idea'.[61] This was the subject-matter of what he called Liberal Education (using 'liberal' in a non-pejorative sense), which meant 'not merely the passive reception into the mind of a number of ideas hitherto unknown to it, but in the mind's energetic and simultaneous action upon and towards and among these new ideas.... We feel our minds to be growing and expanding then, when we not only learn, but refer what we learn to what we know already.'[62] Such 'cultivation of the intellect'[63] required thought and reflection and work and time. This was the proper objective of a university. It was the opposite of the clever-clever smart-alecky ideas in popular circulation.

Lest his point be lost in heavy abstractions, Newman offered several simple analogies to illustrate what he meant. 'If a healthy body is a good in itself, why is not a healthy intellect? And if a College of Physicians is a useful institution because it contemplates bodily health, why is not an Academical Body, though it were simply and solely engaged in imparting vigour and beauty and grasp to the intellectual portion of our nature?'[64]

With an interesting insight to the kind of audience he thought he was addressing, he remarked in another of the Discourses, 'Why do you take such pains with your garden or your park? You see to your walks and turf and shrubberies; to your trees and drives; not as if you meant to make an orchard of the one, or corn or pasture land of the other, but because there is a special beauty in all that is goodly in wood, water, plain and slope, brought all together by art in one shape and grouped into one whole.'[65] So it was also, Newman argued, with cultivation of the intellect.

'One whole ...' This was important. He believed in the concept of universal knowledge: that all 'sciences' or branches of knowledge were part of a totality. He did not, of course, mean that it was possible for a student to learn everything, even in a superlative university. But he kept returning to a little refrain, that a university was *by definition* a seat of universal knowledge. This meant that the major branches of knowledge had to be available in it, so that each might complement the other. Historians, left to themselves, might reach faulty conclusions about the development of a nation or a state if they took no account of geography or economics. Lawyers needed the light of ethics, exponents of literature the lessons of what we would call sociology and so on. Newman, it might be noted, tended to take his examples from the humanities, with which he was familiar; but the point he was making applied even more obviously in the physical sciences where, say, biology had to respect the laws of chemistry and chemistry, in turn, the laws of physics.

In a properly organised university, he continued, the presence of all branches of knowledge would keep each in balance. Every scholar would know, and every student would learn, the boundaries of his particular discipline. In such an ideal situation nobody should have to suffer the annoyance of people making dogmatic assertions outside their own areas of competence. Here Newman was *not* talking about railway carriages and coffee-rooms. He was talking about learned persons in institutions where, for one reason or other, a vital branch of universal knowledge was ignored. This left them open to the danger of pontificating in every direction even though, as he put it, 'men whose life lies in the cultivation of one science or one mode of thought have no more right ... to generalise upon the basis of their own pursuit ... than the schoolboy or the ploughman to judge of a Prime Minister.'[66] Newman's argument carried its own validity, even if he still had come to terms with the implications of popular democracy!

Within this scheme of things he saw theology, man's knowledge of God, as a major branch of universal knowledge. It thrills to this day to feel the passion with which Newman held to this perception against all the countervailing values of his time: the Broad Churchmen, who advised against making a fuss when opinions were divided; the Utilitarians, for whom knowledge was useful only to the extent that it turned out physicians and barristers, engine-drivers, carpenters and clock-makers; the mixture of arrogant liberalism and evangelical sentimentality which made conscience a matter of self-respect and which — said Newman — adopted 'a mere philosophical theory of life and conduct in the place of Revelation'.[67] This mentality he described as 'the ethical temperament of a civilised age',[68] *the* heresy of the nineteenth century.

Here was the true voice of the Oxford Movement. Many Catholics of the time, as Newman acknowledged, must have found this aspect of his case a little puzzling. For them, in their Ivory Tower Church standing defiant to the infidel world, what their religion required was laid down and accepted. Anglicans, by contrast, were compelled to *justify* their insistence on the things of God in the midst of rampant progress, of spreading indifferentism and conflicting schools of thought within their own communion. On the centrality of religion, the Roman Catholic Newman, addressing the Roman Catholics of Dublin, spoke in the authentic spirit of the Anglo-Catholics, Keble and Pusey. It must have been highly stimulating for his audience to be urged to bring intellect to bear on faith, to use reason as a defence — indeed, as an aggressive weapon — in aid of the ultimate verities. The Dublin Discourses here surf-rode upon a wave of Tractarian advocacy: 'if in a certain University, so-called, the subject of Religion is excluded, one of two conclusions is inevitable — either, on the one hand, that the province of religion is very barren of real knowledge or, on the other, that in such a University one special and important branch of knowledge is omitted.'[69]

Nor was it the case, Newman went on, that theology differed from the other sciences because of the type of information sustaining it. 'Are we to limit our idea of Universal Knowledge by the evidence of our senses? then we exclude history; by testimony? we exclude metaphysics; by abstract reasoning? we exclude physics. Is not the being of a God reported to us by testimony, handed down by history, inferred by an inductive process, brought home to us by metaphysical necessity, urged on us by the suggestions of our conscience? It is a truth in the natural order as well as the supernatural.'[70] Some might dispute that, but hardly Christians. In the light of Revelation, Christians simply could not say that a person's knowledge of God was minimal: 'I do not see how it is possible for a philosophical mind, first to believe these religious facts to be true; next to consent to put them aside; and thirdly, in spite of this, to go on teaching all the while *de omni scibili.'*[71]

The need for theology in the curriculum being so obvious to Newman, attempts to omit it or to intrude upon its proper concerns left him totally unimpressed. The politician, faced with the clamour for different concessions from different religious bodies in the matter of education, 'naturally looks about him for methods of eliminating from his problem its intractable conditions, which are wholly or principally religious…. Since his schools cannot have *one* faith he determines, as the best choice left to him, that they shall have *none.'*[72] It had to be asked whether a university, as the seat of universal knowledge, was compatible with this political expedient, whether it was 'philosophical or possible to profess all branches of knowledge, yet to exclude one, and that one not the lowest in the series.'[73] The answer needed no elaboration.

As for the academics who failed to recognise the bounds beyond which they could not trespass without usurping the place of theology, Newman was thoroughly scornful. He dwelt at length on political economy. In so far as this science indicated *how* wealth was to be sought, it was legitimate. But it had no function to represent the amassing of wealth as 'virtuous' or as 'the price of happiness'.[74] Even at Oxford, he said, a professor of political economy had been heard to argue that the pursuit of wealth was a source of moral improvement and that nothing could be more beneficial to 'the lower orders' than the wish to *accumulate* wealth.[75] 'I really should on every account be sorry, Gentlemen, to exaggerate,' said Newman, fractionally restraining himself, 'but indeed one is surprised on meeting with so very categorical a contradiction of Our Lord, Saint Paul, Saint Chrysostom, Saint Leo and all (the) saints … (Christianity) expressly says ''Lay not up to yourselves treasures on earth''.'[76] It should, perhaps, be noted in passing that Archbishop Whately had once held the chair of political economy at Oxford! It was probably of more significance, however, that Whately had been trying to have a work of his own on the general principles of Christian knowledge introduced to the national schools in Ireland. Similar ideas for a faculty of 'General Religion' had been in circulation as a possible approach towards resolving the difficulties inherent in the university question. Newman would have none of it. 'General Religion is in fact no religion at all ... as all branches of knowledge are one whole, so, much more, is each branch a whole in itself... to teach half of any whole is really to teach no part of it. Men understand this in matters of the world. It is only when religion is in question they forget it. Why do not the Whigs and Tories form some common politics, and a ministry of coalition upon its basis?'[77]

Having reached this point, Newman had led himself and his audience by ineluctable logic on to the horns of a grave dilemma. To appreciate it, consider the succession of forcibly argued propositions. Mere opinions were a cheap and flippant phenomenon of the age, without value unless they proceeded from minds *well*-formed and *in*formed. The preparation of a mind to this end involved more than training in a craft or skill, no matter how specialist: you did not necessarily get a well-formed mind by producing a surgeon, an engineer, a high court judge ... or a professor of political economy. You got it from a system of education which exposed the mind to a number of branches of knowledge on which the intellect could exercise itself, speculate, compare with other knowledge, subject to reasoning, follow through to conclusions, enlarge upon, take to a higher level. Perfection of the intellect was the object of all this cerebration and the place where it was conducted was called a university. So far, so good.

But there were obvious consequences. If the acquisition of knowledge meant more than accepting the information handed down by the teacher, the student had to be *free* — free to think his way through what he learned, free to work out what it implied and what further meaning he might draw from it. He could not be spancelled by his professor's attitudes. If he were, his intellect would remain fallow, unproductive, *uncultivated*. The whole tendency of Newman's Discourses supports this view. So does his constant use of the word 'liberal' in connection with the system of education and the kind of knowledge which absorbed his attention. True, by 'liberal' he primarily meant 'not servile'[78]

— that is, not dedicated to a mere practical purpose like learning how to amputate a leg or build a viaduct. But integral to this understanding of 'liberal' was the idea of liberal knowledge *as its own end*. It was not that liberal education had no objective. It was quite the opposite. It had a lofty, most important objective, the production of a cultivated intellect which in turn would redound to everybody's benefit. Said Newman '(if) a practical end must be assigned to a university course, I say it is that of training good members of society. Its art is the art of social life and its end is fitness for the world.'[79] It promised no Napoleons or Washingtons, he added, but 'a university training is the great ordinary means to a great but ordinary end'.[80] Here therefore, was the purpose of liberal education, of equipping the mind to think for itself, of *freeing* the intellect to function *freely*.

There was one restraint. The several branches of knowledge had to respect one another, each keeping within its own competence, acknowledging the light it received from the others. Nobody had all the answers. Theology was certainly to be included among the major branches of knowledge but not even theology, said Newman, was exempt from the law that 'no science is complete in itself'.[81] Theology was therefore part of the balance, part of the liberal education system ... and as a result, surely matter like the rest, open to free speculation and inquiry? A hard question for any Christian, it was especially hard for Roman Catholics reared in the tradition of the Council of Trent, which had delimited so much for them, and living in the polemical — often anti-clerical — nineteenth century when every pressure conspired to force them to rally behind what they thought of as a monolithic corpus of belief, unchanging and unchangeable. Newman phrased the question nagging them: 'You may ask me, Gentlemen, how all this is consistent with the dignity of Christianity, with the merit of faith. You will say that faith is confident, that obedience is prompt, yet without knowing why; that ignorance is the very condition both of the one and of the other. Though we cannot verify by reason, yet we take upon us, on God's word, the very truth to be believed....'[82]

There were answers available to Newman which he disdained. As we have seen, he would not permit the exclusion of religion as a means of avoiding disagreeable controversy. Nor would he have the liberal approach — 'liberal' in the worst sense — which allowed the coexistence of contradictory views regardless of their truth or falsehood: this would have been an indifferentism unacceptable in any serious discipline. He had also ruled out the reduction of theology to 'General Religion', meaning those elements of belief common to Christians of otherwise varying persuasions: this would diminish the whole science to half its scope or less than half, again unacceptable because unscholarly. He offered no glibly prepackaged response of his own. He thought through the dilemma, the seeming dichotomy of freedom and faith. He arrived at his answer and gave it in two parts. The overriding reality was that 'Revelation is all in all in doctrine (and that) Christian truth is purely of Revelation'. 'Revelation', he said, 'we can but explain, we cannot increase ... without it we should have known nothing of its contents, with it we know just as much as its contents and nothing more.'[83] The categorical restriction of theological knowledge to Revelation, although so long an intimate part of Newman's personal faith, seemed superficially to exacerbate the problem; not least, as he remarked, because people were tending to 'scorn any process of inquiry not founded on experiment'. But this really was the backdrop in Newman's mind which threw into relief the larger and prophetic part of his answer. It involved a progression and it went like this:

I deny that faith is a mere unreasoning act ...

We believe what is revealed to us from belief in the Revealer ...

When the Divine Voice quickens us ... we emerge from the state of slaves into that of children...

Children are taught the rudiments of knowledge upon faith; they do not begin with philosophy...

(Eventually) we pass on from faith and penance to contemplation...

To those who have begun with faith (God) adds, in course of time, a higher gift, the gift of Wisdom which, not superseding but presupposing Faith, gives us so broad and deep a view of things revealed that their very consistency is evidence of their Author....[84]

Newman went on:

'Parallel to this Divine Wisdom, but in the natural order ...
is that philosophical view or grasp of all matters of thought,
in which I have considered liberal knowledge to consist, and
which is desirable for its own sake.'[85] Thus he resolved the
dilemma. Faith itself made room in theology for that
freedom of reflection and inquiry and conclusion which are
part and parcel of liberal education in other branches of
knowledge. This in turn implied that, while Revelation could
not be *added to*, its meaning at all times, its significance at
particular times, its message for a given time, were accessible
through the gift of the Spirit which the Church calls
Wisdom. Thus does comprehension of the Master's message
grow. And how could a university, the seat of universal
knowledge, legitimately refuse to recognise that such growth
in comprehension was truly a cultivation of the intellect?

3

'A specimen of English priest'

His extended stay in Dublin during May and June of 1852 left Newman with some bewildered impressions of the Irish and their lifestyle. Their 'great cleverness'[1] took him by surprise. At his first lecture 'the very ticket taker in the room followed my arguments and gave an analysis of the discourse afterwards'.[2] The printer, as we saw, kept trying to improve his text while the chamber-maid at his lodgings was 'supernaturally sharp and subnaturally dirty'.[3] This servant girl spotted exactly which windows he wanted left open, and which shut, and prepared his room each day accordingly. She was, however, guilty of the mortal sin of all Dublin cleaning women then and since: she sorted his papers, put away his books and swept his belongings into drawers. Out of self-protection he had to reprimand her, so 'as I generally seem very cross and very stupid, sometimes both, she puts me down doubtless as a specimen of English priest'.[4] Others were probably doing the same, not least the women in his audience when he opened his Discourse with the salutation 'Gentlemen', not 'Ladies and Gentlemen',[5] pointedly ignoring the Irish rejection of the Victorian convention that only men attended public lectures.

Dorset Street was convenient since he could celebrate Mass in Saint Francis Xavier's, the Jesuit church in Gardiner Street nearby, where he also got breakfast, and he was in short walking distance of the Rotunda. He found self-catering a problem, however, and was taken in — not for the last time — by the blarney of Dublin shop assistants. He bought some tea and found it 'villainous'.[6] He doubted that 'there was one tea leaf in the whole — tho' the man who sold it was very great about it'.[7] He was therefore delighted when Dr James Quinn, a priest whom he had known in Rome, agreed to rent him a room which he could retain as a *pied-à-terre* for use whenever he was in Dublin and where he could leave furniture, books and papers which he did not need to bring to England. The room — very bright, with a large bay window — was in a boarding school run by Dr Quinn at numbers 16 and 17 Harcourt Street, adjacent to St Stephen's Green. The distinguished soldier and author, Sir William Francis Butler, who had been a pupil there at the time, recalled that Dr Quinn was 'assisted by a staff of teachers, nearly all of whom, like their chief, attained celebrity as bishops in the colonial ecclesiastical world'.[8] (Dr Quinn became first Bishop of Brisbane.) They were congenial company for the English scholar, and Newman also appreciated the dignified decor of the Georgian mansion with its 'pagan alto-relievos on the walls'[9] (presumably the stucco-work so typical of Dublin) and the chandelier in his room, not to mention the 'useful books in the bookcase',[10] but there were disadvantages. The mutton, as usual in Ireland, was too tough for his less than robust digestion and he found himself once again at the mercy of a Dublin cleaning woman, this time Dr Quinn's housekeeper, who tidied his 'Discourse papers' according to size, put his linen where she thought best and not where he wanted it, and rearranged his 'pens, pen knife, tooth-brush, boots...'.[11] To her credit, she shut everything neatly away. It did not make for ease of finding and Newman noted that at least one paper he needed for his lectures disappeared forever. Who knows what further illumination of the purpose of a university was lost to the world through the diligence of a Dublin charlady?

The Rotunda Assembly Rooms pleased Newman very much, even though he had to move from one to another of them week by week, according as bigger or smaller premises were needed for various functions. Noises-off accompanied the second Discourse, as the band of the 81st Regiment had been engaged to enliven the St Vincent de Paul Society's bazaar in the Round Room: the effect will be understood by anyone who has sat in the audience at the Gate Theatre while an action-packed film was showing in the Ambassador Cinema. The rooms housing these modern facilities, as it happens, were those in use on that Monday, 17 May 1852. Perhaps it was his lifelong commitment to the poor wherever he found them that ensured Newman's cheerful tolerance of the brass-and-wind recital put on to raise funds for their relief! Despite the laboured sarcasm of a militant Protestant paper which claimed that the attendance had so fallen off at the successive Discourses that Dr Newman would soon find himself, in the words of Thomas Moore's song, like 'one who treads alone some banquet hall deserted', his own correspondence reported good reaction to the later lectures: 'the room full — people seemed pleased'.[12]

Indeed, people always seemed pleased to meet him in Ireland. It was his enduring happy memory of a country where he also suffered much frustration. 'I am being killed with kindness', he wrote home later that summer. '*Words cannot express* the exuberant hearty affection with which all men, the priests and the multitude in the streets embrace me.'[13] This was after the Achilli trial, when the Catholic Irish saw him as a walking martyr for their religion and when such public demonstrations of the regard in which he was held went to his very heart. As he would write later, in Ireland an English Catholic, in spite of the painfully intertwined history of the two islands, 'has but this one imagination before his mind, that he is in the midst of those who will not despise him for his faith's sake'.[14] Emotionally gratifying this might be, but it could also be physically trying. On a short visit to Limerick he had to face what for him were the horrors of feather-beds (in which he was unable to sleep) and five-course dinners (the mutton always underdone) and bone-shaking cross-country journeying by outside-car where no railways ran. It never dawned on his hospitable hosts that their warmth and good-fellowship and rough-and-tumble ways were wearing him down to a state of mental exhaustion. His friend William Monsell, afterwards Lord Emly, had a house at Tervoe deep in the County Limerick countryside which Newman borrowed for a week of rest and silence. It was the saving of him. 'The quiet set me up', he wrote, 'It is the only thing for me ever. I have never been tired of being by myself since I was a boy.'[15]

Irish kindness added to his fatigue but was far from being its only cause. The Achilli affair hung over him the whole of that year. He worried endlessly that if the case went against him it would injure the Catholic Church in the eyes of the British public and that he would thereby create embarrassment and practical difficulties for his innocent co-religionists still suffering the opprobrium stirred up by the restoration of the hierarchy in 1850. The trial began in London on 21 June and went on for three days. The jury brought in a guilty verdict against Newman on virtually every count after a display of anti-Catholic bias by the judge so blatant that the *Times* denounced it editorially. The court did not sit until November to pronounce judgment and was then prevented from doing so by Newman's lawyers, who moved for a new trial. The application involved further proceedings and the case was not finally resolved (without a retrial) until January 1853, when a mere £100 fine was imposed. It was a moral victory but Newman had paid a heavy price in almost unbearable anxiety throughout the previous year.

Throughout most of that year also he had been writing his

Dublin Discourses, a task which continued for months after he
had delivered the first five as public lectures. No other work of
composition in his long life, before or after, proved so arduous
and the repeated record of his anguish wrings sympathy to this
day from any reader who knows the agony of marshalling and
phrasing serious thought upon a serious topic when the will to
do so has to wrestle with a tired and reluctant mind. 'My lectures
have taken me more trouble than any one could by a stretch of
fancy conceive', he wrote in April. 'I have written almost reams
of paper; finished, set aside — then taken them up and plucked
them.'[16] Already plunged into the public exercise, he groaned in
May 'I have just discovered *how* I ought to have written the lecture
… I half thought of lecturing extempore quite a different lecture
— but I am not equal to it.'[17] Later that month: 'I trust I am
doing good in Ireland, but really it is like drawing blood — so
much am I pulled down.'[18] In June, 'These lectures have
oppressed me more than anything else of the kind in my life.'[19]
And yet again, 'As to my lectures, they have cost me no one
knows how much thought and anxiety … nothing but the inter-
cession of the Blessed Virgin kept me up to my work…. For three
days I have sat at my desk nearly from morning to night, and
put aside as worthless at night what I have been doing all day.'[20]
In July: 'These lectures lie like a tremendous load on me…'[21] In
August, to a friend, a *cri-de-coeur* disguised as a joke: 'Do come
— and come soon — and have some long chats — and write one
of my Discourses for me, or at least lighten the writing.'[22]

To the burden of composition in the midst of general anxiety
was added an uncertainty regarding his Irish audience: 'I have
the utmost difficulty in writing to people I do not know, and I
commonly have failed when I have addressed strangers.' Was
he right to talk about Oxford? What would the Archbishop of
Tuam make of it? Theology as a branch of knowledge seemed
a good line to follow. But was he correctly expounding the nature
of Liberal Knowledge? The letters winged to and fro, between
Birmingham and Dublin, Dublin and Birmingham, to Oratorians
whose views he valued, to Dr Moriarty of All Hallows — the Irish
churchman whose intellect he most admired. Scrupulosity and
diplomacy were hard taskmasters for a mind already so troubled:
'thought wears me down',[23] he sighed. There was a strain on
the body, too, for travel had become frenetic: to Dublin early in
May, back to Birmingham for a community celebration three
weeks later, returning to Dublin in three days time; to London

for the trial in mid-June, to Dublin immediately after for a meeting of the University Committee, in the Oratory once more in July and on to Oscott to address the assembled bishops of England and Wales on *The Second Spring*, to Limerick before the month was out, back to England in August to face the staggering legal costs of the trial. As if all this were not enough, his sister Harriett and a much-loved aunt both died that summer. It surprised few of his intimates that he collapsed while giving a talk at the Oratory in September or that his doctor told him in October that he would not have long to live unless he moderated the pace of his activities.

It was indeed more than a middle-aged man, an ascetic and something of a recluse by nature, should have been asked to bear. The strain of it goes some distance to explain Newman's difficulties in coping with the Irish university situation, especially when his personal background and spiritual odyssey are borne in mind. He was English through and through, reared in London, educated at Oxford, a devout Anglican until the age of forty-four and the acknowledged leader of a movement for reform within the Church of England. Most of his adult life had been spent in the self-sufficient world of Oxford common-room, high table and pulpit, a world of polished sophistication where controversies, however acerbic, were conducted in a language and a style and an atmosphere slowly distilled through centuries and absorbed from the very air of the place by those whose windows opened on to its tranquil quadrangles. When Newman removed himself to his retreat at Littlemore he shed nothing of this uniquely civilised, uniquely English, comportment. The companions who joined him there shared for the most part a similar upbringing and similar moulding in the Oxford tradition. Like Newman and with him, their conversion to Catholicism came about in a process of prayer, study, meditation and such influence as they exercised on one another or experienced through the Oxford Movement. As we have seen, they became Catholics without the acquaintance of virtually a single person born into their new faith: 'I am going to those I do not know, and of whom I expect very little,'[24] said Newman. He went, and with him a number of his companions, and together they set up the Oratory ... Littlemore Catholicised, Oxford ministering to another faith and its faithful.

In 1852, therefore, Newman was less than comfortable in a traditionally Catholic milieu. The Oratory ensured that he had men close by him to whom he could relate on the basis of common memories, values, tastes and instincts not shared by the generality of Catholics. He often spoke of the Oratory as his family and it was indeed the haven in every storm. Ireland was utterly alien by comparison: as Catholic as England was Protestant, its people as extroverted as the English were reticent, as gregarious and rumbustious as the English were reserved — the English of Newman's class, at least. The Irish bore the marks of their history as the English bore theirs, but it was a history altogether different, however tragically intermingled with the history of Newman's countrymen. In a hundred little ways they were distinctive and it would be wrong to read Newman's stories of misadventure in Ireland as merely amusing self-deprecation. They were a traveller's tales from a foreign land. Tired, weighed down with worry, baulking at the task in hand and acutely aware that he could not be certain of his hosts' sensitivities, Newman very naturally sought out in Ireland his own kind to advise him, to receive his confidences and to keep him company. Had he been less distraught, he might have been more circumspect.

* * *

Newman's English advisers were something of a job lot, although unquestionably of intellectual distinction. All were recent converts to Catholicism, most were Oxford graduates and had been beneficed clergymen of the Church of England, a few had been Fellows of Oxford colleges (Hope, Allies, Ornsby). It would have been difficult to put together a random selection of people less knowledgeable about Irish affairs — or the affairs of countries other than Great Britain, for that matter, apart from scholars like T. W. Allies, the former Oxfordshire vicar, who had made the Grand Tour in search of information rather than merely to see the sights. Those of them who, for reasons associated with their Catholicism, had recently come to live in Dublin (others would be invited over later by Newman to take up posts in the University) formed a little circle of expatriates who tended to reinforce one another's opinions and shared the same limited range of Irish contacts — and, indeed, of contacts at home in England. It would be altogether wrong to speak of a clique or to see them as representatives of an English interest. They were simply drawn together by natural affinity in a city which, although looking English enough at first sight, revealed itself increasingly to be alien the longer they resided there.

Newman relied especially on Robert Ornsby, who observed well but judged poorly. He was assistant editor of the *Tablet* and a classicist by training. In a long letter[25] to Newman shortly before the lecture series, he shrewdly identified the different elements of 'Dublin Catholic society', distinguishing between the clergy, the upper class or 'Society properly so called', the professional and salaried people or 'citizen class', and the poor. He correctly saw the 'citizen class' as the dynamic group with whom the clergy most closely associated but failed to recognise them as the cadre from which political leadership and public opinion was derived. The source of his oversight was evident from the disproportionate length at which he wrote about 'Society proper', by whom he was not in fact much impressed. These were 'the Castle set', infected with Protestant notions and not all acquainted with the 'ideas familiar to Oxford and England generally'. He obviously saw this as a defect in Irish leadership, assuming this upper class to stand in the same relationship to the people as their counterparts did in England. That he moved mainly in that class himself could scarcely be doubted from his comment that the country was 'profoundly sick and ashamed of its having so long and so often placed itself at the mercy of agitators like O'Connell': only 'the Castle set' among Irish Catholics would have spoken in such terms of the Liberator.

What Ornsby meant by Protestant attitudes among Irish Catholics fell equally wide of the mark. In a succession of anecdotes, he recorded how he met shoulder-shrugging reaction to the high ideals of the Oxford Movement, refusal to be shocked at an author's blasé attitude when his book had been put on the Index, distaste for the spirituality of Alphonsus Liguori, and other examples of a 'general vague liberalism'. It never crossed his mind that this liberalism might have been far from vague, that it might have been a quality integral to the self-confident Irish Church of the day, owing nothing to Protestantism but much to a long history of self-reliance in stubborn adhesion to faith and to a more recent recognition of the intimate connection between human rights, human dignity and the Gospel which underlay the O'Connellite 'agitation'. By the same token, the members of such a Church were unlikely to be interested in importing foreign values, whether from England or the continent. As it happened, continental values ranging from ultramontanism to Italianate devotions were soon to be introduced to that Church through the influence of Archbishop Cullen. At the same time, socio-religious values of English puritanism were to be absorbed as part of the prevailing standard of Victorian respectability: an unhealthy prudery and an emphasis on the stern God of judgement rather than the understanding God of mercy would thereby become features of Irish Catholicism so that, ironically, what Ornsby *thought* was Protestant because it was liberal would be killed off by what was indeed Protestant — but illiberal.

This English observer kept coming back[26] to the Irish ignorance of what a university was: specifically, what Oxford was. He recorded with horror how, having described to one Irishman 'the general finish and refinement of manner which a University should be expected to give, and which in Oxford was a *sine qua non* for all who wished to make their way', the Irishman responded 'Oh, that seems to me like a set of little girls — finicking preciseness.' The 'citizen class' in particular was 'very deficient in education, and of course about as remote from understanding such questions as the University as anything that could be conceived'. He advised Newman on how to prepare his lectures: '... all you can do is to set people a-thinking. They will not understand half of what you say, but you will effect your object better by not hampering yourself with trying to talk according to their capacities, but rather just follow your own ordinary manner....' After which it comes as no great surprise to learn that Ornsby was the source of the information about Irish antipathy to Englishmen! He must have needled quite a few otherwise peaceable natives before he came to terms with the country and its moods.

It would be chauvinistic to deny the degree of truth in Ornsby's analysis. It can be said objectively, none the less, that his neglect or inability to comprehend viewpoints rooted in Irish self-awareness and his assumption that Oxford should be taken as the sole measure of educational excellence (an Oxford in need of much reform, incidentally, according to *English* authorities at the time) were not only narrow-minded but dangerous in a man from whom guidance was being sought on Irish attitudes. He certainly helped to unnerve Newman, whose disquiet about the likely reactions of an Irish audience cannot but have been heightened by a report of this kind. Newman's concern can be detected in the relief he expressed when writing from Dublin to the future Cardinal Manning after the early Discourses had passed off successfully: 'I have been prospered here in my lectures beyond my most sanguine expectations, or rather beyond my most anxious efforts and pains, for I have had anxiety and work beyond belief in writing them, expectations none.'[27]

Another confidant of Newman's was a close friend of long standing, Henry Wilberforce, who had had Tractarian sympathies but had become a Catholic only two years earlier and had been brought to Ireland by Archbishop Cullen to be secretary of the Catholic Defence Association, a body set up to obtain redress of Catholic grievances by parliamentary action. If Wilberforce was not as dogmatic in his opinions as Ornsby, neither did he do anything (or perhaps see the need to do anything) to dissuade Newman from being influenced by Ornsby and he greeted the election of Cullen by the Chapter of Dublin to succeed Archbishop Murray with a 'Deo gratias!',[28] not apparently considering that alternative judgments might have been made on the wisdom of the choice. An alternative judgment had already been made by Archbishop MacHale on the choice of Wilberforce as an officer of the Defence Association; MacHale predictably wanted an Irishman. This may well have been unfair to Wilberforce, but Newman read it as a storm signal: 'it is the Archbishop of Tuam and his party I fear as much as any',[29] he wrote to Ornsby before the lectures, and as we saw he took lodgings rather than risk giving substance to suspicions that an English clique was at work by staying with an English friend — the friend was Wilberforce. This was wise, but he continued to listen to Wilberforce and to seek advice on approaches to the university question from men like Hope-Scott and Allies who had no knowledge of Ireland at all.

He seems to have thought that he was on safe ground with Frederick Lucas, Editor of the Catholic weekly, the *Tablet*. No Irishman could have doubted where Lucas' sympathies lay. He had uprooted himself, his family and his already prestigious (and controversial) journal from London, transferring them all to the Catholic atmosphere of Dublin where he felt he could do much good by championing the cause of the hard-pressed Irish peasantry. Although a Catholic since 1839, his background differed from that of the other converts. He had been a Quaker and so debarred from an Oxford education. Instead he had attended the newly-founded University College, London, specialising in history and economics, helping to set up the debating society and committing himself (like O'Connell) to Benthamite humanitarianism. Surprisingly, in view of his successful career at a non-denominational university, he opposed the Queen's Colleges, holding that there could be 'no real separation between secular pursuits and spiritual duties'.[30] Even more surprisingly, he became friendly with MacHale who proved able to overlook his Englishness when he found him not only sympathetic to the poor tenants and opposed to the government's university proposals but a supporter of Repeal as well. It also helped, with the Lion of the West, that Cullen looked on Lucas with deep suspicion, catching a distant whiff of Young Italy from a man who consorted with Young Irelanders like Gavan Duffy and who favoured the involvement of priests in the campaign for tenant rights. Through that movement Lucas was destined soon to become a Member of Parliament for County Meath.

In Lucas, therefore, Newman had an English adviser with whom he could enjoy rapport, who was close to the realities of Irish opinion and who offered an apparently valuable link to the important but irascible Archbishop of Tuam. 'Lucas was the only friend of the Archbishop I knew',[31] wrote Newman, explaining why he felt that the editor might have had a hand in persuading MacHale to join in nominating him as President of the University. By keeping in with Lucas, however, Newman risked association in the public mind with one strand of Irish politics, which certainly upset Cullen even though Newman in fact took great care to avoid adopting any political stance in Ireland other than on the university question. The advice he received from Lucas was not as ill-informed as that from other English sources, although Lucas also tended to see the 'Castle set' (he called them 'the *respectables* who look with great respect to England'[32]) as the people to win over. Nor did it help that he wrote in his paper with more fervour than discretion, criticising bishops when he felt they deserved it with little regard for their dignity or feelings.

Given the nationalist temper of the day it was inevitable that Newman's connection with these English public men should have created the belief that the proposed university was taking shape under English aegis. It certainly gave its opponents among Irish Catholics the opportunity to allege that this was the case: Cullen warned him as early as February 1852 against 'some ultra-zealous patriots' who were trying 'to get up an agitation against everything English in this country',[33] and shortly afterwards said that, although he approved the offer of a professorship to Allies, there was in Ireland 'a set of newspaper editors and others' who were bent on stirring up anti-English prejudice and 'we must avoid giving them any motive to attack us for a little while longer'.[34] Newman bridled under the repeated hints, reports and warnings. 'I *will* have a certain amount of Englishmen about me, or I will not undertake the Presidency',[35] he wrote to Ornsby in April. To Allies he insisted 'I must have men I know about me, and will' — adding later that Allies should not suppose 'that Irishmen are going to be put about me. I should object to them distinctly, not of course as Irishmen, but as persons whom I did not know, who were not of the same school as myself, on whom I could not rely.'[36] But Irishmen in their turn were beginning to wonder on whom *they* could rely....

*   *   *

Despite the searing mental stress under which he worked at defining the nature of a university, Newman did not neglect the task of shaping the actual university of which he was to take charge. Already he had tried unsuccessfully to interest Manning in the vice-presidency, had dangled the lure of a professorship before Allies and considered doing the same to Aubrey de Vere. From Dorset Street he wrote to Thomas Scratton, yet another Oxford convert, seeking his 'services'[37]: he would later make him secretary to the Catholic University. As the months passed, he became increasingly concerned that nobody else seemed anxious to move the project forward. In particular, Archbishop Cullen had ceased to answer letters and Archbishop MacHale was urging, on the one hand, the erection of grandiose buildings and on the other the minimisation of English involvement. Only Newman seemed to be serious about planning an organisational system so that the University might be inaugurated as soon as possible. He put Cullen's attitude down to a habit of procrastination inculcated in Rome and to a caution (also Roman) against committing more to paper than was necessary. To deal with MacHale he would eventually seek formal confirmation of his rectorship by the bench of bishops and a solemn ceremony of installation. But this was for the future. He had too much on his hands in the crisis-ridden year of 1852 to pursue every objective at the same time.

Matters of more immediate consequence than the University had in fact arisen to concentrate episcopal minds. Cullen's strategy for restructuring the Irish Church had become very clear. Whenever he came across examples of maladministration or even resistance to his own policy among his brother bishops, he would report them to Rome — often with the request that Rome should reprimand the offending prelate. Rome generally complied with the Papal Delegate's advice and Irish bishops were soon receiving requests from Propaganda to explain alleged abuses taking place under their jurisdiction: Cullen would lose the valuable friendship of the elderly Archbishop Slattery of Cashel when Rome asked the old man to comment on the number of apostates in the remote parish of Doon! He intervened in the same way in the appointment of bishops. He blocked the favoured candidate for Kerry by telling Rome that he was 'a boisterous, rough man',[38] unfit to be a bishop. In the case of Ardagh he saw to it that Rome heard of a story going round that a Protestant had been killed by the candidate's horse at a race-meeting in Bundoran — whether the candidate was up or not was unclear. No doubt it was the Delegate's function to keep Rome advised but it remains a little shocking to learn how he could interpose his personal opinion to upset the verdict of senior clergy in the local churches concerned, who could be assumed to know and weigh in the balance the significance of boisterousness and horsemanship.

It need scarcely be said that such intervention was anathema to the Archbishop of Tuam, especially when applied to the western ecclesiastical province of which he was metropolitan. 'A most curious letter',[39] he noted on a missive from Cullen in which the Papal Delegate told him of a message from the Cardinal Prefect of Propaganda asking that action be taken by MacHale to rectify the unsatisfactory state of affairs in some of the western dioceses. MacHale was quite shrewd enough to suspect that the Cardinal Prefect would have moved only if Cullen had asked him to do so in the first place. This, indeed, was Cullen's *modus operandi* and the letters are extant in which he advised the Roman authorities to write back to Ireland with demands, rebukes and paternal recommendations to be acted on by various bishops. Allowing for the need to revitalise and reform certain aspects of Church life and administration in the country, it remains distressing to see how this was done by secretive methods resulting in Roman diktats.

To be sure, it would have been no easy task for Cullen to persuade stubborn, often long-serving bishops to co-operate in pastoral renewal but at least he might have tried — if only to avoid humiliating or antagonising pastors who had shepherded the Irish Church out of penal oppression and, indeed, to show respect for the proper autonomy of the episcopal office. This would have involved listening to his colleagues and making allowance for views rooted in their experience, an approach altogether foreign to his zealous insistence on achieving what Paul Cullen believed to be in the best interest of the Irish Church: as he said on one occasion with unconscious arrogance about the opinions of an elderly prelate, 'it is the good of the Church [that] is to be looked to, not the whim of the good old man'.[40] That 'the good old man' might have had the good of the Church as much at heart as the Papal Delegate never seemed to occur to Cullen, still less that the old man might have been the better informed touching the needs of his own diocese. An inherent danger in Cullen's method was that his personal leanings could lead him astray. A case in point was the attempt which he made to stamp out the 'stations' or house-Masses so common in rural Ireland since penal times. Many bishops resisted him in this — and how fascinating it was a hundred years later to hear their successors at the Second Vatican Council drawing attention to the progressive practice of the Irish Church which had for so long promoted the celebration of Mass in private houses as the Fathers of the Council were then encouraging!

Whatever judgement be passed on the means employed by Cullen to attain his ends, major consequences followed for Newman and for the university project. It would probably have been difficult in any event to secure the wholehearted collaboration of MacHale, whose temperament was always more suited to criticism than constructive activity, but the close association of the Catholic University with Cullen, as well as Cullen's chairmanship of the University Committee and the fact that Newman was Cullen's personal choice to be Rector, all combined to ensure the Lion's determined opposition on any ground he deemed relevant. By the summer of 1852 priests collecting funds for the University in the United States were reporting rumours that the arrangements for setting up the institution and engaging staff had been handed over to Dr Newman by Archbishop Cullen and that this meant it would be under English control. 'If such be the case,' wrote one of the priests, 'the collections in this country may be regarded as at an end.'[41] Another innocently indicated where the stories might have originated when he reported comments that Dr MacHale had despaired of the University and that the Primate (Cullen) had made an Englishman President 'with full powers to appoint all the Professors, English of course'.[42] It was also being said that

Cullen was unduly influenced by Cardinal Wiseman. Later in the year a collector in London wrote to Cullen: 'They seem to know more here about the mischievous opposition of Dr MacHale than is known in Dublin.' For the sake of English Catholic opinion, this priest wanted Cullen to make it clear that 'the illustrious convert Newman' would not be 'cajoled or terrified into the abandonment of the office of president'.[43]

A caveat has to be entered here. MacHale's friendship with Lucas showed that he had no antipathy to Englishmen as such. This was true also in his attitude to Newman. Not only did he support his nomination as President but, in the words of an early biographer of MacHale, 'No one in the three Kingdoms entertained a higher opinion of this great Christian scholar than the Archbishop of Tuam.'[44] It could fairly be said that the Archbishop had a strange way of showing his regard but, rather like Cullen, MacHale would not allow concern for an individual's feelings to obstruct the pursuit of a principle. The principle which he saw at issue in this case was the need to prevent the anglicisation of the University and if Newman's presence could be used as a warning light in the cause, so be it. Other English appointments were in fact being mooted so, by his own norms, MacHale had reason to be anxious. This can be obscured by modern distaste for the more xenophobic of his norms, the crudity of his tactics and the sheer unfairness of invoking Newman's name in an Irish controversy to which Newman was not party.

The controversy ran deeper than the question of University appointments. MacHale was also resisting Cullen's policy against the participation of priests in politics. It might be more accurate to speak of Cullen's opposition to the *overt* involvement of priests in politics. These were the days of the Tenant Right League, the first effective Irish political movement established since the Famine and the death of O'Connell. It secured the election of a number of members of parliament pledged to work for relief of the destitute Irish peasantry. MacHale strongly approved of it and voiced no criticism of priests who publicly declared their support for party policies. Cullen, more subtly, believed that the Church would be injured by visible links between the clergy and a political movement ... at least when that movement's objectives were not directed towards the benefit of religion (for he had supported O'Connell and, quite recently, the Catholic Defence Association). Two further considerations influenced him against the League: former Young Irelanders were among its most active members and it was being impressed on him from Rome that political priests were an embarrassment to the Vatican in its dealings with the British government.

Cullen's efforts to withdraw the Church from public endorsement of the League brought about a situation of byzantine complexity in which MacHale, Lucas, the Young Irelanders and the nationalist press began to represent him as a 'Castle bishop',[45] despite his continuing rejection of any government control in areas (like education) of particular importance to the Church. The Murrayite bishops — still amounting to more than one third of the hierarchy — began to look on him more kindly as a moderating force against what they saw as the nationalist extremism of MacHale and his friends; at the same time, they were not yet prepared to guarantee their support for specific proposals coming from Rome but quite possibly originating with Cullen himself. Faced with the certain opposition of the MacHale faction, enjoying only the qualified support of the Murrayites and being able to count on his own side no more than a maximum of ten bishops (out of twenty-eight), Cullen had perforce to walk warily except in cases where he could summon up a Roman directive to silence disagreement. While Rome was willing enough to propose, it was wise enough not to *dis*pose any more often than it had to. And Cullen knew when not to ask.

The University was now becoming a pawn in the argument over other issues. As the supposed hazard of English control became a factor in civil politics, MacHale moved simultaneously on the ecclesiastical front. As early as February 1852, he twice wrote to Cullen insisting that the episcopal body as a whole retained the right to govern the University and to make all appointments; the Committee chaired by Cullen had only the pragmatic function of making 'preparatory arrangements'.[46] There could be no question, he said, of the bishops delegating their authority to a group consisting largely of laymen and priests, who together might overrule the bishops' intentions. How any effective control could be exercised by the whole bench of bishops was none too clear (MacHale, as usual, had no positive proposals) but the maddening fact from Cullen's viewpoint was that he could not challenge MacHale's assertion as juridically unsound. The *summum imperium* or supreme governing role *had* been reserved to the bishops from the outset. To speak of the Committee as an arm of the hierarchy for the practical discharge of business would be to give a role to the laity of which Cullen himself would be doubtful — as MacHale must have known — while to suggest *sotto voce* that the Committee was merely a front behind which Cullen would make the real decisions might have accurately described the Apostolic Delegate's intention but would hardly have endeared the Committee to the many bishops still unhappy about Cullen's domination of the Irish Church. And they would have been even less happy if he chose to pull rank as the Pope's representative charged with carrying out Roman policy in Ireland, which included the establishment of a University.

It was in this quagmire of Irish civil and ecclesiastical politics that Newman sought to find some firm ground on which to maintain a foothold while trying to build up the Catholic University. He saw clearly the problems created for him by Cullen's procrastination and MacHale's opposition. Whether he fully understood at the time the basis of the power struggle between them or the conflicting tensions of the Irish political situation is doubtful: his search for explanations in Cullen's Roman background or MacHale's nationalist instincts was valid as far as it went but stopped short of the real situation in which the contestants for the moment had checkmated one another so that neither could move in a major way on the university question. Cullen had to avoid any action which might be represented as usurping the rights of his brother bishops. MacHale could not co-operate with Newman as long as the English hazard was being trumpeted about and Cullen was seen to be Newman's main support: in August 1852, in the wake of the Achilli trial, Cullen published a pastoral letter lauding Newman — which can scarcely have enthused the Lion. With mainly English sources for his guidance, and these either ignorant of Irish affairs or *parti pris* like Lucas, Newman was at a loss to know where to turn, or how.

*   *   *

Within the constraints by which his hands were tied, Archbishop Cullen did his best to help the University forward under the stimulus of Newman's lectures. So far it had no premises and the Committee had been investigating the suitability of various properties for sale in the city which might serve at least as a temporary home in which the University could be inaugurated. Property-owners in those unecumenical days were sometimes unwilling to deal with purchasers who wanted premises for blatantly Roman Catholic purposes. Catholics, with generations of experience behind them in exploiting loopholes in the penal laws, were able to cope quite successfully with mere prejudice. Cullen deputed Charles Bianconi to acquire a base for the University and that very astute businessman managed in the summer of 1852 to buy the house in Dublin least likely to become the home of a Catholic institution. Number 86 Saint Stephen's Green was a magnificent Georgian mansion built in the previous century by Richard Chapell Whaley, popularly known as 'Burn-Chapel Whaley' because of his enforcement of anti-papist legislation as a minor legal functionary. His son had been a well-known daredevil rake, long remembered as 'Buck Whaley', given to 'orgies' (his own word[47]) and extravagant wagers like undertaking to walk to Jerusalem (which he did). It was a minor *cause célèbre* when the great house became Catholic property. Nobody on the Catholic side seems to have adverted to the irony of its most distinctive feature, a lifesize stone lion recumbent on the lintel of its doorway: a feature of which the Archbishop of Tuam was surely made aware!

No doubt noticing the pressures on Newman occasioned by travel, illness, Oratorian affairs and the perpetual nag of the Achilli trial (the judgment in which was still awaited), Cullen proposed to him in October that Dr James Taylor be named as Vice-President of the University. Taylor was President of Saint Patrick's College in Carlow and an old friend of Cullen, who would put his name forward to Propaganda in the following year as a possible choice to fill the vacancy for Bishop of Ardagh. Cullen also named Father Michael Flannery to a post which he designated 'Dean of the University'.[48] These well-intentioned moves, which would have provided assistance for the President as well as leaving Irishmen placed prominently near the top of the University's structure, were less than welcome to Newman. While he agreed that the post of deputy to the President/Rector should be held by an Irishman, he felt strongly that he should be entitled to put forward for the bishops' approval a person with whom he was satisfied he could work effectively. Since at that time he knew no suitable Irishman sufficiently well to name him, he thought that the post should be left vacant for the time being. All this he had written to Cullen in one of the letters which went unanswered — or, rather, was answered after several months by a proposal which did precisely what Newman had asked should not be done: namely, offered him a deputy with whom he was unacquainted. As for the Dean, Newman had envisaged no such office. Eventually, Dr Taylor was diverted into the posts of secretary to the University Committee and general manager of the University, where he undertook responsibility for various aspects of administration. Father Flannery served as one of the Deans — head of a hall of residence, not the office Cullen had in mind — until his appointment as Coadjutor Bishop of Killaloe in 1858.

Nor was Newman altogether happy about the purchase of University House, as the Saint Stephen's Green mansion was now to be called. His principal ground of complaint was lack of consultation, for the house sat well enough with his idea for a number of residences which in time would develop into halls and colleges of the University on the Oxford model. University House would make such a residence as well as provide lecture rooms for the University itself. Still, his opinion had not been canvassed prior to the purchase and he might have favoured two smaller houses rather than one so splendid. There was also the question of personal preference. Newman disliked being based in Saint Stephen's Green, the enclosed centre of which was then a plainly laid out private park and not the attractive public garden which Lord Ardilaun would make it some twenty-five years later. More distressing for Newman was the presence daily in and about the Green of Archbishop Whately, who lived across the square from University House and who cut dead his former protégé whenever their paths crossed: a matter of considerable pain to the sensitive former Fellow of Oriel who could remember the burly figure of Whately exercising his dogs in Christ Church Meadows as he now did in Saint Stephen's Green.

MacHale rather than Cullen was responsible for a further cause of anxiety to Newman. His campaign against the English element arose not only from questions in contention between Tuam and Dublin but reflected his genuine belief that the University was to be an Irish institution for the benefit of Irish Catholics. Nobody doubted that it was intended to serve the needs of the people of the country in which it would be situated, but Newman and Cullen had a broader understanding of its purpose also. As the University Committee's appeal to English Catholics in 1851 put it, over Cullen's signature, 'The university is intended for the benefit not merely of the Catholics of Ireland but those of the empire.' The same point was implicit in the Report of the

University Committee published in 1852: 'The idea of erecting a university in this country originated with the Pope. He perceived that while the Church had its numerous universities in other countries it had not one in all the vast territory of the English-speaking world.'[49] The bishops of England and Wales believed that the advantages of the University would be 'incalculable'[50] because it would provide the young Catholics of their countries with a suitable means of education.

Newman himself stressed again and again that it was to be a 'Catholic University of the English tongue for the whole world'[51] and 'a University for the Catholics of Ireland and of other countries which speak the English tongue'.[52] Indeed, given his Oxford background and his profound reflections on the nature of a university, it would be hard to imagine Newman entertaining any narrower vision. A university for him certainly had a physical location but its student body and teaching staff might be drawn from anywhere — as was the case in Louvain, the example set before the Irish bishops in the very first Papal Rescript on the subject back in 1847. It was with this concept in view that he saw nothing wrong in offering academic posts to Englishmen for whose scholarship he could vouch. Nor did he confine his search to England. As will be seen he tried to lure the famous (and ultimately notorious) theologian, Ignaz Doellinger, from Munich and Orestes Brownson from the United States — even though Brownson had been a virulent critic of some of Newman's published opinions. Newman's concern was to seek out the best, wherever they might be found ... not only because he wanted the best for his students but because the best students would not be attracted to the University unless the professors and lecturers were men of distinction. The University Committee had been thinking on similar lines when it urged the clergy in 1851 to get in 'the contributions of all' so that the University could be opened 'with a certainty of success, by engaging the services of some of the most eminent men of Europe in arts and sciences and literature'.[53]

A number of effective (and some spurious) arguments could be advanced on MacHale's side as well. The whole question had arisen because of the Queen's Colleges, a purely Irish issue. The Roman documents had been sent in response to requests for guidance on the provision of higher education for Irish Catholics. Nothing in these documents specifically prescribed the kind of university outlined by Newman and the University Committee (the Committee would be written off by MacHale, in any event, as the mouthpiece for whatever interpretation found favour with Cullen). Most of the money was being raised in Ireland, and could it seriously be suggested that the impoverished Irish in the wake of the Famine should set up a major institution for the benefit of people from better endowed nations? Was it not the case that what the country needed was training in the skilled professions — medicine, engineering, physical science — and how could this be guaranteed except in an Irish institution set up and run for the purpose of meeting Irish wants? How could the institution be expected to respond to the needs of the country, in general or in detail, unless it were run by Irishmen? The desire to protect the youth of Ireland from proselytising and Protestantising influences had been stressed in various appeals to the people and in the appeals to American Catholics: these appeals could only be construed as soliciting help for an *Irish* objective and the critical American reaction to the news of English involvement showed that they were so understood by the Irish in the United States. And anyway, was it not a fact that Dr Newman was hiring more Englishmen?

This was dangerous reasoning from Newman's point of view. Some of it could in fact be easily refuted. More of it could be shown to be compatible with the broader understanding of a university. Neither point greatly helped, however, for the argument was presented on a different plane from that of Newman. People who thought first of the functional needs of Irish society, of the hazards of anglicisation and the attractions of self-government had adopted perfectly valid objectives. But they were objectives which had nothing to do with the pursuit of knowledge as its own end and, to that end, opening the minds of young people to the best scholarship available. Of course, the cultivation of the intellect would have been, in the most profound sense, cultivation of the national interest because 'training good members of society'[54] — we might say, producing well-balanced citizens able to think and discriminate — was just as important as training doctors and engineers. The best results of this order were naturally to be anticipated from a university conducted on the best principles, and the best principles did not admit of utilitarian or nationalist limitations. But that was a rarified argument, difficult then as now to convey to people conscious of objectives which they deem more practical and practicable. Fully aware, and kept aware by his English informants, of the

MacHale-leaning nationalist emphases, altogether unsure of Cullen's mind for want of communication but knowing from experience that the Archbishop of Dublin was apt to take decisions on his own initiative which others had to live with, Newman struggled through the remaining personal problems of 1852 and into 1853 with no assurance regarding the future of his Irish commitment.

Feeling the better for a holiday at Abbotsford, the former home of Sir Walter Scott, Newman put his frustrations frankly in a letter to Cullen in January 1853. A meeting of the University Committee was scheduled and he asked that it should clarify what he was being instructed to do and what powers he would be given to do it. This was necessary before he next came to Dublin. 'At present I could do nothing at all, though I were ever so much on the spot, and ever so anxious to make progress, for I have no work committed to me.'[55] He wanted to know whether he was to act on his own or together with others, what objects he was to keep in view and whether his 'conclusions' (meaning decisions) were to be final or to be open to revision by the Committee. Three weeks passed, the last stages of the Achilli trial were disposed of, and still no reply came from Cullen. Newman wrote again; again no reply. Cullen's discourtesy in failing to acknowledge the letters cannot easily be excused, but neither could he have been expected to pay much attention to the university question in those weeks. He had a political crisis on his hands.

A new British administration had been formed just before Christmas. Needing the support of Irish members of parliament, the Prime Minister, Lord Aberdeen, had appointed two of them, John Sadlier and William Keogh, to government office. Like many politicians in the burgeoning Irish Party which had grown out of the Tenant Right League, they had given election pledges not to join a government unless it yielded to Irish demands. The Party's strategy, like that which would be brilliantly implemented by Parnell thirty years later, was to hold itself independent of all British factions and use its numbers to achieve the best deal it could for Ireland by bargaining with whomsoever needed its support. The nationalist press denounced Sadlier and Keogh for abandoning this principle and selling out to Aberdeen. On the very day that Newman first outlined his frustrations to Cullen, MacHale declared the election pledges to be morally binding. The Bishop of Kildare, however, declared for Sadlier. Shortly afterwards, the Bishops of Meath, Cloyne and Killala came out for the Party and therefore on the side of MacHale, but the Bishop of Elphin rallied to Keogh. With bishops adopting political positions, priests could scarcely be restrained and angry comments were made from many a pulpit. Worse than that, and reflecting the state of affairs among the bishops, priests were taking up opposite viewpoints and quarrelling among themselves.

* * *

Cullen, who had been trying to extract priests, and the Irish Church overall, from open involvement in politics, found his efforts put seriously in jeopardy. It happened that he favoured the Aberdeen government, with which he believed he could negotiate in the Catholic interest, and he was accordingly not going to join in condemning the defectors — not that he would have done so publicly, in any event, since he wished to set a good example to the other bishops and the clergy in the matter of overt political involvement. But he had to look for ways of calming the storm, explain what had happened to Rome, talk to Lucas in the hope of weening him over (he talked, but to no avail). He had also to secure his position *vis-à-vis* MacHale, whose status as a patriot prelate standing by his people against the ancient enemy was enhanced by these developments, just as Cullen appeared all the more to have gone over to the 'Castle set'.

Cullen's strength lay elsewhere. It had been consoling for him to learn of the Pope's attitude from a Roman informant, who noted that Pius IX had told a British government envoy the previous summer 'that Dr McHale could not be checked; that they wrote to him and would renew their orders — But of Dr Cullen he said I do not believe anything against him: I have documents in my hands to show he is *loyal* and *faithful*'.[56] This was remarkably accurate. The envoy's report to the British Minister in Florence[57] had the Pope saying in regard to the Archbishop of Tuam that 'of him, & of those who acted like him, the Holy See would certainly not undertake the defence. He highly disapproved of their conduct, & was well aware of the mischief they caused.' By contrast, the Pope remarked 'that Archbishop Cullen, and other Bishops, had by every means endeavoured to inculcate obedience to the laws, & moderation, and Christian charity, & his Holiness read to me some extracts from a pastoral

of the former addressed to the clergy of the diocese of Dublin
...'. The Pope himself, although Cullen may not have known it,
had in fact written to MacHale in October, admonishing him to
'take to heart the use of ... priestly prudence' and to be in future
'most careful to abstain from anything which may appear in any
way to depart from the prudence which befits a bishop'.[58] That
was all very well, but if Cullen's Roman backing was to prevail
at home when the Lion took to growling and roaring on behalf
of his people, the Apostolic Delegate's support in the hierarchy
had to be reinforced at every opportunity that offered. In these
New Year weeks of crisis, Ardagh fell vacant. This called for more
advice to Rome and reports on the candidates....

At a distance from all this and only thinly informed about the
intricacies of the Irish situation, Dr Newman little realised how
slim his chances were of attracting the notice of the Archbishop
of Dublin for some time to come. In the silence, rumours
flourished. At one stage the gossip had it that Newman was about
to be made a bishop in Nottingham or Liverpool. Then it was
said that the government had put out feelers to Cullen, seeking
a compromise on the Queen's Colleges. It was even suspected
that the status of Trinity might be changed. In Rome Monsignor
Talbot of the Curia was heard to ask whether Newman was really
suited to be Rector and some people in Dublin got the notion that
the University might be reduced to the lesser status of a college.
Lacking direct contact with Cullen, Newman gave more credence
to the stories than he would otherwise have done and spent time,
which could have been better used, in writing memoranda to
himself and letters to his friends discussing the implications of
what might or might not be about to happen. (He particularly
did *not* wish to be a diocesan bishop and he felt strongly that any
abandonment of the Catholic University idea would be injurious
and disrespectful to the Holy See.) Indeed, much of 1853 was
frittered away on matters more trivial than Newman should have
been engaged upon. He gave a series of lectures in Liverpool on
the Turks — a subject remote from his special competence — and
in the autumn had to plumb the depths of diplomacy to soothe
the ruffled feathers of Faber and the London Oratory over a silly
question of who-said-what-to-whom regarding the transfer of one
of the Fathers from London to Birmingham. Other Oratorian
business had to be attended to also, including the completion of
the new church in Birmingham and the transfer of the London
community to their new house in Brompton. It was just as well

that he had some distractions, for he had packed his bag at Easter in the confident expectation of an early summons to Ireland. And nothing happened.

He was not altogether forgotten. The luckless Dr Taylor, spurned as Vice-Rector, was dispatched to Birmingham to explain that Dr Cullen was asking each bishop to appoint Newman his vicar-general: this device, employed by the Belgian bishops in the case of Louvain, would have enhanced the Rector's authority to act in the name of the bishops but nothing came of it. Instead, at a Dublin provincial synod in June the suffragan bishops deputed the Archbishop to act for them in University affairs and Dr Taylor held out the hope to Newman that the same arrangement might be arrived at in the other ecclesiastical provinces so as to produce a four-man team which could efficiently represent the whole hierarchy. This would come about eventually, but by a different means than through provincial synods.

Nothing was done in the short term, which was hardly surprising since the main purpose of the Dublin synod had been to approve resolutions prohibiting political meetings in churches and the denunciation of named persons from the pulpit as well as exhorting priests to stay away from political meetings wherever held. These were the decisions demanding energetic implementation rather than urging other provinces (including Tuam!) to be guided by the example of Dublin on the university question — which was far from the top of the agenda on most bishops' desks in 1853. The latter half of that year found the Archbishop of Dublin still occupied with politics and episcopal appointments. Rome wanted information on the events in Sligo where a defeated by-election candidate had alleged clerical intimidation and a further election had been held in which the Bishop of Elphin was thought to have had at least an indirect involvement through his senior clergy. Kerry and Dromore needed coadjutor bishops, and just about now came the alienation from Cullen of the Archbishop of Cashel and the Bishop of Waterford. The Apostolic Delegate's hands remained full indeed.

*   *   *

Although he could do very little, Newman kept turning over in his mind and discussing with his friends the desirable organisation of the University and who might be invited to join its staff. Teaching would be provided by persons in three academic grades: professors, lecturers, tutors. Each would have radically different functions. Professors would be given an effective role in University decision-making (from which they were excluded at Oxford) but would be little enough involved in the day-to-day process of teaching the students. They would present series of lectures, many of which would be public. It was hoped that they would enhance the reputation of the University through their eminence in their own fields and the authority which would attach to their public addresses: the Discourses delivered by Newman in Dublin were a good example of a distinguished scholar offering an authoritative lecture series addressed to an educated public — a public which might, of course, include students but was not meant to consist of students exclusively or even in large measure. The ongoing courses for students of the various disciplines would be given by lecturers properly so-called, who would not be professors except possibly in the initial years before a full staff had been built up and it would be convenient to merge the two functions; Newman hoped that some of the lecturers would acquire high repute and thus make themselves worthy of permanent chairs. Lastly, but in Newman's scheme of things most important of all, would be tutors, the teachers associated with the individual halls of residence who would supervise a student's development, intellectual and moral, through personal contact. The 'secondary teachers' (lecturers and tutors) would be 'the real strength of the institution',[59] according to Newman.

As we have seen, he had already sought to persuade Allies and Scratton to accept University appointments. He now went after Wilberforce, Ornsby and a number of Oxford graduates (as well as at least one Cambridge man) still in England, mostly for the 'secondary' posts to which he attached such significance. Among his personal acquaintances only Aubrey de Vere (an Irishman), Allies and Wilberforce seemed to him worthy of chairs; it was now that he gave serious thought to Brownson and Doellinger, who might be given chairs but would really function as guest lecturers. One major problem faced by Newman was that he felt it absolutely necessary to confine the teaching posts to Catholics. As he saw it, 'while you have professors of different religions, you never can have a *genius loci;* and the place is no longer a university'.[60] If this seemed an extreme view, he had a practical point as well: he felt sure the Holy See would 'never agree to any plan which mixed up Catholic youth with Protestants, let alone the Professors'.[61] Another, and most frustrating, problem was that he could not conclude the terms and dates of appointment with those who reacted favourably to his invitation. He had to apologise to Allies that he could not safely advise him to move house to Ireland while to others he wrote about 'hitches in the progress of the university, which just have the effect of keeping me from having any part in its preliminary proceedings'.[62]

Some small progress was made at a meeting of the Committee in October, which agreed to allow Newman to hire tutors at a salary of £200 a year and placed £2,000 at his disposal for other purposes. The decision scarcely ranked as momentous and included no formal invitation from the bishops asking their President/Rector to proceed with setting up the University. Still, the Committee asked him to come over. Typically for Newman, the request which he had been awaiting most of the year came at a very bad time when a number of engagements clamoured for attention. He went to Liverpool on 3 November to talk about Turks (running one lecture on after another), immediately left for Holyhead and Ireland, spent a day inspecting University House and meeting members of the Committee, Dr Moriarty and Archbishop Cullen, got back to Birmingham to preach at the first diocesan synod, went to Clifton and back to Birmingham again — all in atrociously bad weather. Inevitably he had to take to bed with a severe cold but staggered up to preach at High Mass sung by the Bishop of Birmingham at the opening of the Oratory's new church. The month's activities were part of the 'gadding to and fro'[63] he so complained of and they left him with little positive impression from his brief foray into Dublin. On Christmas Eve, by now harbouring dark thoughts of resigning his University position, he wrote to Cullen asking that he be admitted as Rector of the University in a formal way as soon as possible by the administration of appropriate oaths.

A cautionary note from Dr Taylor arrived after Christmas saying that Cullen wanted him to do nothing for the moment since the bishops had still to be won over and some difficulties concerning the lease of University House had to be disposed of. Newman's reaction was to sit down and write himself a memorandum to clarify why a public act of recognition by the bishops was necessary. He did not even advert to the presidency with which he was already conferred, presumably seeing it merely as a nomination to the University's senior executive office: in modern terminology, a job without a job description. What he wanted was an exact indication of the duties with which he was charged, endorsement of his authority to decide what was needed to bring the University into being, and recognition of the University itself as a public institution rather than a private centre of higher education like the college of a diocese or a religious order. Interestingly, he envisaged 'students, professors, members coming from different and often distant parts, in the present instant [sic] including Catholics in England and North America',[64] and he noted the practical point that he had begun to engage teachers who should not have to wait for confirmation of their employment until after they had sold their houses and come to Dublin. These considerations satisfied Newman that, unless positive developments took place without delay, he would have no option but to resign.

As usual, he consulted his friends. Hope advised a little more patience. Lucas thought he should call on a number of bishops in person to show that he accepted their right to be involved in the University equally with Cullen (regarding whom, he wrote, 'the word "little Pope" is sometimes heard among grave clergymen'[65]). Cullen at last sent a note himself to say that he would 'attend to the wishes expressed in your letter' but he would first have to consult some other bishops. This was encouraging, but even more exciting was the letter Newman received from Cardinal Wiseman. He had written to Wiseman, who was on an extended visit to Rome: 'I ask nothing ... but a *locus standi* if it be but an inch of Irish ground or the point of a needle — but unless they let me come in I can do nothing.'[66] The Cardinal in reply told him that, with the 'hearty concurrence' of the Archbishop of Dublin, he had advised the Pope 'to create you a bishop *in partibus,* which would at once give you the right to sit with the bishops in all consultations, would raise you above all other officers, professors, etc., of the University.... The Holy Father at once assented.'[67]

This was splendid news. Unlike the rumour that he was to be made a bishop with diocesan responsibilities in England, the elevation now mentioned (which would make him a titular bishop without a diocese) did not threaten to remove him from the University; instead, for the reasons set out by the Cardinal, it would hugely strengthen his hands on University matters.

Wiseman had also arranged for a Brief to be sent from Rome

approving the University, confirming Newman as Rector and making other dispositions to enable the project to proceed. Not even the most recalcitrant bishop would be able to oppose the directives or the sentiments of a Papal Brief. Although Newman could not help worrying a little lest the Cardinal should over-exert himself and have details settled in Rome which needed to be thought through in Dublin, the clouds really seemed to be lifting. Word got out (via the Bishop of Birmingham) about the proposal to give Newman an episcopal appointment and congratulations began to flood in. It was in a cheerful frame of mind that Newman took the advice of Lucas and set off on his winter journey to the Irish provinces, blissfully unaware of the scaffolding, schoolgirls and bandboxes awaiting his arrival.

He was also unaware of Archbishop Cullen's reaction to the news from Rome. Since the previous year Cullen had been contemplating a formal 'canonical' meeting of the bishops, ostensibly to regulate the affairs of the University but with the ulterior motive of re-uniting the divided hierarchy — a purpose which he felt might be achieved on the University question to the benefit of the far more delicate political issues around which so much unseemly controversy raged. Wiseman's intermeddling in Rome had been helpful to the extent that the Papal Brief would be a focus of unity. Cullen had no intention, however, of permitting the English Cardinal to be seen to be making provision for the Irish University — as MacHale would certainly represent what was happening, despite Wiseman's anticipation of the complaint with the argument that a Cardinal, when in Rome, had a duty to advise the Pope on any matter which might arise touching the government of the Church. As for making Newman a bishop, Cullen might voice 'hearty concurrence' in principle. But now? And at Wiseman's behest?

4

'A university is not founded every day'

The year 1854 got off to a bad start for the Archbishop of Dublin. After initially favouring Newman's friend, David Moriarty, the superior of All Hallows College, for appointment as Coadjutor Bishop of Kerry, Cullen swung against him from a tactical motive: he saw a pillar-to-post transfer of existing bishops as a better way to strengthen his support within the hierarchy. Rome for once disagreed — or failed to appreciate his convoluted reasoning — and named Moriarty to fill the vacancy. By February Cullen was lobbying Propaganda to prevent a similar upset in the northern diocese of Dromore, where it seemed likely that another friend of Newman's, Professor Charles Russell of Maynooth, might be made coadjutor. Russell would not do, the Archbishop told the Roman authorities, because he was too fond of travel and had several impoverished sisters to provide for. The solidly well-to-do background of the Russells, who in the next generation would produce a Lord Chief Justice of England, was hard to detect in Cullen's reference to the 'great misfortune for a Bishop to be surrounded by poor relatives'![1] Be that as it may, and by extraordinary coincidence, the only Irish churchmen with whom Newman enjoyed a close acquaintance and sympathetic rapport were both opposed by Cullen as candidates for episcopal appointments within a few weeks of each other and at the very time when Newman himself was on the brink of being raised to the same dignity. Cullen energetically set about blocking this development also.

Newman was scarcely the kind of recruit to the bench of bishops Cullen had in mind when he determined to convert the Irish episcopal body to unequivocal ultramontanism. This might have been reason enough to seek deferral of the appointment, which Cardinal Wiseman believed he approved in principle, until a clear Cullenite majority had been built up within the hierarchy. A more urgent consideration, however, had arisen to trouble the Archbishop of Dublin. The involvement of priests in politics had worsened with reports of inflammatory tenant-right addresses from pulpits in County Meath and a controversial by-election in

County Louth, where Catholic clergy were found in the camps of both candidates. In the event, the government candidate won in Louth, to the satisfaction of Cullen who doubted the commitment to religion of his Tenant Right League opponent, a Catholic with wide popular (if insufficient voting) support. Cullen's position on political priests and on the League was now generally known. The League, the Young Irelanders, Lucas, the MacHaleites and the nationalist press were openly calling him a 'Whig'[2] and a 'Government bishop'.[3] If he was to succeed in his objective of withdrawing priests from the political arena, he could not allow his allegedly pro-British image to harden further. He could not risk being represented as an ally of the 'English interest'. He had to extricate himself from the charge of delivering the University into English control.

Cullen thought it dangerous, therefore, that the Cardinal of Westminster should be seen to dabble on a visit to Rome in the affairs of the Irish University. By the same token, it seemed desirable to prevent Newman from acquiring a status which the Lion of Tuam would claim as proof positive of English infiltration promoted by the Apostolic Delegate. Accordingly, while Newman was making his way from town to town in the south of Ireland, Cullen first wrote to the Rector of the Irish College in Rome, reminding him (and through him, the relevant Curia officials) that the *Rector Magnificus* of Louvain was not a bishop. He then drew up a careful letter to the Vatican in which he combined admiration for the famous English convert with an account of the anti-English sentiment so common in Ireland, gently hinted at Wiseman's endearing but ill-informed exuberance and stressed the need to launch the University without a display of pomp inappropriate to 'the poverty of Catholics in general'.[4] All things considered, he suggested, it would be better to put off the elevation of Dr Newman for the time being. Rome accepted the advice and shelved the idea. Given Cullen's difficulties, it was understandable.

Far from understandable was the discourtesy of both Wiseman and Cullen in neglecting to tell Newman about Rome's decision. He never heard of Cullen's letter, which has come to light only in recent years, but the reversal of intention which it achieved in Rome caused him very great embarrassment for the word had got out (through Bishop Ullathorne of Birmingham) that he was to be honoured. The newspapers carried the story. He received many letters of congratulation, gifts, offers of mitres and playful comments by his Oratorian colleagues on the ancient sees *in partibus infidelium* of which he might be declared bishop: the London Oratory, none too seriously, was 'all for Ptolemais'.[5] The awkwardness of having to send back the presents and stop friends from addressing letters to 'The Right Reverend Dr Newman'[6] when the weeks and months brought no further word on the subject was bad enough. Much worse, in the atmosphere of Victorian England, must have been the demonstration of insensitive and off-hand treatment visited by the Catholic authorities on their best-known convert from the Anglican Church. The episode left Newman pained and bewildered. 'The Cardinal never wrote to me a single word, or sent any message to me, in explanation of the change of intention', he recalled, '... Nor did Dr Cullen, nor Dr Grant [Bishop of Southwark], nor Dr Ullathorne, nor anyone else, ever again say one single word...'.[7]

According to his own charitable testimony, the unhappy experience faded from Newman's mind over the years for he had welcomed the prospect of being a bishop solely because it would have been useful in his conduct of University business. He must have wondered, but refrained from asking, whether it was moral cowardice or thoughtless arrogance that lay behind the failure to tell him what had happened. He even saw a good consequence in the way it all turned out: had he been a bishop, he reflected, he might have been unable to resign the Rectorship when he felt there was no more he could usefully accomplish. Others, either personally or vicariously, showed signs of guilt. Cullen was the first. Newman remembered later how, on 29 April 1854, the Archbishop showed him the Brief in which, after instructing the Irish bishops to make arrangements for opening the University, Pius IX referred to the Rector's 'outstanding gifts of character and intellect', his 'reputation for holiness and doctrinal learning' and his 'defence of the Catholic religion'.[8] Speaking 'in an awkward and hurried manner',[9] Cullen alleged that these polite compliments were the mark of distinction which the Pope had been expected to confer on Newman. Coming from the man who had blocked the distinction actually intended, this was lame indeed. Manning tried to revive the proposal in 1859 with the consent of Bishop Ullathorne, and in his own right when he succeeded Wiseman as Archbishop of Westminster in 1865, but without success. The original purpose — to strengthen the hand of the Rector — had lapsed with the resignation of Newman, who himself scotched Manning's second effort by begging him to desist.

While Newman may indeed have resumed his busy life without thinking much more of the embarrassment he had undergone, it would be disingenuous to suppose that it had no effect on his future attitudes. His relations with Cullen and Wiseman certainly became more distant and less trusting. An unconnected happening twelve years later evoked a reflection which surely owed something to the disappointment of 1854 (as well, perhaps, as to the behaviour of the Anglican episcopate towards the Oxford Movement): 'I think Bishops fancy that, as justice does not exist between the Creator and His creatures, between man and the brute creation, so there is none between them and their subjects. So that they only look out to see *how* clergy and laity accept those acts of theirs which in one *not* a Bishop *would* be unjust — e.g. whether the aggrieved accept them as an opportunity for gaining merit with humility, cheerfulness, submission ...'.[10] As a generalisation the remark may itself be unjust, but many can bear witness to this day that Newman's prophetic insight catches exactly the mind and values of ecclesiastics who too readily ride roughshod over personal rights — not to mention feelings — in the interest of what they judge to be a greater good, as if the end can justify the means or as if the Christian patience of those who suffer somehow exculpates the infliction of suffering.

*   *   *

His winter tour undermined the high spirits in which Newman had set off from Birmingham. The Jesuit provincial was right, he concluded: no class existed in Ireland from which university students might be drawn in large numbers. This, at any rate, was what everybody believed, which meant that he could evoke little enthusiasm for the idea. This, however, made no difference to his own commitment, since he still considered the Catholic University to be a project for the English-speaking world rather than Ireland alone. Although he had no more authority to make provision for the project than when he sent his protests to Cullen the previous Christmas, he knew from the Archbishop that a Brief was expected from Rome confirming his appointment as Rector, which would enable him and the Irish bishops to proceed, and he had his expectation — an apparent certainty — of being made a bishop himself for the precise purpose of enabling the University to succeed in spite of local foot-dragging. It was reasonable, therefore, to resume his tentative planning and he wrote to friends in England that he would not be home for several weeks yet.

This was less than convenient. Much Oratory business awaited his attention in Birmingham, from mundane decisions about the decor of the house to guidance for the temperamental master of novices on what to do regarding young entrants to the congregation. There were money problems to be sorted out and Faber was pestering him to come and preach at the imminent opening of the Brompton Oratory church. The pressure of these demands wore Newman down, not because he found them an intrusion on the great University question but, on the contrary, because they nagged his conscience. Throughout virtually his entire life as a Catholic, even when a Cardinal in advanced old age, he considered it his first duty to care for his 'family' of Oratorians and the work they had undertaken. Hence his anxiety in Limerick on discovering that his colleagues in Birmingham had misunderstood his instructions because he was not there to explain. In his anguish he rushed them a letter stutteringly phrased and punctuated: 'I am conscious to myself, that my heart is with you all, and no where else. Husbands and wives write to each other daily, when separated — When I come to a place, like Limerick, I say, "I wonder whether any letters from Edgbaston, will be lying for me." I write you to you [sic] when ever I have half an hour, and wish to find sympathy in you ...'.[11] The University, not the Oratory, was the intrusion on Newman's lifework.

Is it fanciful to imagine that gnawing scruples over what he should be doing had a physical consequence? His digestion, always delicate, seems to have given him particular trouble in the weeks after his Irish tour. Dr Quinn's table, though hospitable, had not improved. Newman had to write to his confessor in Birmingham for dispensation from the Lenten fast when he found that too often he could not continue once he had started with the one meal at which meat was permitted each day and he needed to try again later. He wrote also to Stanislas Flanagan, asking him whether there was a 'Club House' in Dublin which he might join as 'the best way ... for securing my dinner'.[12] As an Irish gentleman and former Guards officer, Father Flanagan was well-informed. He advised 'the Stephen's Green Club, which is the opposite side of the Green to the University.... Into this, altho' I think any other priest would be blackballed, *you,* I feel sure, would be admitted. It is not the crack Club of Dublin, but it is, of course, a most respectable one. Myles O'Reilly and the O'Ferrals (I believe) are members. *I* know shoals of its habitués — I wish you *were* a member, because I am of the opinion it would be the most efficacious way of gaining over to your views those who are now your opponents. It would serve all the purposes of dinners, without the bore and loss of time ... [but] perhaps the Archbishop might not like it.'[13] Whether frightened off by this revealing insight to the prejudices of Dublin society at the time or apprehensive of upsetting Cullen, Newman appears to have abandoned the idea of joining a club. Another factor, in a man as edgy as Newman about personal encounters, could have been the proximity of Whately a few doors away along the Green. Ironically, Whately's palace now houses the Kildare Street Club, which Flanagan would have known in its original premises and probably had in mind as the 'crack' establishment of the day. In any event, Newman settled down as best he could to live with his scruples, bad dinners and — it may be — want of the kind of company in which he would have felt most at home.

Myles O'Reilly, as it happened, was among the first people whom Newman approached when he got down again to making plans for the University. He invited him to accept a lectureship, apparently without specifying the subject since O'Reilly himself suggested political economy. The potential lecturer went off to consult his friend Thomas O'Hagan, the future Lord Chancellor of Ireland who had already turned down the offer of a professorship from Newman. O'Reilly must have decided against acceptance since his name does not feature in later staff lists. A more successful and much more important invitation resulted from a conversation which Newman had at this time with the antiquarian, Eugene O'Curry, who wanted his help in retrieving some Irish manuscripts from St Isidore's, the Irish Franciscan house in Rome. At Newman's request, he accepted the chair of Archaeology and Irish History at the University, where his lectures were to have a seminal influence on the development of studies in the literature and customs of Gaelic society. MacHale's suspicion of English influence in the University looks distinctly misplaced when the English Rector's enthusiastic sponsorship of O'Curry (which extended to funding his publications and having Irish-language type specially cast for him) is weighed in the balance. It surely merits an honoured niche in the annals of Gaelic scholarship for the most English of English churchmen!

Recruitment was to occupy much of Newman's time for the rest of the year. He had managed to post a number of invitations while travelling around the country and replies were now coming in. Denis Florence MacCarthy, a Young Ireland poet recommended by Bishop Moriarty, agreed to be professor or lecturer in poetry — meaning, said Newman, 'Poetry as a science, an art, an historical fact etc, etc, just as another might be Professor of Ethics, or of Politics, or of Political Economy'.[14] Peter Le Page Renouf was a Channel Islander, tutor to the son of a French aristocrat, and with some reluctance he accepted the offer of a lectureship in French language and literature: 'My favourite and persevering study is Christian Antiquity', he pointed out.[15] His wishes would eventually be met for, after a year as lecturer, he was promoted to the chair of Ancient History and Geography. Ornsby of the *Tablet* was already helping with the Greek and Latin curricula — he later turned down an offer of the University Secretaryship, which went to Scratton, but settled for the Professorship of Classics.

Others took longer to rise to Newman's bait, either because he could offer them no binding contracts until he was empowered to act by decision of the bishops in mid-May or because the men he approached needed to elucidate the scope of the subjects he wanted them to cover. Thus, his convert friend from Oxfordshire, T. W. Allies, decided in June to take up a lectureship in the philosophy of history but Newman was still explaining in September what this involved ('the science of which historical facts are the basis, or the laws on which it pleases Almighty Providence to conduct the political and social world'[16]) and as late as November Allies was wondering whether it would be correct to suppose that 'instances of the philosophy of history are the *De Civitate Dei*, in some degree; Bossuet *sur l'histoire universelle*; Guizot, civilisation in Europe and in France'.[17] Modern philosophers of history would confirm that Allies was on the right track, which says something for his grasp of what he called 'a science almost new, about the meaning of which even people are not agreed'.[18]

Hoping to satisfy local and episcopal preferences, Newman chose Irishmen for appointment where possible. This meant checking credentials since he could not vouch for them himself. 'I am *very* anxious to get some *good* information of the points of

Mr Butler the Mathematician', he wrote to the University Secretary in August, ' ... Who can definitely speak of him? *What were his honours?'*[19] 'I WANT INSTANTER SOME PARTICULARS OF YOUR COUSIN TERENCE'S CAREER', he shouted in untypical capital letters to Stanislas Flanagan in October, adding more calmly 'A few words will do.'[20] In the event, Butler gave up his post as a Chief Inspector in the National Board of Education to become Professor of Mathematics and Flanagan, well-known as a railway engineer in Lancashire and on the continent, became Professor of Civil Engineering. At Cullen's request more delicate enquiries were made in the case of possible appointees to theological posts. To a Roman canonist living in Paris Newman wrote, 'Monseigneur de Dublin ... désirerait savoir si ces Messieurs sont imbus des préjugés Gallicans',[21] and he received the reply concerning the 'Messieurs' in question that 'Mr Lahire de St Sulpice est ultramontain; c'est un homme solidement instruit.... Mr Faillon ... n'est peut-être pas aussi décidement [sic] ultramontain... mais ses doctrines sont sûres ...'.[22] For whatever reason, neither these nor other continentals enquired about were engaged at the outset. The religious chairs went to Dr Edmund O'Reilly, SJ, a former Maynooth professor and in Newman's judgement 'one of the first theologians of the day',[23] who was named Professor of Dogmatic Theology, and Dr Patrick Leahy of St Patrick's College, Thurles, who was appointed not only Professor of Exegetics but (by the bishops, not by Newman) Vice-Rector as well.

Newman tried valiantly to persuade Doellinger to take up a position in the University. The German scholar replied in his quaintly fluent English that he would like to help in an 'undertaking, which if the old antipathy between the Anglosaxon and the Celtic race doth not frustrate it, will be an invaluable benefit to the Catholic Cause.' He had, however, 'not yet been able to discover a way by which, without neglecting duties nearer home', he might make himself 'serviceable at Dublin'.[24] Newman refused to take 'no' for an answer. 'Now you cannot be *certain*', he wheedled in August, 'that a little time hence, say this time two years, you might not be able to help us — At least then let me enter your name *now* as Professor of Ecclesiastical History — when the time actually comes, you can but withdraw it.'[25] Newman's scrupulosity would appear to have had its limits! He failed to get Doellinger but was more successful with Aubrey de Vere, who also tried to avoid committing himself.

'Because you cannot promise to do any thing *now*, is no good reason why you should not do something in a year to come — and no reason you should not *promise* you will do something then', urged Newman, '... why will you not let me offer you the Professorship of Medieval History on the terms that you do not begin to lecture until November 1855?'[26] De Vere wriggled. Poetry, he said, was the only chair for which he was 'even tolerably qualified'.[27] Poetry by now was not available (MacCarthy had accepted) but, oddly enough, qualifications mattered little to Newman if a big name could be netted. De Vere was a big name, and in 1855 he yielded, becoming Professor of Political and Social Science.

Newman was embarrassed by the paucity of the salaries he could offer, as can be seen from his cumbersome proposal to Renouf: 'If I offered you the Lectureship of French Literature for 3 years ... at £150 a year *at least*, would it be worth your acceptance? ... Dublin is a very cheap place to live in ... what your work would be and what your remuneration, it is impossible to calculate at first.'[28] To Allies, who had employment in London, he suggested payment by fee. He could come over to Dublin to give two courses of lectures a year, said Newman, but 'the emolument would be very little at first. Say the course was one of 10 Lectures, and we paid your expenses of journey, and gave you £50 a course, this would be no more than the rate of paying an (Oxford) University Sermon.'[29] J. B. Robertson, who had been offered the lectureship in German Literature on the same terms as Renouf, came up with the bright idea that he might qualify for an enhanced salary if he took on a second lectureship as well. 'Undoubtedly every one has a right to his due remuneration, and I was ashamed of offering you the poor sum I did', wrote Newman.[30] Robertson settled for a lectureship in geography but went on to become Professor of Modern History and Geography.

In all these cases Newman held out the hope that better pay would be available when the bishops approved the arrangements he had set in motion or when the University had established itself on a firm basis. Surprisingly, he assembled a worthy staff list from the beginning on his inauspicious policy of live-horse-and-you'll-get-grass. It may fairly be assumed that the prospect of association with a man so renowned and respected was the spur to those who joined him in the venture. Certainly it was not the money on offer. After reference to Cullen and Archbishop Dixon of

Armagh at the end of September, salaries were fixed at levels close to Newman's predictions. Cheques issued for the quarter 1 November 1854 to 1 February 1855 showed the professors' pay to be £300 a year and lecturers' £200 or £150, depending on the subject taught. It was envisaged that tutors would be paid on the same scale as lecturers. Academic salaries might well have been higher had control of the University's finances been consigned to a committee of laymen, as Newman wished. The bishops were understandably obsessed with their role as trustees. They had raised the funds for the University by appealing to the generosity of their impoverished people. They set their faces against any squandering of the mites of the poor: Cullen, it will be remembered, had urged this as a reason for avoiding the expense and pomp of making Newman a bishop. He would blame the Rector in later years for wasting money by hiring too many staff. Such an attitude within the hierarchy did not make for enlightened views on disbursement of the moneys collected.

Newman had another objective in wanting lay involvement. He saw it as a way to overcome the lack of interest in the University which he met with in various parts of the country and, perhaps, as a way to encourage the growth of that class which he found inadequately represented in Irish Catholic society, the class which would aspire to a university education for its children. 'I wished the gentry whose sons were to be educated by us to have the financial matters of the institution in their own hands',[31] he recalled in old age. Even if the word 'gentry' betrayed Newman's personal limitations, his general argument convinces: 'I thought that such an arrangement would conciliate the laity and would interest them in the University more than anything else. [Instead] They were treated like good little boys, were told to shut their eyes and open their mouths, and take what we gave to them, and this they did not relish.'[32] The observation was psychological, and good psychology at that, but, although Newman may not have known it, it conveyed a profound historical message as well.

Here was the watershed between post-Famine Ireland and the world of Daniel O'Connell, not to mention Archbishop Murray. Leadership of the Catholic people had passed from the gentry, the professional classes and finally the people, to the Church. Even the politicians of various colours (not excluding the British administration) vied for clerical support. The senior clergy were in no mood to surrender that leadership. The argument between

105

Cullen and MacHale had nothing to do with the rights of the laity. It concerned where in the Church the leadership function rested: in the newly-centralised authority of Rome, represented in Ireland by the Apostolic Delegate, or corporately in the national bench of bishops.

Alone among lay Catholics now, Young Irelanders held out against Roman pretensions, believing as they did in a pluralist society where the members of all religions would be treated equally and mixed education at university level would be one of the ways to replace sectarian bitterness with harmony. Cullen mistrusted them deeply because of these views, which contradicted the fundamental assumptions of the ultramontane mentality and sounded in his ears too like the ideals of Italian revolutionaries for comfort. 'The young Irelanders desire to destroy all the power of the priests', he wrote, 'they seem to act just as the Mazzinians did in Italy — Evviva Pio Nono, when they were going to crucify him.... When I hear of the sanctity of some of these gentlemen, I always recollect the novenas and general Communions of the Romans in 1848.'[33] So much for Catholic liberalism and the legacy of O'Connell. So much, too, for the general body of the laity, whose supposed fickleness he denounced in his moment of reminiscence. For Cullen, only episcopal leadership was safe, and the bishops themselves were subject to the leadership of Rome.

MacHale gave his blessing to the Young Irelanders, at least in their latest manifestation as the Tenant Right League, partly because they stood for Irish control of Irish affairs and the entitlement of Irish priests to voice their opinions about what touched their people's interest, and partly because their policies — so attractive to the bulk of the Catholic people — were the Achilles' heel in the hardening Cullenite domination of the Irish Church. But nowhere in MacHale's support of their cause was there mention of the laity's role *as laity*. He supported them because they advocated the policies which *he* approved and in consequence were useful allies in his campaign to make the opinions of Tuam prevail over those of Dublin and London ... and, if need be, of Rome itself, for when it came to Irish affairs he knew that Rome allowed itself to be guided by the Apostolic Delegate, the Archbishop of Dublin. If a vision of Church can be assigned to him, beyond a mere determination to resist external pressure in what he believed to be for the good of Irish Catholicism, it was an episcopal/collegial understanding. The corporate view of the bishops was to prevail in the local Church, not that of one bishop alone: this he consistently urged over many years.

To say that MacHale had no conception of the laity's right to be heard as *members of the Church* would be factually true, but it would be reading history backwards to think that he consciously formed an attitude on the question. No more than Cullen did he doubt the leadership role of the bishops. The controversy concerned how this should be exercised, collegially by discussion issuing in majority decisions or subserviently by collective endorsement of Roman decisions. MacHale could not accept the second position for he never saw the bishops as agents or vicars of the Pope. This was in no sense anti-Papal, and it would be sustained in the distant future by the Second Vatican Council, for the collegial vision went beyond the local Church to embrace the relationship between all the local Churches and the Church Universal, between all the bishops and the Bishop of Rome. Once more, we must beware of attributing attitudes to a nineteenth-century prelate which took definitive shape only in a later age. Such attitudes *take* shape, however, because somewhere, by someone, and then by others, they are first inchoately perceived, then argued over, thought through and — it may be generations later — receive precise phrasing at last. On the function and authority of bishops, we can say no more than that John MacHale had a view which belonged within the emergent understanding of the Church and it differed from the view of Paul Cullen. It rested upon a higher regard for the episcopal office.

Two objections can be made immediately. MacHale gave unstinting support to O'Connell and O'Connell was not a man to be led by a bishop or any number of bishops. Did the Lion of the West (and it was O'Connell who dubbed him 'the Lion') therefore then concede leadership to the laity? The question forces a bygone situation into a modern mould. Like Cullen in Rome, MacHale saw the benefit to Catholicism of O'Connell's political priorities and, like Cullen, he backed them. Perhaps more than Cullen, he saw them also as beneficial to *Ireland,* so that a patriotic instinct strengthened his ecclesiastical judgment. In the absence of a serious conflict of opinion between the Lion and the Liberator, no basis exists for reading into their relationship a MacHaleite stance on lay initiative in matters of concern to the Church. What can be said with certainty is that after O'Connell had died, MacHale acknowledged the mantle of leadership on no shoulders other than those of the collective episcopate.

The second objection, the more real, touches the extent to which MacHale in fact believed in this collective leadership, which he used unmercifully to batter Archbishop Murray, and after him Cullen. That he harangued and browbeat his brother bishops to secure a majority for his personal views cannot be denied. When Cullen provided them with an alternative focus, MacHale's majority dwindled and eventually disappeared. The logic of his concept of episcopal authority should then have required him to yield. He never did. He became the defender of minority opinion, which in another might have been admirable but in MacHale was a contradiction, and he would carry his new perception into a General Council of the Church when, at the First Vatican Council, he stood out to the end against the majority who favoured defining the doctrine of Infallibility. We need not go as far as the man who said that if the issue had been the infallibility of the Archbishop of Tuam, MacHale might have come to a different conclusion! The fact remains that his collegial vision stopped short of bowing to collegial viewpoints contrary to his own. He was scarcely alone, of course, among public figures then and since who modified or reversed their beliefs when brought face to face with the logic involved. It could be argued that the senior authorities of the Catholic Church have been doing this in our own day when faced with the logic of the Second Vatican Council. In more humble walks of life, the practice is known as moving the goalposts. MacHale was adept at it and thereby gave Cullen good reason for his case that a strong Roman hand was needed to prevent the Irish hierarchy from treating every decision arrived at, not as settlement of the question at issue, but as the springboard for launching another destructive debate. On the evidence, the Lion cannot be credited with prophetic insight since he failed to be guided by his own principles, but it would be fair enough to suggest that the case he put together against Cullen incorporated messages more profound than he knew on the nature of the Church.

The tension between Dublin and Tuam was stretching to a breaking point which would be reached in Rome as the eventful year of 1854 drew to its close. Newman was largely unaware of the mounting crisis during the spring and summer, while he was occupied in enticing, cajoling and talking the persons he considered most suitable on to the University staff. He none the less found himself confronted in various ways with the episcopal attitudes involved in the controversy. MacHale complained that Newman had presented the hierarchy with a *fait accompli* when he informed the archbishops of the provisional appointments to chairs and lectureships. Cullen graciously signalled his approval of the names, saying 'I place so much confidence in your judgment and prudence that I cannot hesitate one moment in giving my sanction',[34] but Newman would later note the difficulty he had in putting forward some of those on his list. MacCarthy, O'Hagan and O'Curry were former Young Irelanders: Dr Cullen always compared Young Ireland to Young Italy; and with the most intense expression of words and countenance, assured me that they never came right, never.'[35] Just how the Rector trundled these names successfully past the Archbishop is unclear. Only three months later Cullen was writing to him from Rome, 'I trust you will make every exertion to keep the University free from all Young Irelandism.'[36] As for a lay finance committee, Newman might as well have bayed to the moon for all the response he got. Yet he formed an academic staff almost entirely lay from the beginning, which was a considerable achievement, and for the most part Irish, which went a distance towards pleasing the bishops. It may not be far from the truth to detect an unspoken degree of compromise on every side in the steps taken to ensure that the University was equipped with a worthy teaching body, calculated to attract students of talent and ambition.

*   *   *

As a grace-note to the selection of staff, Newman also sent letters to persons of rank or distinction in Ireland, Britain, America and the continent soliciting permission to enter their names on the University 'books'. They would thereby become Associates of the University, in effect honorary graduates who would be presumed to have that interest in its development which the real graduates might be expected to show in time as their numbers grew. No functions were assigned to the Associates: '… they will be simply names on our books. I mean the owners of them will have no trouble or expence' [sic],[37] Newman told Manning. In practice, therefore, the display of interest requested went no further than allowing themselves to be seen to be 'associated' with the University. The elusive Doellinger gave the Rector *'carte blanche* in this respect'[38] as also, perhaps surprisingly, did Archbishop MacHale. The Comte de Montalembert gave his name upon receiving a letter from Newman in which the Rector made no reference (he may have been unaware of it) to the Frenchman's past acquaintance with Ireland and O'Connell. Most of the Irish, British and American bishops went on the list together with a number of Catholic peers and scholars, including the future Lord Acton, the great liberal historian. Some Irish gentry, on the other hand, refused to be entered for reasons ranging from their belief in the Queen's Colleges and dislike for the apparent clerical control being exercised by the bishops over the new University to a simple wish not to fall out of favour with the Government. The list of Associates was published but it would be difficult to point to any good that came of it. The exercise illustrated Newman's anxiety to buttress the University with every possible source of prestige on which he could draw. It revealed as well his continuing assumption, as he put it to Montalembert, that he was 'setting up a Catholic University of the English tongue, which it is to be hoped, will be of service, not only to Irishmen of the upper and middle class, but to the Catholics in England and the United States also'.[39]

Just how sanguine Newman was about receiving students from abroad became evident from the arrangements he put in hand for accommodation. As we have seen, he wished the students to be lodged in halls of residence, which would eventually become endowed Colleges like those making up the University of Oxford. Each house would have some twenty students, its dean or head, its tutors and one or two university lecturers, all living in: 'one of them should be called St Patrick's ... another St Lawrence's, another St Columba's, etc. Each of them should have its private Chapel ...'.[40] To this tidy plan, which he had been mulling over for several years, he now added the idea of putting what he called 'the Nations' in separate halls. The Irish would go into one. The '60 to 100 Yankees'[41] he was expecting in due course would go to another (how this intention could be reconciled with the desirable complement of twenty he did not say; perhaps they would not all come in the one year) and he was determined to have 'an English house of *my own friends*'.[42]

Although there were medieval precedents for such a scheme (in Oxford, Balliol College had originally been for Scottish students and Jesus College for Welsh) it sounded in the nineteenth century uncommonly like the Irish, English and other national colleges for clerical students attending the Roman universities. This was hardly a precedent to appeal to Newman, who emphatically insisted in another context that a university was not a seminary. His reasoning was pragmatic. He needed the English house, as noted earlier, to provide him with a base where he could feel at home, a vital protection against the awkward uncertainty he suffered in the presence of strangers. He furthermore saw an advantage to the parents of poorer families, most of whom would be Irish, in being able to fix different fees for each house. The English students, who would lodge in his own house, would come from relatively wealthy families and could be charged up to £100 a year. In the Irish house, he thought £50 might suffice, although at that price he felt it would be 'in every sense a rough place'.[43] (These estimates were in fact very close to the fees levied when the University opened; no 'American' rate was struck, for the transatlantic influx sadly failed to materialise.)

By July, however, the housing arrangements were no more than plans on paper — and, as will be be seen, Newman was pledged to open the University on 3 November. So far, he had only one premises, University House at 86 Saint Stephen's Green. He was still living in lodgings himself at Dr Quinn's school. On 5 July he wrote to Henry Wilberforce: 'I want to rent a large house ... as large a house, say in Eli [sic] Place, Hume Street, Leeson Street, or Harcourt Street, as I could get for £60 to £80 a year with £20 rates and taxes.'[44] His idea was to fit out a bedroom and sitting-room for his own use, turn another room into a chapel and engage a husband and wife as living-in servants. The remaining rooms he would let to a secretary, students or lecturers. 'If you think it possible', he rather casually requested Wilberforce, 'just look out for a house as you walk through the streets.'

By mid-August it seemed that suitable buildings had been found, not one but two houses, 21 and 22 Ely Place, which could be had from the same landlord for little more than Newman hoped to pay for one house alone. It was a bargain not to be missed. Then, without explanation, the offer to let them at a rent was withdrawn. It reflected sadly on the religious animosities of the day. Newman's colleague from the Oratory, Father Ambrose St John, happened to be in Dublin and had visited Ely Place to see the properties. Shortly afterwards he received a letter from Newman: 'Our negociation [sic] about Numbers 21 and 22 is all off. Scratton thinks a priest (you) going there had something to do with it.'[45] Eventually, a mere week before the University opened, Newman rented 6 Harcourt Street, which he called Saint Mary's House, and proceeded to fit it out in accordance with his plans. The name of University House was in due course changed to Saint Patrick's. Meanwhile, a number of senior pupils in Dr Quinn's school became students at the University and the school at 16 Harcourt Street became a further house of the Catholic University under its existing name of Saint Lawrence's. Only Saint Patrick's remains university property today (under yet another name as Newman House of University College, Dublin). Saint Mary's is the headquarters of Conradh na Gaeilge. St Lawrence's has long been converted to business use. Number 22 Ely Place, interestingly, housed for a time the editorial offices of the Christian journal *Alpha* which, being ecumenical, compensated in some manner for the discriminatory decision regarding the tenancy made in less happy times!

In other ways also Newman worked hard in these months to build up the status of the University before a single class of students had been assembled or a single lecture delivered. It would not be too much to say that he had become mildly obsessed with the notion that students would come in numbers only if the overall education to be acquired at the University and the intellectual quality of its lifestyle each promised to be superlative, and if a certain sophistication was going to be the hallmark of its activities. Seeking out the right names as associates and lecturers (a man's general reputation mattering more than his competence in a particular field), as well as establishing a collegiate system, were part of this remarkable ambition to mould the University's character in advance of its physical existence. His early thoughts on a university church — shades of Oxford! — betrayed the same concern. A church would proclaim the Catholic principles which the University served and would be a focal point uniting the students from the several faculties and halls of residence. Degrees would be conferred there and its Sunday afternoon sermons — Oxford again, but now ending with Benediction — would 'bring the University, as a University, once a week before the public',[46] and he wanted careful consideration to be given to the forms of dress to be worn by clergy, academics and students alike. There would be a choir and 'I want the whole *imposing* ... with thrones, pulpits etc all very grand'.[47] This he specified in March 1854, when the bishops had yet to give him licence to proceed with organising the University itself and the only prospect of acquiring a church was the hope that the diocese might make one available. For Newman, whose personal taste in dress was unostentatious and who always relied on words rather than gesture to convey his message, such concern with ceremonial meant he was seizing a further opportunity to ensure that the University would evoke respect from the moment it came into being. As it transpired, he had to begin without a church — but the project would be heard of again.

The establishment of scholarly 'institutions'[48] to promote special areas of learning struck Newman as another effective means of conferring prestige on the University without awaiting the graduation of the first classes or even the induction of the first students. These foundations could be put in hand as soon as he had engaged the University professors, whose responsibility they would be. His enthusiasm for the work of Eugene O'Curry probably reflected the consolidation of this concept in his mind: Newman certainly hoped to create what would be called in the next century a School of Celtic Studies, with an emphasis on Irish language, art and archaeology. An institute to study the development of Irish economic resources, an astronomical observatory and a medical school (in association with a hospital) were among other proposals which Newman, in May 1854, advised the bishops should be set up under the aegis of the University and be intimately associated with it through the involvement of its senior staff.

These institutions would meet a need which arose because Newman had theorised it into existence in his Dublin Discourses. He had been so anxious then to stress the nature of a university as the centre in which liberal knowledge was *acquired,* tempered through the relationship between the various disciplines or branches of knowledge, that he could find no place in its ordinary proceedings for *research* — examining received knowledge in a critical spirit, seeking fresh information, setting up hypotheses, testing them by analysis and eventually arriving at new or additional knowledge or a deeper understanding of what was already known. Yet the knowledge available was manifestly incomplete. In the physical, political and social sciences, the nineteenth century saw knowledge being enlarged daily. It was scarcely a development from which the university could opt out, being the very home of knowledge. Indeed, although the analogy is inexact, Newman's views on the development of doctrine sat uneasily with any disparagement of research. But as ever,

Newman was precise, speaking strictly of the university's primary role, its service to the undergraduate and its function to turn him into a useful citizen.

The place of research, the importance of which he fully admitted, was within the teaching or graduate community. It arose after the university had discharged its primary duty. It was more correct to locate it in institutions separately identifiable, although in fact parts of, the university which created the stimulus to research by providing the education upon which it was built. This would meet a vital need also among the teachers, who risked mental atrophy if they could not participate in the development of their own disciplines. The distinction between university teaching and research was possibly made sharper than necessary by Newman's relentless logic. In reality, since the teachers and researchers were so often the same people, and many students were in the process of growing into researchers, the distinction was one of activity rather than location: a medical school obviously incorporated both functions, and the university itself only a little less obviously. To meet the distinction which he made, Newman's 'institutions' need have been no more than postgraduate departments.

It remains revealing to note, at a time when specialised institutes in Ireland have just been granted the title of 'university' which they long craved, that the apologist *par excellence* for the university saw research in specialised fields as a more esoteric occupation than the work which a university was by definition required to discharge. It was for this reason that he believed a university could build up its prestige through founding 'institutions' which would be associated with it in the public view, and which conveniently did not depend on a body of undergraduates to justify their establishment. At the same time, an 'institution' like a medical school or a scientific foundation, especially if it were involved in teaching as well as research, benefited in its turn from association with a university. Said Newman in his Eighth Discourse, 'there will be this distinction as regards a Professor of Law, or of Medicine, or of Geology, or of Political Economy, in a University and out of it, that out of a University he is in danger of being absorbed and narrowed by his pursuit, and of giving Lectures which are the Lectures of nothing more than a lawyer, physician, geologist, or political economist; whereas in a University he will just know [*recte* 'know just'?] where he and his science stand ... he is kept from extravagance by the very rivalry of other

114

studies, he has gained from them a special illumination and largeness of mind and freedom and self-possession, and he treats his own in consequence with a philosophy and a resource, which belongs, not to the study itself, but to his liberal education.'[49]

Whether experience has proved this to be the case or not, can be left to the witness of university teachers. Newman was never at his best in making hairline distinctions or asserting a belief rather than arguing it. What matters is that he acted on his faith in the value of 'institutions'. Early in May 1854, and without waiting for the bishops' meeting which was about to take place, he wrote to an old acquaintance, Manuel Johnson, Director of the Radcliffe Observatory at Oxford, to ask whether he knew of a Catholic astronomer who might be employed to set up an observatory in Dublin. In further correspondence he told Johnson that 'For reasons, which it would take too long to explain, it is desirable to make a *show* ... It has struck me then to set up certain institutions or schools which will have their worth in themselves, and will command respect, while the real University (i.e. the bodies and minds of its constituents) is growing in number and in intellect under their shadow.'[50] The observatory would be one of these institutions. Stubbornly, despite all the other matters demanding his attention, Newman persisted in an unsuccessful search for an astronomer to the end of the year, asking Johnson for advice on instruments and their cost as well as drawing on his friend's knowledge of the Observatory at Bonn where he thought a suitably qualified Catholic might be found. Newman's concentration on an observatory, rather than other 'institutions' which might have been more usefully encouraged, was all the more surprising since Dublin already had an observatory at Dunsink, the superintendent of which was the famous mathematician, Sir William Rowan Hamilton — although Johnson was unimpressed by the the achievements of Dunsink, whatever he thought about Hamilton's work on quaternions.

In the event, a different 'institution' became the most immediately successful feature of the Catholic University, and remained for generations its outstanding service to higher education in Ireland. On 11 June Newman heard that an established medical school was about to be put on the market. It had been opened nearly twenty years earlier on the site of the eighteenth-century Crow Street Theatre, which faced on to Cecilia Street in the warren of pre-Georgian alleyways between Dame Street and the Liffey. Known as Cecilia Street Medical School, it had been quite satisfactorily run by the Dublin Apothecaries' Hall but was now being sold because two of its best professors had resigned simultaneously. Newman contacted Cullen, who put no obstacle in the way of buying the school, but the problem arose once again of concealing the official Church interest in the purchase of property. Negotiations were concluded in mid-July and the University acquired the school for £1,500. Only MacHale objected — on the ground that Newman had merely informed the archbishops and not consulted them. This was in fact the case so far as Tuam, Cashel and Armagh were concerned and Newman's plea in reply, that he believed such a purchase to be within the authority delegated to him, was somewhat disingenuous since he had written to Cullen on 12 June to say that 'Unless then I hear any thing from your Grace to the contrary, I shall proceed to make an offer.'[51] In Newman's defence it can be said that realistically he *had* to have Cullen's approval since, with Cullen's backing, he could outface any other opposition but if Cullen objected, he could not proceed: apart from anything else, Cullen's counter-signature was needed before a cheque could issue! Also, because of the need to keep the identity of the purchasers concealed until the latest possible moment, general consultation would have been impractical. None the less, the wily old Lion had only to sniff the air to know how the wind was blowing. He growled for the record but made no attempt to undermine the acquisition.

Although the Medical School came fully equipped, Newman delayed opening it for a year. He needed the time to engage Catholic professors, whom he deemed to be absolutely necessary. It was not that he objected to students attending lectures on medical subjects given by Protestant professors, but rather that he could see no way to appoint Protestants to chairs in the Catholic University. He considered opening the School as the University's Faculty of Medicine in the autumn of 1854 with such Catholic staff as he could assemble, while allowing the students to take courses elsewhere which could not be supplied within the Faculty for want of Catholic staff. Alternatively, he thought of letting out the School for a year so that the University would not be responsible for the courses provided there. In the end he decided simply to wait until he had found adequate staff who were suitably qualified, professionally and denominationally, for the School to be conducted entirely from its own resources. This took a year and the School accordingly opened in the autumn of 1855.

To the modern mind Newman's intransigence about the religion of his staff members, even when their subjects were far removed from religiously contentious fields (anatomy, for instance, or geography), inevitably savours of bigotry. His position has to be understood from two perspectives. In the first place, the unity of all knowledge, the inter-relationship of its various branches and the inability of compromising the truth, as he had elaborated these principles in his Dublin Discourses, gave a philosophical *rationale* to his rigid stance which owed nothing to prejudice. Secondly, denominational exclusiveness was the norm rather than the exception in the milieux of his experience: only members of the established Church could hold chairs or fellowships in Oxford and Cambridge. Catholics were still excluded from senior posts in Trinity College, Dublin. At the practical level of medical institutions in the Irish capital — hospitals and medical schools — he recorded the following year that, outside the Catholic University, 'of one hundred and eleven Medical Practitioners in situations of trust and authority, twelve are Catholic and ninety-nine Protestant'.[52] In being true to himself he was therefore rectifying an intolerable imbalance. It may, however, be suggested that, notwithstanding the temper of the times and the undoubted logic of his personal attitude, Newman missed an opportunity which Archbishop Murray would have seen and seized. Catholics could have claimed their rightful place in Irish society without elbowing aside their compatriots of other faiths, and had they been tolerant in this (as O'Connell also would have wanted) many of the tensions of later years might have been averted. Newman, far-seeing in so much else, was altogether blind to the prophetic wisdom of Emancipation Catholicism in Ireland, which was not yet dead despite the resolute efforts of Archbishop Cullen to bury it once for all.

*   *   *

Newman undertook his preparations at this increasingly hectic pace because, between April and June of 1854, the formal procedures had been completed to permit the University to open. In April the expected Brief arrived from Rome, approving in fulsome terms the appointment of Newman as Rector, setting out the purpose of the University and instructing the Apostolic

Delegate to summon a synodal meeting of the bishops to agree the necessary arrangements so that classes might begin at an early date. The bishops met from 18 to 20 May. On 4 June, at an impressive ceremony in the Metropolitan Church of St Mary, soon to be the Pro-Cathedral, Archbishop Paul Cullen presided over the official installation of the first Rector of the Catholic University of Ireland, Dr John Henry Newman of the Oratory. Each of these events had its own significance and taken together they amounted to as massive an endorsement of Newman's authority and as wide an indication of his duties as he could have wished. The dark uncertainty of the previous Christmas had lifted ... or so it seemed. The excitement and anticipation infusing the Rector can be sensed from the first issue of the *Catholic University Gazette*, the eight-page weekly journal launched in June and edited by Newman — as if he hadn't enough to do! 'A University is not founded every day', he wrote. Most universities emerged slowly from schools or colleges or monasteries, but in Ireland 'this great institution is to take its place among us without antecedent or precedent.'[53] People were unconscious of the need for it, it was misunderstood, was the object of prejudice and lacked 'any counter-balancing assistance whatever, as has commonly been the case with Universities, from royal favour or civil sanction'.[54] Yet it was about to happen. Rarely has anyone so exulted in challenge.

He did not arrive at this summit of confidence without last-minute qualms. The Papal Brief troubled him, for it seemed to see the aim of the University as the production of graduates not only well-versed in secular subjects but well-grounded in their faith. Newman, by contrast, had argued that 'knowledge is one thing, virtue is another';[55] knowledge was the stock-in-trade of liberal education and 'Liberal Education makes not the Christian, not the Catholic, but the gentleman';[56] the end of a university course was 'training good members of society'[57] whom it made fit for the world. There was in fact no fundamental contradiction. The problem lay once more in Newman's extraordinary precision of thought. Pius IX could not begin to match him in this and wrapped up the objectives of University education by stating a pastoral *desideratum*. Newman had distinguished between intellectual and moral objectives, siting the first within the ambit of University teaching and the second within the family atmosphere of the embryonic colleges, the houses or halls of residence where the tutors would exercise a beneficial supervision. Since both he and the Pope resorted to metaphysical concepts in stating their views, Newman felt that somehow an alternative doctrine was being proposed and he expunged from the later editions of his Discourses (published as *The Idea of a University*) some sections which might have been said to conflict with the formal philosophical terminology of the Papal Brief. Whether he tampered with his text *because* of this possible clash is open to argument, but the fact remains that he did so. It was quite unnecessary since he and the Pope shared the same perception of what a Catholic university might hope to achieve. Newman merely analysed more fully how it was to be done and distinguished between the purposes served by the various activities encompassed by university life.

The Papal Brief also exacerbated the fear, which had been nagging Newman for some time, that the bishops intended the University to be no more than a college. By stressing religious formation and good conduct the Pope seemed to expect the University to do the work which Newman believed to be a college responsibility. But this definition of collegiate duties, although reasonable and perceptive, was peculiarly Newman's own, an echo of Oxford controversies in a receding past. The Pope was not presuming to enter into Newman's mind, still less disputing Newman's theories. He was simply issuing a pastoral reminder. Unfortunately, the Vatican officials who drew up the document varied the word used for 'university', saying sometimes 'Universitas', sometimes 'Gymnasium' and sometimes 'Lyceum'.[58] To Newman's extraordinarily sensitive mind, this stylistic practice implied an uncertainty regarding the status of the Irish University and went a distance towards convincing him that the bishops, few of whom had any experience of a true university, were indeed disposed to think of it as a lay seminary or an expanded diocesan college — that is, a secondary boarding school. His anxiety was groundless. Whatever annoying restrictions the hierarchy, and Archbishop Cullen in particular, might envisage to limit either the Rector's or the students' freedom of action, they stopped far short of undermining the essential character of the University.

The synodal meeting held in Dublin in May drew up a list of decrees which assumed that, in virtually all respects, the University would be established and conducted on Newman's principles. This fact removes any suspicion of serious deviation by Newman from the values set out in the Pope's document. The astute scholarship of men as different from one another as Cullen and Moriarty would have quickly identified any departure from officially approved standards and neither they nor most of their colleagues would have admitted deviant attitudes into their synodal decrees. At the same time, the decrees revealed no concern to restrict the University within the limits more appropriate to a college. In view of the criticism which can validly be made of the treatment visited on Newman by the bishops, justice requires it to be said that he sometimes suspected them, or individuals among them, of intentions which they never harboured or (as in the present case) of influencing Rome in a direction which they never contemplated. The major influence detectable in the 1854 decrees was that of Newman himself. While the bishops retained the *supremum ius* or ultimate authority (as the Belgian hierarchy did in the case of Louvain), the full administration of the University, control over its academic standards (through the power to confer degrees), the right to appoint the administrative staff and to 'designate' the professors for definitive appointment by the bishops together with power to establish halls of residence and to appoint their deans were all vested in the Rector. There were to be five faculties (Theology, Law, Medicine, Philosophy and Letters, and Science), which between them, as these disciplines were defined in the nineteenth century, covered the entirety of subject matter with which universities anywhere were expected to concern themselves.

Only on the relatively minor question of the Vice-Rector was Newman denied a voice where he felt he should have it: the bishops reserved this appointment exclusively to themselves and, having done so, immediately named Dr Patrick Leahy of Thurles to the post, as noted already. On the other hand, the hope of being able to function efficiently was much enhanced for Newman by the decision that if no meeting of the hierarchy were held in a given year the Rector was to present his annual report to the archbishops, who were also to receive the names of persons to be granted honorary degrees. These seemingly pragmatic arrangements meant that the Rector could dispose of ongoing business with the trustees by dealing with four people instead of nearly thirty, and would be spared the hazard of becoming the victim of quarrelling within the hierarchy where he had feared that a minority might be numerous enough to defy majority decisions. Of course, there was always the Lion ... but it looked as if he would normally find himself in a minority of one. In fact the informal committee of archbishops was soon to be given exceptional recognition by Rome, in a way which would weaken further the influence of MacHale, when it was decided that the archbishops were to act permanently for the trustees and, for good measure, that the Apostolic Delegate would have a casting vote in the event of a two-against-two deadlock on any issue to be determined.

Newman meanwhile could rejoice over the many hurdles cleared by the synodal meeting. Not only had he got the University structured as he wanted but, now that the wide powers of the Rector were confirmed, he could proceed along the lines set out in a memorandum which he had submitted to the meeting and which it had noted without comment. This document reasserted and elaborated the objectives of the University.[59] It would be 'for the Catholics of Ireland and of other countries which speak the English tongue'. It would help 'to provide a series of sound and philosophical defences of Catholicity and Revelation' and 'raise the standard ... of the schools ... throughout the country'. Here Newman was repeating his familiar theme on the need to improve the quality of Catholic scholarship to combat the intellectual indifferentism of the age. He stressed it also in the wish to put 'young men of rank, fortune, or expectations ... on a level with Protestants of the same description'. This was not elitism, but the drawing of battle-lines: he had ambitions too for students of law and medicine, for 'youths destined to mercantile and similar pursuits', for 'promising youths in the lower classes' whose talents he wanted to develop — modern readers may find the class distinctions distasteful, but by Victorian norms this amounted to a step towards equal opportunity.

He added his thoughts on university organisation, including the importance of halls of residence and a university church. He had a fully developed scheme for segmenting the study-course. The first two years would be spent on the basic humanities like Latin, Greek, logic and mathematics. Students leaving after this would have had a grounding in liberal education, certified by the degree of Scholar. Those who stayed for another two years would concentrate on specific subjects, some of them of a quasi-professional nature: metaphysics, economics, law, history. They would qualify for the degree of Bachelor. Three more years would lead to post-graduate degrees — Master of Letters or Science; Doctor of Theology, Law or Medicine. If Newman at this stage put his emphasis on arts subjects, this simply reflected what could be set in motion without delay and what in any event was to be the starting point for all students, regardless of their ultimate specialities. His determination to provide Bachelor and higher degrees in engineering, science and medicine was clear not only from his forward planning but from his efforts throughout 1854 to recruit teaching staff in these fields and the energy with which he would pursue the purchase of Cecilia Street Medical School. It should also be said that if the breakdown of the seven-year course appears unoriginal, the reason is that Newman's formula *anticipated* the approach adopted by many universities in the twentieth century. Some followed his guidance; others arrived by similar reasoning at the same conclusion. In either case, the prophetic quality of Newman's vision is evident: he saw the needs of the age and responded to them.

The sole remaining action required to admit Newman formally to possession of his charge was to have him take an oath of office, as he had told Cullen he was anxious to do when he wrote to him at Christmas. This was carried out after the special High Mass sung by Bishop Moriarty in the Metropolitan Church on Whit Sunday, 4 June, when Newman made a profession of faith before Archbishop Cullen and promised obedience to the Irish hierarchy. The Rector hastened to let his friends know the good news. 'The church was more crowded than ever known. The Archbishop ended with a very touching address to me', he wrote to the Oratory.[60] 'I took the oaths yesterday, the feast of Pentecost', he told Acton.[61] 'We have begun on the most suitable of days', he said for the Pope's information in a letter to Monsignor Talbot of the Roman Curia, 'and I trust we shall put ourselves under the patronage of the Sedes Sapientiae.'[62] Similar messages went to Bishop Ullathorne of Birmingham and to Cardinal Wiseman. Cullen was no less pleased. He wrote to the Vice-Rector of the Irish College in Rome, 'We shall be most cautious to banish all strange doctrines and Gallicanism from our university. Dr Newman is thoroughly Roman. We inaugurated him with great *éclat* on Pentecost Sunday. *Sit faustum felixque.'*[63] In his sermon at the installation, which Newman so appreciated, he had exhorted the Rector to 'teach the young committed to your care to cultivate every branch of learning, to scan the depths of every science, and to explore the mysteries of every art; encourage the development of talent and the flight of genius; but check the growth of error, and be a firm bulwark against everything that would be prejudicial to the interests of religion and the doctrines of the Holy Catholic Church.'[64] For once, Newman could scarcely have put better what he proposed to do.

Thus the Papal Brief, the synodal meeting and the outcome as Newman saw them. In his Saxon innocence he assumed that the Brief was chivvying by Rome to expedite the University project and that the meeting had been called for the purpose for which it was said to be called. In fact he was looking at the tip of an iceberg. What he did not know was that in the previous December, when he was himself having such difficulty in getting Cullen to answer his letters, the Archbishop had written to the Rector of the Irish College, instructing him to suggest to the Curia that Rome should direct the Irish bishops to hold a canonical meeting (that is, one required by higher authority in due form, the decisions of which would be binding when endorsed by Rome) in order to remove the obstacles in the way of launching the University. These obstacles, he explained, were all raised by the Archbishop of Tuam who was putting about stories — abetted by the Young Ireland newspapers (the *Nation* and the *Freeman's Journal*) — that the University Committee was 'hostile to the interests of Ireland' and wanted 'to introduce an English spirit'.[65] The request appeared to be a change of subject. All that autumn Cullen's correspondence and actions had to do with the question of priests in politics and the related question of filling episcopal vacancies with churchmen who would support the Apostolic Delegate's opposition to priests in politics. So why his sudden renewal of interest in the University? True, according to Wiseman, the Pope was becoming impatient with the absence of progress on the project, but his concern had not seemed to percolate down to the Archbishop of Dublin. True also, MacHale attacked the University Committee as he attacked any enterprise with which Cullen was associated, but the burden of his criticism in 1853 had been directed against Cullen's political stance rather than his attitude on higher education. Yet the Archbishop of Dublin unilaterally, as it were, reactivated the University question with Rome at a time when the putative Rector could glean no information about it whatsoever.

The reason became apparent when the canonical meeting suggested by Cullen and ordered by the Papal Brief assembled in the Marlborough Street Presbytery in Dublin on 18 May 1854. It had been called in line with Cullen's advice to make provision for the University. Even Newman caught a whiff of trouble. On 20 May he noted 'This is the *third* day the Bishops are sitting —

and I hear not a word what they are doing. I fear there are sad disputes, but I cannot tell of course.'⁶⁶ There were disputes indeed. The agenda for the meeting listed an item on political priests prior to discussion of the University question. MacHale protested, quite correctly, that this was not what the meeting had been summoned for. When Cullen persisted, MacHale claimed that the issue had been raised in order to censure his conduct. This was also correct, at least to the extent that Cullen intended to make it much more difficult for bishops to follow MacHale's example in supporting political priests. Had he arranged for a meeting explicitly on this matter he might have faced serious opposition, for not only was the dwindling MacHale camp against him but he could not be sure of the line that the Archbishop of Cashel, the Bishop of Waterford and perhaps others whom he had offended by interfering in their affairs, would adopt. On the University question, however, the Pope's position was now so definite that even those who doubted its wisdom were not going to resist its implementation. By holding a meeting about the University and at it introducing what really concerned him — the controversy surrounding political priests — Cullen cleverly forced a choice between himself and the obstreperous Archbishop of Tuam. Factions could not readily form, MacHale's unhelpful obstructiveness alienated sympathy and most of the bishops were glad enough to have binding directives to help dampen the over-ardent political atmosphere in their dioceses. Cullen got his way: overt electoral politics were debarred from the pulpits and chapels of Catholic Ireland, and priests were forbidden to inveigh against one another on political issues. After this, the University proposals had a relatively easy passage.

Relatively only, in the eyes of Cullen — although Newman was very pleased. Having set up an episcopal meeting with the help of Rome and used it successfully to achieve a major objective, the Archbishop of Dublin proved incapable of accepting other decisions by the same assembly when these diverged in the smallest detail from what he thought desirable. His report to Cardinal Fransoni makes it clear that he never envisaged the meeting as a means to arrive at consensus. He intended using it to achieve as much of his immediate programme for the Irish Church as he could. In so far as it failed or refused to meet his wishes, he would wheel in the Roman steamroller to quash or alter what his brother bishops had agreed. For example, he did not like the qualification which they incorporated in some of the rules drafted for the University, that these should remain in force 'as long as it seemed good to the hierarchy'.[67] He was unhappy as well about the obligation requiring the Rector to report annually to a meeting of the bishops. The latter decision, he maintained, would make an ordinary (non-canonical) meeting necessary, at which the former decision could be invoked to change the rules. Accordingly, he advised Rome to order that the synodal decrees should remain in force for 'five or seven years' without alteration and that for the purpose of ongoing business the four archbishops should be empowered to act throughout this time in the same manner as the decrees allowed them to do if an episcopal meeting were not held, but that Rome should also nominate 'someone among them to decide when the votes were equal'.[68] Rome acceded in November, with dramatic consequences, as will be seen, imposing a six-year embargo on changing the 1854 decisions, giving the archbishops the authority recommended by Cullen and giving Cullen himself the casting vote. The bishops were further told that it would be sufficient for them to meet every three to five years rather than annually and that their next meeting was to be in canonical form under the presidency of the Apostolic Delegate.

By such methods Paul Cullen bent the Church of the Catholic Irish to his will and made it for the most part an adjunct of ultramontane Rome. There are those who admire his skill. It must be doubted that Newman would have admired it had he known that he and his University were mere pawns called into play to serve a strategy for checkmating the Lion of the West. As for the hospitable and kindly men he had met on their own ground the previous winter, the bishops of half-a-dozen dioceses, what were they to think of their responsibilities now? Were they no more the shepherds of their flocks, witnesses for and teachers of their people? They had seen their role thus, rooted in faith and shared tribulation and a newly awakened consciousness of human dignity. Where was the dignity in finding their views acceptable on what was best for the Irish Church in so far as they coincided with the mind of the Archbishop of Dublin but overruled behind their backs on his say-so when they diverged from what *he* thought best? It is easy to say that what Cullen asked Rome to do made for greater efficiency. How often in the history of the Church must it be asserted that the end cannot justify the means? It may be said that it was his duty, as Apostolic Delegate, to advise the Pope. Why then go through the pretence of consultation when he meant from the outset to proffer his own recommendations, with or without the bishops' approval? And why resort to deceit by disguising under the cloak of papal authority what in fact were his personal judgements? This is not to decry the art of politics, statesmanship or diplomacy. It is to say that such professions are other than the pastorate. Their use by Cullen brought about a deficient understanding of Church that would long prevail in Ireland among clergy and laity alike.

'Not so bad as landing on the Crimea'

Aware of no more than rumbles of dissension in the hierarchy and grateful that these had done little apparent injury to his plans, Newman continued after his installation with staff recruitment, house-hunting, discussion of curricula, drafting examination papers in classics (with the help of Ornsby) and mathematics (with Butler) for 'exhibitions' or scholarships in these departments which, he daringly announced in the *Gazette*, would open on 'the Feast of St Malachi next, Friday November 3rd'. He added that 'the schools of medicine, of civil engineering, and of other material and physical sciences will be opened at the same time, or as soon after as possible'.[1] To appreciate the act of faith involved it should be remembered that he had not heard at this time that Cecilia Street was coming on the market or that suitable houses could be found other than 86 Saint Stephen's Green, and he had not until now been able to enter into formal contracts with the professors or lecturers whom he had provisionally engaged. It helped, although he knew only what he could glean from Lucas, that the Archbishops of Dublin and Tuam had very different problems on their minds: this gave him a free hand when he most needed to be spared from interference.

Incredibly, throughout this busiest of years he managed to meet many demands in Britain as well as Ireland. He crossed the Irish Sea no fewer than ten times. He discharged Oratory business from Dublin and University business from Birmingham, wrote letters counselling converts and giving spiritual advice to Anglican correspondents from whatever address he found himself at. He would take any trouble to avoid disappointing a friend. He attended the opening of the Brompton Church at Faber's urging and on 1 May caught the evening boat from Kingstown to be present at the consecration of a convent chapel near Birmingham, returning to Dublin on 4 May. On 23 May he left Ireland again, visited Saint Beuno's in North Wales, travelled to Birmingham, London ('to catch the Cardinal'[2]), Saint Edmund's College at Ware in Hertfordshire, Ushaw in Yorkshire, thence 'to Holyhead by Manchester and Chester' and on 3 June 'arrived in Dublin 7 a.m. in time to say Mass'[3] — and, of course, the next day to be inaugurated as Rector. Most of July and August he spent in Birmingham, as he normally did to permit his colleagues to take holidays, although this year, when he returned yet again to Ireland, a number of them joined him by rotation at a holiday cottage which he borrowed from the Jesuits for September and October. Called Mount Salus, this was (and still stands) near Dalkey, on the hill high above the village with dramatic views of Dublin and Killiney Bays, Howth Head, Kingstown Harbour and the Sugar Loaf peaks beyond Bray.

For Newman it was a busman's holiday, with preparations for the opening of the University taking up much of his time. He enjoyed his stay there none the less in 'enchanting weather'[4] and extolled the scenery with unusual enthusiasm: 'a most *beautiful site* looking over the sea, and its healthiness is conveyed in its name';[5] 'Tastes so differ, that I do not like to talk, but I think this is one of the most beautiful places I ever saw';[6] 'I never saw a place out of Italy and Sicily like it for beauty of rock and sea.'[7] The views of the coastline especially impressed him, although he rejected comparisons with the Bay of Naples, and he remarked how the 'houses innumerable ... being all of stone ... and the ground being very irregular, they do but furnish and set out what would otherwise be bare and rugged'.[8] He enthused over the 'hills, of rock and heather mixed ... affording endless rambles'[9] but these were literally his downfall for, while hill-walking, he tore a tendon in his left leg which caused him much inconvenience for several months. He was not the only Oratorian to come to grief in Mount Salus. Father Ambrose St John succumbed to 'the worst attack of asthma he ever had', and Newman wondered whether 'this most beautiful place, from its purity of air, may not have had something to do with it'.[10] He none the less thought it so healthy a location that he offered rooms to Faber for any of the Fathers who might be 'invalided in the cholera'[11] then rampant in London.

Archbishop Cullen was meanwhile preparing for a visit to Rome. Unknown to MacHale, he was making arrangements also for a stay in the Eternal City by the Lion of Tuam. Cullen's report to Cardinal Fransoni on the synodal meeting had perturbed the Curia officials and Monsignor Kirby, Rector of the Irish College, heard they were about to summon MacHale to Rome to explain his conduct. Cullen hastened to block this move. Through Kirby, he told the Curia that an open move against MacHale would evoke protest and opposition in Ireland; it would be better to get the Lion to Rome on some innocuous pretext. The opportunity presented itself when the Pope decided to invite a number of bishops from around the world to meet in Rome and advise him on the course he should adopt in defining the doctrine of the Immaculate Conception. It would be appropriate, Cullen suggested, to invite the four archbishops of Ireland. He was certain that MacHale would attend. This would create the opportunity to hold discussions in Rome on the affairs of the Irish Church and to confront MacHale with the bad impression made by his behaviour. For the second time in a year, MacHale was to find himself lured into a pejorative situation by a seemingly innocent request to come to a meeting. On each occasion Cullen laid the trap. Tuam clearly could not match the masterly tactics of Dublin.

Whether Cullen comes the better out of the comparison must be a moot point. There is something poignant in the cornering and wounding of MacHale by a succession of ploys. The Lion was in so many respects a man of the age: he (and interestingly, his theology) made a very favourable impression on Montalembert, Lacordaire and Lamennais when he met them in Rome in 1832, during the crisis which ended in the suppression of *l'Avenir*. On the way home he visited Doellinger, who wrote to Lamennais that 'this excellent man makes us even more bitterly aware of what we lack: bishops with the learning, the noble courage and the independent spirit of an Irish prelate'.[12] In Ireland, such sympathies were naturally reflected in his rapport with O'Connell. He was, of course, his own worst enemy. His pugnacious and negative approach alienated other bishops who might have been his friends and his sheer rudeness deeply offended the thoughtful and concerned among them, especially Archbishop Murray. A Roman manipulator like Cullen disliked his manners and his views, and would have been deeply suspicious of his theology had he known about the good opinion formed of him by Lamennais and Doellinger — each of whom abandoned Catholicism because they could not accept ultramontane attitudes of the type quintessentially represented by Cullen. Newman, by contrast, respected MacHale's openness, despite the trouble it caused him, and reported after their first meeting in Maynooth that 'the Archbishop of Tuam shook his hand with so violent a cordiality, when I kissed his ring, as to punish my nose'.[13] Ever responsive to — if often bemused by — Irish warmth, the English Rector would have found this more reassuring than the fainéant urbanities and long silences of the Archbishop of Dublin. The Lion had long been asking for a bloody nose himself, but he deserved better than to be snared.

Cullen felt more than justified, however, in moving against MacHale by the means he knew best when political priests returned to the news in September, the strictures of the synodal meeting notwithstanding. Father Matthew Keefe and Father Thomas O'Shea, curates in Callan, County Kilkenny, had been founders of the Tenant Right League. O'Shea had already been in trouble with his bishop, Dr Edward Walsh of Ossory, for speaking from party platforms in New Ross, Drogheda and Dublin, all of them places outside his own diocese where the bishop's authority over the private activities of his priests was a little uncertain. Cullen was said to have urged Walsh to censure O'Shea during the Louth by-election in February, which raises the intriguing possibility that the bishop enjoyed Newman's arrival in Kilkenny as a welcome break from the tiresome fuss created by his clergy on the one hand and his Metropolitan Archbishop on the other. He may have been in search of fresh air when he dragged his English visitor to the top of his unfinished cathedral! However that may be, it was Keefe, the other curate in Callan, who started the trouble in September by writing a letter of complaint to the member of parliament for County Kilkenny, who not only replied but sent the correspondence to the local paper. Keefe had been less circumspect than O'Shea, for this was political activity within his own diocese and the bishop was able to reprimand him at once and instruct him to keep out of politics for the future. This brought O'Shea back into the arena to defend his colleague against what he claimed was unwarranted episcopal interference. The bishop then ordered O'Shea to get out of politics. The independent Irish party and the Tenant Right League rallied to the priests and announced a three-pronged appeal to Rome: by the two curates against their bishop, by clergy from a number of dioceses against the policy of the hierarchy which they associated with Cullen, and by Catholic members of parliament against the official Church attitude in Ireland on political priests. Cullen and MacHale had meanwhile set off for Rome (separately) with the sound of battle ringing in their ears. They had no sooner arrived than word came of the proposed petitions to the Holy See. Lucas, they learned, was coming out to prepare the ground....

In the long run, these developments were not to help Newman. They hardened Cullen's suspicion of the laity and his determination that the only safe course in the affairs of the Irish Church was to keep the reins firmly in his own hands. MacHale *pari passu* renewed his resolve to combat the growing influence of Cullen and, to that end, to beat the nationalist drum with vigour. His complaint, sent just before his departure for Rome, that Newman should have consulted the archbishops before buying the medical school and a protest in the same letter that consultation should have preceded the offer of even provisional appointments to professorships, was a broadside on both fronts: addressed to Newman and therefore a reprimand to English presumptions about who controlled the Irish University, but simultaneously challenging decisions which he knew or suspected that Cullen had sanctioned. MacHale's obstructionism was now blatant. Cullen's dead hand would show itself in time. To MacHale therefore Newman sent as curt a reply as his innate politeness to a bishop would permit, stating simply the authority of the Rector as he understood it and the impossibility of making progress if he had to consult as often as MacHale required. When, however, Cullen wrote to him stressing the need to treat everything as provisional for the moment, to hire as few professors as possible and for one year only, to have some of them take on the responsibilities of two departments and in particular to use the available talents of the Vice-Rector, Dr Leahy, in teaching the classics, Newman replied with circumspection. He explained that he could not expect reputable academics to settle in Dublin for short temporary appointments and that setting up a new institution was a different task from presiding over one already existing: 'unless I begin in my own way I cannot promise I shall succeed in making any beginning at all'.[14] It was a plea for understanding which the Rector clearly assumed would be granted, for two days later he forwarded his list of appointments to Cullen without the deletions implied in the Archbishop's advice.

The suggested employment of Leahy, incidentally, would have obviated the engagement of the Englishman, Ornsby, and of James Stewart, a Scot who was to lecture in ancient history: the Archbishop, for good measure, had remarked on the unpopularity of 'the Scotch' among Irish Catholics.[15] Newman suspected that the whole purpose of Cullen's advice was to keep down the number of 'English' appointments in order to minimise the grounds for objection which MacHale was bound to look for in the list. He was unwilling to allow such extraneous considerations to influence his plans for the University and in this instance, it must be said, Cullen graciously conceded the unspoken argument and gave his blessing to the full complement of appointees, as also did the Archbishops of Armagh and Cashel. Newman's obstinacy thus facilitated the further isolation of MacHale which Cullen had been working to contrive since before the Synodal meeting. These were the last exchanges before the opening of the University which now, in October, was imminent. Newman could be well satisfied that he had got his way, even if he had to fight every inch of it. The war then in progress between Britain and Russia gave him the analogy to describe how he felt in a letter to Bishop Ullathorne of Birmingham: 'we are now just on the brink of an experiment, which, though not so bad as landing on the Crimea, is in a little way parallel to it'.[16]

* * *

With Newman, the bizarre kept intruding on the important. With less than four weeks to go to the launching of his great project, word came from Birmingham that Brother Frederic, an Oratorian laybrother, had proposed marriage to a young woman not only on the Oratory premises but while wearing the habit. Although laybrothers were free to leave the Congregation at any time — and then, of course, marry if they wished — Newman understandably found his conduct outrageous. It offended against good order because it took place in a celibate household and it threatened scandal — for in the atmosphere of Victorian Britain anything which seemed to show Catholic clergy falling short of the standards which they adopted in public was likely to be seized upon as an example of Roman hypocrisy. Charitably, he did not order Frederic's immediate expulsion but decreed that 'while he is in our house and under our shadow, he must observe most perfect chastity — which in a certain sense courting is not'.[17] He then arranged for him to come to Dublin as a servant, first in Mount Salus and then in Harcourt Street, and reported back to Birmingham, mystified, that the former religious 'sings in the kitchen with astonishing compass and volume'.[18] The ascetic

Rector did not quite appreciate the uplift of love in a young man's heart!

In retrospect it seems a cheerful little story with a happy ending, for Frederic (after reverting to his pre-Oratorian name of Thomas Godwin) married his lass, set up home in Birmingham and did many chores on-and-off for his former brethren in religion. But it prompts the thought that Newman, for all his commitment to the University, remained too intimately involved with the Oratory for his own or the University's good — or, indeed, for the Oratory's good. True, the Oratory was his home and its community were his family. It was altogether natural that he should return there often and no doubt these visits (if visits they can be called; he would himself have seen Dublin as the place visited) rejuvenated his spirit and gave him the strength to return to the frustrating anxieties of his Irish mission. It remains extraordinary, none the less, that he concerned himself so much that autumn with the domestic affairs of the Oratory and, indeed, with other non-essential items of English business.

His correspondence from Mount Salus includes comments on the use of a room in Birmingham for teaching purposes; the provision of tuition for schoolboys; whether the hired tutor's room should be papered (he was against it) and the need to paint the 'Congregation Room'; the removal of curtains from confessionals in the Oratory church and the best manner in which to hang a crucifix; directives on paying the choristers, introducing a prayer for the Queen and hiring various persons as servants. There was fall-out from the Frederic crisis: the priests in the congregation were urged to remember that laybrothers were gentlemen too, and there were questions about replacing Frederic in the choir — 'the greatest loss of Frederic will be in the singing',[19] wrote Newman, unaware that the talent he so praised would soon be enlivening the kitchen in Harcourt Street. The Oratorians had just acquired a country cottage for their use at Rednal outside Birmingham and Newman gave instructions about the title deeds, the plumbing, the pony (which was not to be ridden) and preparing the vegetable garden ('break up the ground for potatoes'[20]). He wrote also about legal problems regarding a legacy left to the Oratory and what to do with the money if they got it. He discussed how best to set up Catholic Sunday Schools in England, read and commented on publications by some of his friends and gave precise orders to one of the priests about a retreat he was to give in Bristol.

All these letters were sent in the ten weeks immediately before the University opening. They sustain well enough the familiar picture of Newman as a man of consummate energy and organisational flair, able to bring his mind to bear on matters of the smallest detail and on the most profound philosophical problems alike. A more realistic assessment would be harsher. Either he could not bear to relinquish a jot of authority as *paterfamilias* of his community or he had a low opinion of his Oratorian colleagues' competence to cope with practical responsibilities. His readiness to respond to any query put to him by acquaintances in England suggests that he saw his native country as his primary field of mission even while so heavily involved in Ireland. As his Anglican friend, Dean Church of St Paul's, would write: 'his chief interests were for things English — English literature, English social life, English politics, English religion. He liked to identify himself as much as possible with things English ...'.[21] Which surely was no fault in an Englishman, but there may have been fault in indulging his interests at a time when the charge he had accepted from the Irish bishops called for unremitting attention. In the same way his mother-hen fussiness over every aspect of life in the Birmingham house may have been unexceptionable in an Oratorian Superior: 'My separation from the Oratory is a greater and greater trouble to me', he would later remark.[22] But many decisions could and should have been left to persons delegated to make them while he got on with the job in hand.

Newman recognised the possibility of delegation. 'I wish you to exercise a supreme discretion', he wrote to Stanislas Flanagan[23] in regard to some of the works at Rednal. He said it very rarely, however, and it would have been an innocent colleague who thought that such a licence would protect him against his Superior's relentless dabbling from afar in the administration of the community and its property. The habit helps to explain the attitude of his critics in the London Oratory, who considered him to be dictatorial and thought his Birmingham brethren fawned on him overmuch. The brethren themselves went a distance towards confirming the critics. Excellent pastors though they were (and the pastorate was clearly their vocation), men like Ambrose St John, Edward Caswall and William Neville seemed often to crave direction rather than act on their own initiative. True, they were all younger than Newman and some of them had been with him at Littlemore, so the filial relationship went deeper than formal religious obedience. Their Oxford contemporary, Mark Pattison, was probably unfair to those of them whom he described as 'not intellectually equal companions' of Newman: 'it was a general wonder', he wrote, 'how Newman himself could be content with (their) society'.[24] Pattison remembered them as youthful post-graduates in Littlemore and neglected to mention that, once they became Catholics, Oxford set a barrier to their further advance in the university. The fact remains that their voluminous correspondence to and from Newman leaves the impression of young men who never grew up and were content to remain happily in thrall to their master. No doubt it was fascinating and, for some, satisfying to live in the permanent shadow of genius. But might there not be significance in the fact that Newman offered none of them a post in his University? Perhaps he, too, had taken their measure. Perhaps that was why he withheld responsibility from them and persisted in treating them as children to be worried over by an anxious parent.

It has to be said that nothing essential was left undone in the weeks before the opening of the University by reason of the Rector's involvement with non-University matters. Still, the amount of time he could spend at a crucial period on such extraneous questions lends credence to the complaints later made by Archbishop Cullen that the University suffered because of Newman's failure to give it wholetime care. Newman could plead that he had never considered the University to be a purely Irish institution, that he had not made it a commitment to the exclusion of his other concerns and that he had intended no more than to help in getting it started. None of this altered the central fact that his mind was much of the time half-elsewhere, and some of the time unnecessarily so. It is a fact which should never be forgotten when judging his performance as Rector during the first four years of the University, notwithstanding the sympathy we feel for him in the tribulations which the task brought on his rapidly greying head. We may stand in awe of the polymath and the man of action. We do not have to admire without qualification his over-indulgence of polymathy or his excess of activity when either distracted him from important duties which others relied on him to discharge.

*   *   *

On Friday, 3 November 1854, the feast of Saint Malachi of Armagh, the Catholic University came into being with all the absence of extravagant display that Archbishop Cullen would have considered proper to a poverty-stricken people. No ceremonies took place and, as Ornsby recorded in the *Gazette,* 'no crowds assembled to behold a spectacle'.[25] The literal opening of the University House doors in St Stephen's Green to admit the students who had passed the entrance examinations served to symbolise the opening of the University itself, for University House incorporated the lecture-rooms of the University as well as the hall of residence to be called Saint Patrick's. Nothing else was done to mark a day which in retrospect can rightly be called momentous, since in the opening of those doors was the remote beginning of University College, Dublin, for many years now the largest university institution in the country and the lynch-pin of the National University of Ireland. But that lay far in the future in 1854, when it was felt achievement enough to have launched the Catholic University with its proud complement of 'above twenty'[26] students.

The undergraduates had come through entrance tests conducted by the Vice-Rector, Dr Leahy, the Professor of Classical Literature, Ornsby, and the Lecturer in Logic, Dr D.B. Dunne, a layman, formerly of the Irish College, Rome. Although only the classical and mathematical schools had been officially established at this stage, Italian and Spanish literature were taught from the outset as well as compulsory French. A base of liberal education from which all students were to advance was therefore in position and functioning. Newman explained it at a reception for students and staff in University House the following Sunday. The students had come, he said, to prepare for their respective professions but a University education would do more for them than that. It would fit them for every place and situation in which they might find themselves during their lives. With cultivated minds they would be able to meet adversity or good fortune calmly, with grace and propriety. They would not be thrown off balance. He apparently avoided the word 'gentleman' (the text of his address has not been preserved and we must rely on Ornsby's report) but the sense of his remarks conveyed the selfsame message about the purpose of liberal knowledge as he had elaborated it in the Discourses two years earlier. He was not upset by the paucity of their numbers, he added. Time would remedy that. He concluded with a rather far-fetched analogy, comparing those who had entered the University on Saint Malachi's Day, 1854, with the English soldiers at Agincourt: he quoted the lines which Shakespeare put in the mouth of King Henry V, ending 'We few, we happy few, we band of brothers'[27] — and therefore omitting the reference to 'gentlemen in England now a-bed'. (It was not the best play to provide an appropriate thought. Newman could scarcely have quoted its stage Irishman, Macmorris, protesting 'by my hand, I swear, and by my father's soul, the work is ill done'![28])

Among the more interesting freshmen was Daniel O'Connell, a grandson of the Liberator, who on the strength of his antecedents was granted an exhibition or scholarship giving him free board in the University House and exemption from fees for the four-year University course. Another, who Newman liked to tell people with wry amusement was residing at his house in Harcourt Street, was 'a French Viscount ... a youth of about 17 — Mr Renouf's pupil'.[29] The Vicomte Louis de Vaulchier was the son of Renouf's aristocratic employer who thought so highly of the tutor that he insisted on leaving the young man in his charge even if it meant sending him to Dublin. He was not to be the only student from a titled family in the house. Sir Reginald Barnewall, tenth Baronet and of old Anglo-Irish stock, arrived in mid-November: a sickly boy, he had to have bread soaked in boiled milk for breakfast. After Christmas came Frank Kerr, grandson of the Marquess of Lothian, whose special wants were also catered for. Newman explained to his father, Lord Henry Kerr, 'I shall not give him a fireplace in his *own* room, but will take care, tell Lady Henry, that he is never in the cold.'[30] While the Irish bishops would scarcely have envisaged students of the University coming from such a background (and more were to come, both from England and the continent), they fitted into Newman's concept of a centre of learning which would attract an international clientele by its reputation. In English Victorian terms, this could also work in reverse: reputation was strengthened by the social standing of the clientele. It may have mattered little to the Irish (although there were those among them who would be impressed by social rank) but Newman remained always conscious of the need to create status for the University by every stratagem that offered. He lured upper-class students, thinking they would help in the same way as the names of distinguished scholars on the staff and public dignitaries among the Associates might help by giving an air of quality to the enterprise.

Most of the students, as might be expected, belonged to the solid Irish middle-classes. Those of them not living with Newman or in Dr Quinn's establishment were lodged in Saint Patrick's — University House — under their Dean, Dr Flannery, and their Tutor, Dr Dunne. Their daily routine was simple: Mass at 8.00, breakfast at 9.00, lectures from 10.00 until 2.00; the rest of the day, apart from dinner at 5.00, at their own disposal for leisure or study. The Dean might make further rules in the interest of good order but regimentation was kept to the minimum. Newman told the students they were 'verging on manhood',[31] that the University authorities reposed confidence in them, believed their word, and hoped to be met by a similar spirit of confidence. They had more company than their numbers might suggest for many 'externs' attended the lectures: these were students who had not taken the entrance examinations but still wished to benefit from the courses. Some of the residents in Newman's house (Frank Kerr, for example) were externs. The students gave little trouble but, like their counterparts everywhere, got plenty of fun out of life.

Newman soon found himself faced with the dilemma of reconciling his lenient views on discipline with the exigencies of life as it was lived. In their first term a number of students took to frequenting a well-known billiards saloon in the city. It was so respectable, he reported to Stanislas Flanagan (whom he liked to consult on Irish *mores*), that 'priests play there in private'.[32] What worried him was that the students might get into the wrong company or pick up 'undesirable betting news'.[33] Should he licence the saloon and forbid the students to go elsewhere? He hated to prohibit categorically, partly because he believed it created a sense of grievance rather than conviction and partly because martinet dictation had no place among Oratorians, who promised obedience but stopped short of vowing it. He resolved the question of the billiards saloon by spending £160 on converting an outhouse behind the Saint Stephen's Green premises into a billiard room for the students' own use. He appears to have taken no steps to prevent them from attending the theatre or riding to hounds: as late as 1857 the students themselves, in drafting the rules of the Historical, Literary and Aesthetical Society (now the Literary and Historical Society of UCD), felt it necessary to ban members in top-boots from attending its meetings and the first known point of order raised in this famous debating society concerned the propriety of Count Etienne Zamoyski — another colourful import from the continent — attempting to join in the proceedings while wearing his scarlet hunting jacket.

Cullen and others were to charge Newman with laxity in his supervision of students which they seemed to think should have been similar to the discipline of a boarding school. The Rector, however, was acting in total consistency with what he had laid down in his tenth Discourse. There the passage rejecting literary censorship in a university followed from an argument which went: 'If then a University is a direct preparation for this world, let it be what it professes. It is not a Convent, it is not a Seminary; it is a place to fit men of the world for the world. We cannot possibly keep them from plunging into the world, with all its ways and principles and maxims when their time comes; but we can prepare them against what is inevitable; and it is not the way to learn to swim in troubled waters, never to have gone into them.'[34] In his first rectorial report to the archbishops (for the academic year 1854/55) he elaborated: 'I believe it to be the truth, that the young for the most part cannot be driven, but on the other hand, are open to persuasion ... they are to be kept straight by indirect contrivances rather than by authoritative enactments and naked prohibitions ... nothing is more perilous to the soul than the sudden transition from restraint to liberty ... boys who are kept jealously at home or under severe schoolmasters until the very moment when they are called upon to take part in the business of the world, are the very persons about whom we have most cause to entertain misgivings ... we could not do worse than to continue the discipline of school and college into the University, and to let the great world, which is to follow upon it, be the first stage on which the young are set at liberty to follow their own bent ... a certain tenderness, or even laxity of rule on the one hand, and an anxious, vigilant, importunate attention on the other, are the characteristics of that discipline which is peculiar of [sic] a University.'[35]

Playing billiards, going to the theatre, hunting: they sound as innocent as the boating and swimming expeditions which the students got up as soon as summer came round and were scarcely encounters with 'the world' of the kind that went into the moulding of responsible adulthood. But saying that is to take a modern measure to the nineteenth century, then nearing the climax of its obsession with prim respectability. Almost any participation by the young in group enjoyment could be represented as decadent behaviour or at least as behaviour which wasted the serious Christian's time and talents. This extraordinary yardstick of respectability, with its Protestant evangelical roots, had begun to permeate Irish Catholicism in which an inferiority complex was replacing the self-confidence of earlier years. Irish Catholics were concerned to show themselves no less moral than the English bourgeoisie and upholders of the same strict standards of behaviour. It was an attitude which sat well with the reforming zeal of the Cullenite Church: the Papal Delegate's disapproval of much harmless clerical conduct, especially if the cleric in question was being put forward for a bishopric, at once jumps to mind. Cullen's own confinement for so long within the narrow authoritarian limits of seminary and curial life in Rome made for no broader understanding and it was not surprising that the Archbishop should have wanted far more rigid constraints put on the students. 'But then, what can I do', he is recorded as saying, 'when Dr Newman just listens to me without speaking, and then says "I will think about it", and then everything goes on as it was before?'[36] That Newman stood his ground against the temper of the times both in Church and society, in Ireland as in England, was a tribute to his obstinacy, his clarity of vision and his sensible appreciation of the needs of young people. And in fairness to Cullen it must be added that, although he would go on complaining, he never interfered with the liberal regime of his distinguished Rector.

When the regime was instituted on Saint Malachi's Day 1854, the Archbishop was, of course, far away and occupied with very different matters in Rome. Student discipline had not yet become a question in his mind. But he took time to drop a note to Newman to congratulate him on the start which had been made. He was happy with the number of students — he probably knew that forty more were pledged to come above the twenty present for the opening. He had encouraging news to record: 'The Pope and Cardinals make continual enquiries about you ... Dr Hughes, [Archbishop] of New York, says that many American families will send their children to you ...'. He noted as well that 'The Regulations made at our meeting last May have been sanctioned by the Pope for *six years* in order to have time to see how they will work', but omitted to say that they had been qualified in other ways also and that the changes were made as a result of Cullen's unilateral recommendations. He added 'His Holiness has also given the power of conferring degrees.'[37] To Newman, this letter must have sounded satisfactory indeed, especially since it was no longer an intimation of good will such as he had received in the past but comment on a functioning institution. It confirmed his relief at being past the preparatory stage at last. 'All is going on well'.[38] 'We are getting on very well',[39] 'We are going on very well here — and ought to be most thankful for the success which has hitherto attended on us'[40] — thus the refrain in his letters to the end of the year. 'I rejoice, and am most thankful, to say that the Catholic University is progressing as well as ever I could expect', he wrote from Birmingham at Christmas.[41] He had already sent a letter to Archbishop Cullen reporting the success of the five Inaugural Lectures, the growth of interest in the University ('We have now above 60 names down for matriculation') and his hope 'to build a Church or Chapel out of my own money'.[42] It was winter, but spring was in the air.

Of the Inaugural Lectures it was, naturally, Newman's own on 9 November which attracted most attention. Afterwards published as *Christianity and Letters,* its theme was the centrality of a faculty of arts to any university, notwithstanding the traditional place of theology, law and medicine or the contemporary advances in 'Chemistry, Electricity and Geology'[43] as well as other disciplines. The lecture lacked altogether the universality and depth of the Dublin Discourses and was rather the clever elaboration of two questionable propositions than a profound insight to the relationship between learning and religion. It asserted that the Graeco-Roman world and its European descendant had 'a claim to be considered as the representative Society and Civilization of the human race, as its perfect result and limit',[44] and went on to argue that Christianity 'waited till the *orbis terrarum* attained its most perfect form before it appeared; and it soon coalesced, and has ever since co-operated, and often seemed identical, with the Civilization which is its companion'.[45] Only a very Victorian superiority complex, not elsewhere noticeable in Newman, can explain why he felt it appropriate to underscore the significance of the classics and literature by the use of dubious concepts which any modern missionary priest, let alone any anthropologist or philosopher of history, would indignantly reject. The lecture, however, long continued to be a favourite among admirers of Newman and perhaps the annealing effects of two world wars were needed to expose its deficiencies.

He concluded on a more homely, if disingenuous, note by recalling that his connection with the University began after the Holy See had formally approved the project. Accordingly, said Newman: 'It is my happiness to have no cognizance of the anxieties and perplexities of venerable and holy prelates, or the discussions of experienced and prudent men, which preceded its definitive recognition on the part of the highest ecclesiastical authority. It is my happiness to have no experience of the time when good Catholics despaired of its success, distrusted its expediency, or even felt an obligation to oppose it.'[46] Only by assuming that certain prelates were neither venerable nor holy, or by treating the earlier Briefs from Rome as 'definitive recognition', or by disputing the goodness of certain Catholics (including the Jesuit provincial and the Bishop of Limerick), could the Rector have justified these comments. More kindly, it might be suggested that his generous and forgiving nature induced a kind of amnesia so that, in the relief of finding the University actually in being, a veil fell across his memory of the tribulations and discouragement he had so recently suffered. It was in fact less than a year since he had contemplated resigning. Perhaps subliminally the trauma still made itself felt, for he left his hearers with a hint that he might soon relinquish his charge. 'It is enough for one man', he said, 'to lay only one stone of so noble and grand an edifice; it is enough, more than enough for me, if I do so much as merely begin what others may hopefully continue.'[47]

The remaining Inaugural Lectures delivered on successive Thursday evenings through the term, were given by Leahy, Ornsby, Marani (the lecturer in Italian and Spanish) and a reluctant Allies who agreed to undertake the task only after relentless wooing by Newman. All were heard, according to the *Gazette*, 'with the deepest interest by an assembly so crowded, that it became a matter of regret, that the University was unable to place at their disposal a larger room for their accommodation'.[48] If the academic staff were thus put to work from the outset beyond their classroom duties, so were a number of the students who sat examinations for exhibitions or scholarships confined to 'candidates of Irish birth'.[49] Awards of £35 and £25 were announced in both classics and mathematics. Newman himself spent much time on money matters. 'I have great anxiety lest I should not make both ends meet', he wrote. 'My expences [sic] are near £1050 a year.'[50] He cannot have been too greatly worried, though, for he toyed with various costly ideas — a chapel for his own house and further thoughts on a church for the University — and the Irish Father Stanislas Flanagan at the Birmingham Oratory helped him with his estimates of income and spending. He continued to seek competent staff. Among those with whom he kept up a correspondence that winter were Henry Hennessy, the physicist, and John Hungerford Pollen, the artist, each of whom would provide valuable services to the University in years to come.

* * *

Much meanwhile had been happening in Rome. Newman, back in Birmingham for Christmas, got a flavour of the atmosphere there in a letter from Cullen confirming yet again that the Pope had approved the decisions of the Dublin Synod regarding the University, subject to a trial period of 'five or six years' when no change in the rules would be allowed. As a consequence, he told Newman, 'during that time at least the presentation of professors etc will depend on you'. Dr MacHale had made every effort 'to prevent the confirmation of those regulations', continued Cullen. 'He says now he will have nothing to do with the university — so much the better — but I fear that he will excite a storm....' Then Cullen added 'Of course *Haec omnia inter nos sint* — It is as well not to let Dr Leahy know this matter, lest Dr Slattery should be displeased.'[51]

The secretive mentality (and a twinge of conscience?) revealed in the gloss on his remarks points up the manipulative tactics favoured by the astute Archbishop of Dublin. He told nobody more than he chose to tell, and he told that much only at a time of his choosing. On the face of it, it is unclear why old Archbishop Slattery of Cashel should have been displeased, or concerned at all, at the news of MacHale's annoyance. The reason lay in what Cullen kept from Newman: precisely *why* MacHale had been so angry. The Lion had learned at a meeting in Propaganda of the full extent of the changes in the synodal decrees engineered behind everybody's back by Cullen, which effectively handed over total control of the University to the Papal Delegate. Had Slattery known this, he would probably have sided with MacHale, for he was already incensed over the Delegate's interference in the affairs of his diocese. Cashel as well as Tuam was now relegated to a secondary place in University matters through Cullen's influence with Rome and the decision-making authority of the bishops as a body had been further undermined. Slattery would indeed have been 'displeased' and he would have had the support of Leahy, as Cullen probably knew, not only because the Vice-Rector was a Cashel priest (who would succeed Slattery as Archbishop in 1857) but also because he agreed with the clerical critics of the Delegate's dominance in Irish church affairs. They had 'a good & just cause', Leahy wrote to Slattery the following February, but they were presenting it badly and 'they are no match for the wiley [sic] and artful man they are opposing'.[52]

Whatever about Leahy's views, it suited Cullen to hold back the full story in December when he was trying his utmost to have MacHale once and for all put under restraint by Rome. It was no time to provoke others to ally themselves with the Lion of the West. In fact at this stage it looked as if Cullen's wiliness was beginning to flag. Not only were the Archbishops of Dublin and Tuam both in Rome, each with prelates in support (Dixon of Armagh and Murphy of Cloyne with Cullen, Derry of Clonfert and McNally of Clogher with MacHale), but Lucas had also arrived to publicise the protests by priests and members of parliament against the policies of the Papal Delegate: there were signs that Lucas might secure tentative approval from some English bishops, and even from Cardinal Wiseman. Remarkably, perhaps, all these parties had ready access to the Pope as well as to Monsignor Barnabo, the Secretary, and therefore effective head, of Propaganda during the illness of Cardinal Fransoni. Rome could not doubt the reality of tensions within the Irish Church nor the existence of opposition to Cullen which went beyond the personal antipathy between himself and MacHale. His triumph on the University question might yet prove to be a pyrrhic victory, for it gave his critics an ideal opportunity to expand on his overbearing disregard for his brother bishops.

MacHale was quick to seize the opportunity. He had already semi-publicly distanced himself from Cullen during the weeks leading up to the proclamation of the Immaculate Conception as a dogma of the Church on 8 December: the MacHale party refused to lodge at the Irish College where the Archbishop of Dublin was staying and made their excuses to avoid attending a reception which he held there for the English bishops. Even Newman, despite his innocence in such matters, picked up the rumour of MacHale boycotting a dinner at the College. Barnabo can therefore have been little surprised to find Dublin and Tuam deeply divided at a succession of meetings which he held with them before Christmas. The vehemence of MacHale's reaction on hearing of the University arrangements, however, took him aback. This was during the same meeting at which MacHale challenged Cullen's interference in the affairs of the diocese and province of Tuam and complained about the unnecessary extent of his legatine authority. To the Lion all these grievances were aspects of what he saw as the fundamental usurpation of episcopal rights by the Archbishop of Dublin, whose alteration of the synodal decisions regarding the University showed how little effective control the Irish hierarchy could exercise within the Irish Church. Cullen represented his actions as merely carrying out the wishes of Rome. MacHale, knowing full well who implanted ideas about Ireland in the Roman mind, kept up his denunciation until an exasperated Barnabo referred to 'a democratic spirit' within the Irish episcopate.[53] MacHale and his two colleagues indignantly rejected the implied accusation of anti-papal disloyalty, said they would not listen to that kind of talk and that it was 'the privilege and duty of the Pope alone to lecture bishops.'[54] They left Barnabo with no option but to terminate the meeting.

The pyrrhic victory now was MacHale's for, although he had yielded nothing and had registered damaging ripostes to Cullen's apologia, he had demonstrated at first hand in the presence of a senior curial official the irascibility and intemperate attitude which made him so difficult a man to deal with. The table-thumping shouting match tolerable in an Irish committee room was altogether out of place — and worse, was totally alienating — in the atmosphere of polished diplomacy which marked any discussion in a Vatican office. Instead of sympathy from the Roman authorities, MacHale received a demand after Christmas from the Pope through Fransoni (and therefore far above Barnabo's level) to explain in writing the continuing dissent in the Irish Church, and in particular to say why he was so negative in his stance on the recent statutes approved by the Irish bishops in synod. MacHale had little difficulty in composing a masterly reply, for he was largely going over old ground, but he failed entirely to appreciate the subtlety of the Roman request for a statement in writing. Rome laudably hoped to restore peace in the Irish Church. What it needed from the Archbishop of Tuam was some hint of compromise, not yet another contribution to confrontation. In the end he found himself ordered directly by the Pope to tell the bishops of the Tuam province to publish the Dublin statutes as amended: an outcome no doubt doubly satisfying to Cullen, for it not only meant that his plans — including his plans for government of the University — would be brought into force but it ensured that the amended version was seen to issue from the Pope himself which veiled over the part played by the Archbishop of Dublin. MacHale left Rome in early February before worse could befall him, and in this gave further offence to the Pope who had expected him to remain until all the contentious issues had been resolved.

Lucas fared little better. It helped him not at all that his case was associated by the Curia with the Archbishop of Tuam whose position on priests in politics, of course, paralleled that of the protesting clergy, laity — and media. Cullen had successfully been making the point that he had to fend off the attacks of Gavan Duffy's *Nation*, a paper much honoured in Tuam, while the Pope in speaking kindly to Lucas had distinguished between his good work for religion as a member of parliament and the immoderate impatience which he sometimes showed as Editor of the *Tablet!* But where Lucas really foundered was on the misjudgement of the priests who voiced their objections against Cullen as a condemnation of the synodal decrees and who demanded that certain rights be granted to protect them against arbitrary transfer from parish to parish as a punishment if they challenged a superior. The trouble with this line of protest was that it sought redress against the Papal Delegate by methods which would have diminished the authority of *every* bishop. MacHale, for one, could not concur in this, and other bishops on his side of the national argument took the same view. So, apparently, did many priests, for the numbers willing to sign the memorial to the Pope fell dismally short of what had been hoped for. The protest by members of parliament also found few supporters. This left Lucas isolated, not to mention the two priests from Callan, whose appeal against the Bishop of Ossory he was promoting together with the wider complaints.

With hindsight it can be seen that Cullen's position was stronger throughout than his critics realised, either MacHale or the people represented by Lucas. During these years a growing concentration of power in the papacy matched the rapidly growing status of the Pope within the Church. It was significant, for example, that the Pope sought the bishops' advice regarding the Immaculate Conception only on the manner in which the proclamation should be made and on its wording. The questions whether the Immaculate Conception was dogma and whether it should be defined he reserved to himself. The centralised papacy, together with is curial departments, felt affronted by any Catholics who challenged its dispositions or dispositions made by churchmen (like papal legates) acting on its behalf and by its licence. MacHale, Lucas and all associated with them were thus swimming against the tide in asking Rome to endorse greater freedom of action as the right of bishops, priests or laity if it meant freedom from direct or indirect Roman control. Newman faced similar resistance in arguing that the rector of a university should enjoy a certain minimal autonomy, and would meet a more virulent resistance in the years ahead when he dared to advocate the rights of the laity in the Church. Ironically, it was not the least of MacHale's miscalculations that he withheld his support from Newman on narrow national and personal grounds, because he judged him to be Cullen's English pawn. Newman might have become a prestigious intellectual defender of some at least of the Lion's attitudes had he been approached with more under-standing. Not that they would have prevailed ...

Notwithstanding the temper of the times, it must be said that Rome gave as fair a hearing as it could to MacHale and Lucas, even to the extent of requiring Cullen to sit down with them in an attempt to settle the discord. It was the injudicious behaviour and reasoning of the complainants which confirmed Pius IX and his officials in their instinctive suspicion of their 'democratic spirit'. Cullen, by contrast, was a Roman himself, shared the Roman outlook and agreed with its priorities. In short, he spoke Rome's language, and could claim to have acted in Rome's interest exactly as he and Rome understood it. In Rome, as in Ireland, he could represent criticism of himself as criticism of the Pope ... which he truly believed it to be. Not surprisingly then, after much deliberation, Rome decided in Cullen's favour on every subject in dispute between him and the Archbishop of Tuam, including the major issues of priests in politics and (once more) the arrangements for the University. It decided to censure MacHale gently and privately for the controversies he had fomented in good faith. More bluntly, the Callan priests were told to obey their bishop. It was thought better to say nothing to the politicians of the Tenant Right League or the parliamentarians.

Some less attractive features of the centralised Church can be detected in these gradations of treatment when the facts are related in slightly different terms. Thus, the papal authorities avoided by silence any argument with those politically-minded Catholics least susceptible to clerical control. They chose to handle with care the Lion of Tuam, who could still cause trouble. They showed no consideration for the feelings of the priests who laid their grievance before the Holy Father but who could be reprimanded with impunity. They vindicated totally the prelate who embodied the Roman ethos and sustained him in all that he had done. By now it was June.

Newman had long been optimistic that, whatever was happening in Rome, His Grace of Tuam would not prevail. The Rector was happy with the provision made for the University the previous May, felt reassured by Cullen's letters and was especially anxious that the successful beginning made in November should be continued in the New Year. He was less concerned at this stage with Cullen's views on control of the University than that he should be kept interested in the fledgling institution and committed to its growth. Newman accordingly became almost obsequious for a time in his dealings with the Archbishop in faraway Italy. When Cullen wrote to suggest that an 'Academia' — a sacred concert of celebratory hymns, verse and prose — be organised by the University in honour of the Immaculate Conception, the Rector rushed off letters to Faber and Ornsby seeking material in English, Latin and '*all* languages'[55] (Cullen wanted O'Curry to look for old Irish litanies), but neglected to tell them whose idea it was. Did he perhaps want to avoid the reputation of being at the Archbishop's beck and call? He also asked Ornsby to send the *Gazette* to Cullen but warned that 'we must be very careful what we insert'.[56]

In January he hastened to promise Cullen that he would do his utmost to keep politics out of the University and he flatly denied a rumour which Cullen had heard about Newman himself persuading people that the Archbishop was 'a slave to the Government'.[57] In fact, Newman went on, 'I have said "I know nothing of politics ...". And I have uniformly protested, that *you* had nothing to do with politics either.'[58] In this he exaggerated somewhat his own ignorance of affairs as well as the Archbishop's detachment from them, but his concern can be understood since Cullen believed that Lucas, Duffy and others were saying the Archbishop would throw the Church behind the government if the government would grant a charter for the University — and some might jump to the conclusion that Newman was the source of such an allegation. As for the Archbishop's *bête noire* of 'Young Irelandism', which had pursued him to Rome in the person of the Young Irelanders' friend, Lucas, Newman stressed that the former Young Irelanders on the University staff were 'admirable persons now' and 'far from any political spirit...'.[59] Lucas was 'under a simple delusion' if he thought Newman had said Cullen was betraying the Irish Church.[60]

Newman thus took great care to to dissociate himself from the gossip reaching the Archbishop's ears, but he worried none the less. Might it be that he would be prevented from engaging the best-qualified staff, despite the synodal decrees, since nationalists would object if the appointees were English, and Cullen if they had a Young Ireland background? He consulted Manning, who felt on the whole that he was unduly perturbed but that if problems were going to continue because of 'the national element' it might be a good idea to relocate the University in England, which was 'even more central to the Anglo-Saxon race than Ireland'![61] His anxiety having led him into Manning's cloud-cuckoo-land, Newman sensibly got down to recruiting again without noticeably bothering about the personal history or nationality of his potential professors.

Inevitably, of course, he became caught up in other matters, from administering spiritual direction to the excessively spiritual Father Bernard Dalgairns in Birmingham to writing articles about the Crimean War under the guise of letters to a newspaper. At least he had a little more time for such activities now, with the University running smoothly under the direction of its competent staff.

This also meant that, following his return to Dublin in mid-January, the Rector could concentrate on his grand strategy to enhance the status of the University in the public mind. He set out to do this by making it as far as possible a public institution. He devised a further series of lectures, some to be at a popular level and others more academic, for persons who wanted to learn without becoming wholetime students. The course dealt with aspects of Irish, French, Spanish and Italian literature as well as archaeological and philosophical themes. Students at the university could attend, but he felt it would be wrong for him to send young men 'with pencil and paper to take down notes' if ladies were present.[62] Clearly, his Oxford-bred sense of propriety died hard despite the refusal of Dublin, which he had already encountered at his Discourses in the Rotunda, to be bound by such unreasoned convention.

The engagement as professors of men distinguished in their own fields had, of course, been part of Newman's plan from the beginning to boost the University's reputation. This could now be combined with the prospect of early expansion. The Medical School was to be opened as soon as suitable staff had been recruited and the Rector straight away set about finding competent men among the Catholic medical doctors practising in Dublin. While this search was in train he made the first provisional appointment to the proposed Faculty of Science by naming the well-regarded mathematician from Cork, Henry Hennessy, to the chair of Natural Philosophy (i.e. Physics). Hennessy was a meteorologist and climatologist, a member of the Royal Irish Academy and soon to be one of the first Roman Catholics elected a Fellow of the Royal Society. He was a worthy catch.

A more remarkable coup by Newman that spring, however, was persuading the poet Aubrey de Vere, after much discussion, as noted above, to accept the unlikely professorship of Political and Social Science. De Vere came from a Protestant landed family long established in County Limerick and with connections in the English Lake District, where he came to know and virtually worship William Wordsworth: a taste and experience which he shared with the future Father Faber of the London Oratory. He first met Newman in Oxford and heard him preach in Saint Mary's, where he noted that the great man's 'reading is beautiful, a sort of melodious, plaintive and rather quick chaunt ... He looks like a very young man made old by study.'[63]

He would later recall him resembling at that time 'a high-bred young monk of the Middle Ages, whose asceticism cannot quite conceal his distinguished elegance'.[64] He met Newman again at Littlemore and was himself received into the Catholic Church in 1851 by the recently converted Henry Manning. Respected in Ireland for his trojan work on behalf of famine victims, he had become renowned by 1855 in England and Scotland as one of the foremost literary critics of the day.

It fell to de Vere to add to those unpredicted mishaps which kept intruding on Newman's best-laid plans. Already limping with a swollen leg (the consequence of his Dalkey accident), after Easter the Rector suffered such pain from bad teeth that he said he could eat only grass until a dentist remedied the problem. Now de Vere arrived to stay with him in Harcourt Street, prior to delivering his inaugural lecture, and promptly went down with scarlet fever. A student in the house caught the infectious disease as well and Newman had to send away all the others living there lest an epidemic should break out. Although grateful for the care he received — 'Newman found time to sit by my bedside occasionally, and delight me with his conversation'[65] — it distressed de Vere to see how the head of the University had to cope personally with such trivial occurrences and even, when normality returned, 'that he should carve for thirty hungry youths'.[66] The poet thought that 'subordinates' should take care of these matters but recognised that the shortage of servants arose from a shortage of money.

Not that the chores worried Newman, who ran a cheerful household. One servant still there was the amorous Frederic who remembered 'jolly recreations which might be termed musicals or extempore plays or charades ... amusement of the highest and most innocent order. They would bring me up bodily to sing a favourite bass song ...'.[67]

6

'Raise up something good'

As we have noted, Newman hinted in the very month when the University opened its door that his work in Ireland was complete. He felt that no more could be asked of one man than to transform an idea into a living reality. He also considered this to be the limit of the commitment he had made to the Irish bishops. Thereafter Birmingham, the Oratories and the English Church would progressively occupy more and more of his thoughts, although it would be over a year before he directly broached the question of retirement and several further years before he finally succeeded in detaching himself from the tenacious Irish hold on his services and his name. As long as he retained the rectorship, however, he continued to build upon the foundations he had laid by expanding the courses offered at the University and by ensuring that the University made a tangible contribution to the welfare of the Irish Catholics among whom it was established and by whom it was funded.

Developments which were manifestly beneficial to the wider public included the launch of the medical school and the inauguration of evening classes. Less obviously, but perhaps more profoundly, for Newman an educational institution offered special opportunities to help people come to a richer understanding of their religion. In a piquantly perceptive essay (analysing Newman's influence on the Dubliner Frank Duff, who founded the Legion of Mary), Dr Finola Kennedy has pointed to Newman's comment that his University Sermons at Oxford were the best things he had written although the least theological. This was to see beyond the function of education as defined in the Discourses and to suggest that a university setting could be employed to promote the evolution of an informed laity — and the greatest lack in nineteenth-century Catholicism, to Newman's mind, was a laity who really knew what their faith meant and demanded of them. This consideration encouraged him to proceed with the plans for a church building which would not only meet the specific needs of the University but at the same time be a centre for inculcating an intelligent perception of Catholic belief.

Of all the appointments made by Newman in 1855 none was to leave a more permanent impression on the city of Dublin than his choice of John Hungerford Pollen as Professor of Fine Arts. This was an honorary (i.e. unpaid) position but it carried with it the salaried post of architect and decorator. The salary would be splendidly earned.

The thirty-four-year-old Pollen had not intended to take up a career in the arts. As the second son of a Wiltshire squire, he had gone to Oxford from Eton to prepare for the Anglican ministry. He visited Saint Mary's to hear Newman preach on the development of doctrine, a new and exciting theory at the time. 'There and then', he said afterwards, 'did I first begin to learn reflection.'[1] Like de Vere, he was much moved by Newman's reading: years later, after listening to a Shakespearean actor recite from *Henry V*, he jotted in his diary 'If I could have heard John Henry Newman! *There* were the reading! Appreciation of the author, without studying the effect upon the *hearers*.'[2] He became a Fellow of Merton College, was duly ordained, adopted Tractarian views in the controversies of the day and gave much of his time to tending the victims of cholera in Leeds. He was also able to indulge a taste for travel and with his elder brother visited Egypt, the Middle East and various European cities: his considerable talent for sketching and painting ensured he brought home a substantial pictorial record of his journeys. Merton recognised the young clergyman's ability and engaged him to decorate the College chapel — a most unusual commission to give a Fellow. He used bright colours instead of Victorian brown and, in the face of strong objections, included a figure of St Gregory wearing the papal tiara.

He saw these artistic activities, however, as no more than the indulgence of a hobby until he converted to Catholicism in 1852, followed shortly by his brother. Their baronet uncle, the senior member of the family, thereupon declared them disinherited and announced that he would refuse ever again 'to hold friendly communication' with either of his nephews.[3] It was a melodramatic reaction but sadly all too real in its effect. Pollen's conversion had automatically cost him his fellowship and related Oxford perquisites. He now was to lose his inheritance and other anticipated sources of income as well. 'I have serious thoughts', he wrote to a friend, 'of turning my pencil to account. It is my old and very strong taste, and almost the only opening to a livelihood.'[4] His Oxford background and misfortune for conscience's sake would have commended him to Newman in any event. As it happened, his views on the style and decoration of churches closely coincided with those of the Rector and he became available for employment providentially at the moment when the Rector needed an architect to design a church for his University.

The abiding memory of Newman in his Oxford pulpit, which men like Pollen and de Vere retained to the end of their lives, explains why it mattered so greatly to him to have a University church. The formally-prepared spoken word — preaching and lecturing — was Newman's special talent and the preferred instrument of his pastorate. As he put it in a lecture on 'Literature' to the Arts Faculty, 'thought and speech are inseparable from one another',[5] and again, 'When we can separate light and illumination, life and motion, the convex and the concave of a curve, then it will be possible for thought to tread speech under foot, and to hope to do without it...'.[6] For Newman speech was indistinguishable from writing: no difference of style marks off his spoken Discourses from those which appeared only in print, and it was specifically of preaching rather than writing that he said: ' 'Til a man begins to put down his thoughts about a subject on paper he will not ascertain what he knows and what he does not know; and still less will he be able to express what he does know.'[7] He knew not only from the testimony of those who had sat in congregations and audiences to hear him, but also from events traceable to his preaching, the force of ideas presented with such clarity. They had inspired the Oxford Movement, defused anti-Catholic feeling in England, given Ireland the principles upon which it was decided to construct a university. And within a university preaching was particularly appropriate for it helped to concentrate the mind on profound concepts and stimulated students to ponder them.

For Newman, the most profound subjects would be religious and it was only fitting that Divine Worship should be associated with them. This meant preaching in a *place* of worship. While manifestly inspired by the Oxford tradition, he saw a special virtue in adapting it to Dublin. As early as March 1853 he told Ornsby that he planned to have a University church in which there would be 'a High Mass and University Sermon every Sunday'.[8] Preachers would be invited from all parts of Ireland and England, which 'would be a set-off to the professors being laymen'.[9] To this, as noted already, he added other objectives: the church would be a unifying focal point for the students from different faculties, it would be used for solemn corporate ceremonies like conferrings and the sermons would not only be instructive to the general public but would ensure that the public were regularly alerted to the University's existence. Above all, the church would underscore the Catholic character of the University, 'the indissoluble union of philosophy with religion',[10] and would promote respect for the institution to which it belonged by the imposing quality of its decor and the very dress worn by its functionaries. For Newman, then, the church would contribute to the thought, unity and Catholicity of the University; it would offer a means for the University to serve a wider public than its own student body; it would increase the regard in which the University was held. It was central and indispensable to his vision.

Although his first idea had been to 'knock up' a temporary church in the garden of University House, he had no fundamental objection to taking over an existing church or even sharing one with a parish. Saint Mary's was, after all, a parish church as well as the University Church of Oxford. Also, to use an existing building in Dublin would save the construction costs; so that whatever money he had could be spent entirely on decoration. More than a year before, Archbishop Cullen had suggested that the newly-built Church of Saint Audoen in High Street might be available for an Oratory if Newman wanted to establish a house of his Order in Dublin. With Cullen's approval, he now approached the clergy of Saint Audoen's, hoping they would allow him to use it as a University Church. He was quite happy that it should continue at the same time to serve the surrounding parish in the heart of the Liberties, the old city within the walls.

Saint Audoen's appealed to him for many reasons. Not only was it sited, in the words of the *Catholic Directory*, 'in one of the leading streets of Dublin attracting from far and near the attention of its frequenters',[11] 'but it was well removed from Saint Stephen's Green which, as we have seen, was not at all Newman's favourite quarter. He, too, felt it would enjoy many 'frequenters' because the Church of Ireland cathedrals of Christ Church and Saint Patrick's were close by. These had 'the two fashionable choirs' and he concluded that 'if people came to them, they would come to us'.[12] The comment reminds us how Victorian congregations savoured the liturgical incidentals of worship. The music mattered — and so, indeed, did the preaching: Ornsby approved the idea of a church because 'there is such a rage in Dublin for hearing sermons'.[13] It was, however, the architectural style of Saint Audoen's which pleased Newman most of all. 'A fine, bare, Italian Church', he called it.[14] It was in fact the masterpiece of Patrick Byrne, architect *par excellence* of the Catholic Revival in Dublin. Byrne used the classical tradition of his native city to construct churches of nobility and beauty with the minimum resources (not by accident was Saint Audoen's 'bare'!). By the sensitive treatment of a single feature — the apse of Saint Paul's, Arran Quay; the lunette-pierced barrel vault of Saint Audoen's — he imposed Roman grandeur on what essentially were plain meeting-halls. Until he succumbed to popular demand, Byrne confronted the rampant neo-Gothic of the day with uncomplicated exquisitely-proportioned statements of artistic values that reached back from the streets of Dublin through Palladio's Vicenza and the basilicas, Christian and pagan, of Rome to the temples of the Acropolis. To Newman, the concept was hugely satisfying.

It was not that Newman disliked the Gothic. On the contrary, he thought it, in its original manifestation, 'endowed with a profound and commanding beauty such as no other style possesses'.[15] But this, he argued in his Fourth Discourse, derived from a spirit long dead by the nineteenth century. To pretend that it could be resuscitated was a kind of heresy, making the style an end (to assert the superiority of the medieval spirit) rather than a means (for giving expression to a living spirit). Why the classical style should have a permanence beyond the spirit which brought it into being in the Mediterranean lands so long ago, Newman failed to explain. He may merely have been rationalising a personal preference. 'I cannot deny that however my reason may go with the Gothic, my heart has ever gone with the Grecian',[16] he had written years before, and he had extolled 'the Italian style' for its 'simplicity, purity, elegance, beauty, brightness ...'.[17] His theory of aesthetics may have been questionable. The taste underlying it was not.

Saint Audoen's actually represented only part of what he liked in a church — dignity, order, stateliness. He also responded to colour, the warm, hieratic, shimmering colour of Byzantine interiors. He found both features combined in the loveliest churches of Rome: Santa Sabina on the Aventine, Santa Pudenziana, San Clemente (in the care of the Irish Dominicans) and a score of others, some dating from the fifth century, some from the ninth, some from the eleventh. All were 'basilican' in the basic Roman manner with an oblong ground plan, a semicircular apse beneath a 'half-dome' roof for the altar at one end, none of them very large. Usually the Roman sunlight, filtered through windows of millefiori glass, filled them with an even creamy whiteness, the perfect foil for fading frescos and sumptuous mosaics, the mosaics as gold and blue and purple and green as the distant day when the artist had painstakingly set them into the roof or curving wall of an apse. Floors and pulpits had their colour, too, contrived with marble inlay and polished stone. Such was Newman's ideal, and not only because of its inherent beauty. He thought these churches practical for the purposes which he considered important. Music and preaching, in his opinion, were most effective in a building of moderate size and simple shape, unbroken by massive pillars, wide aisles or deeply recessed side-chapels.

The negotiations for Saint Audoen's broke down in April 1855 when the clergy could not see their way to give the Rector all he wanted — he would have left only the nave for the parishioners who, after all, had raised the money to pay for the whole edifice (they were the first parish to inaugurate a weekly penny collection for church-building). This freed Newman to build his own church, not in the garden of University House but in that of the house next door, 87 Saint Stephen's Green, the lease of which he was able to acquire at short notice. Meanwhile, John Hungerford Pollen arrived in Dublin in response to the offer of a professorship from the hero of his Oxford days, whom he had seen and heard but with whom he had never spoken. Newman had approached him the previous winter through the father of his fiancée, also a convert clergyman, whom he told that he needed 'a person like Mr Pollen' as Fine Arts Professor 'to give the subject a Christian character and separate it from the sensuality which is often considered part of it, without running into the extravagances of the Ultra-Puginians'[18] (these last were the neo-medievalist promoters of the Gothic not only as a style but as the model for every last detail of construction and embellishment). He made another approach through Allies and wrote also to suggest that Pollen might decorate a University church for him (perhaps he intended at the time to take the bare look off Saint Audoen's). This typical persistence in pressing a request persuaded Pollen to ignore his doubts about his own competence. The artist accepted both the professorship and the commission, crossed over to Ireland in early May and called to Harcourt Street, where Newman entertained him to 'a plain but very good dinner'.[19]

157

The meeting of minds at once became apparent. It was scarcely surprising. Pollen's travels had taken him to Constantinople and Venice, to Venice a second time, to Ravenna and to Rome. This was the world of Byzantium and Byzantine influence, awash with colour as the Fellows of Merton were to find to their discomfort when their young colleague and his paint-pots brought their chapel to life. Venice stirred him deeply, especially Saint Mark's, the greatest embodiment of Byzantine decoration in the West: it was, incidentally, to have the same effect on Newman in 1856 — 'St Mark's is the most wonderful building we ever saw, and far exceeds St Peter's ...'.[20] As to architectural form, Pollen so admired the Italo-Byzantine basilicas that he would devote an entire series of lectures at the University to examining how the style had evolved. Basilican buildings, he said, exhibited 'elements of consummate grandeur', but they needed 'the help of colour' and 'colour is like melody, [it] can be learnt by the eye only, and felt...'.[21] With such sentiments, he came to Dublin attuned to the Rector's taste. Nor is there any sign that he was discouraged by his patron's modest ambition. 'My idea', Newman wrote in old age, 'was to build a large barn, and decorate it in the style of a basilica, with Irish marbles and copies of standard pictures.'[22] As a concept, this repeated the objective he set before himself a few years earlier when having a church put up for the Oratory in Birmingham. He succeeded to a degree on that occasion, and with no Pollen to guide him, if we are to judge from the critical puzzlement of his friend, Ambrose St John, who said the Oratory church was 'in style something between a Basilica and a Tithe Barn ... it is like nothing else on earth, and consequently cannot be taken for a Methodist chapel'.[23] Happily, we can note Father St John's description without going into *his* theory of aesthetics!

For Pollen, the basilican style made its impact entirely through interior arrangements (by contrast with the Gothic which he thought, perhaps oddly, was 'mostly external in its beauty'[24]). A 'barn' therefore suited him very well for it gave him ample wall surfaces to work on and unrestricted internal space to fill. Also, it could be got up quickly. He outlined his design in June 1855. Incredibly, the church, already substantially decorated, was opened on Ascension Thursday, 1 May 1856. Purists might argue whether it was strictly basilican, for Pollen had to adapt to the severe limitations of the site, but nobody could question its basilican spirit. An outer hall, with its hint of an atrium or, it might be, the narthex of a pilgrim church where the faithful composed themselves physically and mentally before entering the sacred building, led into a darkened space overhung by a gallery supported on a little copse of slender pillars reminiscent of the retrochoir in Wells Cathedral, which Pollen knew intimately. Beyond it, along the walls and all about the sanctuary, glowed richly tinted marbles in profusion, golden mosaics, frescos and precious stones ... or at least what seemed to be such. A choir-loft stood beside the sanctuary on high arches thrust upwards by a row of pillars similar to those at the back of the church. A lattice-work screen, all gilded, topped its balustrade, evoking eastern mystery and ensuring that the singers would not visually distract attention from the celebrants below. The body of the church was free of all obstruction, having no aisles or columns or recesses to block the view to the sanctuary or to distort the voice of a preacher in the marbled pulpit set over against the right-hand wall.

All was glorious in this jewel-box of a church but, when completed a few months later, it was the great sanctuary space which caught and held the eye. The curve of the apse, marble-panelled beneath a blind arcade and a frieze of roundels, embraced an immensely dignified altar of which the frontal centrepiece was a Byzantine (we would say Maltese) cross with a Christ-Triumphant, the Evangelists and Doctors painted on it as they might have been in medieval Italy. Tall candlesticks flanked the high crucifix, and shading the whole was a *baldacchino* or canopy of miniature Byzantine domes projecting from the wall just below the apsidal half-dome. The half-dome was, indeed, as Pollen claimed, 'noble'.[25] All over its proportionately vast expanse, and echoing the apse of San Clemente, trailed a 'mystic vine', with birds in its branches while a rabbit, two deer, a lamb and other creatures reposed or romped beneath. The vine entwined itself into a succession of circular motifs, each framing a saint and all surrounding the central figure of the Virgin as *Sedes Sapientiae*, the Seat of Wisdom. Newman had written to an acquaintance on the day after his installation as Rector, 'I trust we shall put ourselves under the patronage of the *Sedes Sapientiae*.'[26] Here was it wonderfully done. 'The more I looked at the apse', Newman remarked to Pollen, 'the more beautiful it seemed to me — and, to my taste, the church is the most beautiful one in the three kingdoms.'[27]

But how was so much achieved in so short a time? We can only surmise that Newman's vision sparked the artist's genius, so that inspiration was not long delayed. That inspiration went beyond design. Much of what was seen, and is still seen, had to be contrived by Pollen from base materials. Wood was made to look like beaten gold; ceramic in places substituted for marble; 'mosaic' was created by roughing over the surface of a painted picture, the 'frescos' were done in oils and the 'precious stones' (Pollen's term[28]) were rock crystals of the same mineral from which the humble fluoride of our water supplies and toothpaste is derived today. The windows, close under the roof, were particularly good, admitting as bright a light as Dublin had to offer and softening it with the opaque quality of the glass, yet this glass was no millefiori or Venetian concoction but simply 'bull's eyes'[29] — knobbly chunks, translucent but not transparent, which were normally treated as waste to be melted down or given to the poor!

Like Patrick Byrne, Pollen was constrained by limited finance. The result may be partly illusion, but is never fraud. Pollen used the available materials to the best advantage imaginable in his day. A modern artist or architect would probably let the same materials be seen precisely for what they are, timber or stone or oil-paint. That was not the Victorian way. Victorian architecture was imitative of one inherited style or another. Newman did not order a church *simpliciter*. He ordered basilican form and decoration — and kept specifying all manner of detail while it was under construction. Pollen did not set out to produce the kind of building for which his materials were best suited. He aimed rather to come as near to an Italianate basilica as he could with the materials to hand. There was neither failure nor dissimulation in not doing what he had not been asked to do. There was brilliant success in discharging the commission he received.

Nor was it all a matter of improvisation. Whatever his amateur background, Pollen was by now a fully professional artist, well versed in contemporary French and German techniques for achieving antique effects by nineteenth-century methods: in particular, he had taken careful note on his travels of such work going on in Munich. Nor were his materials always ersatz. The capitals of his columns were alabaster, as they would have been in Rome. Much of the marble was not only genuine but, as Newman requested, obtained from various parts of Ireland: Cork, Kilkenny, Connemara, Armagh. The University, according to Pollen, wished 'to set the example of developing ... the natural capabilities of Ireland; and, geologically, the most valuable of these are the various veins of marble'.[30] (It seems possible, incidentally, that this emphasis originated with Sir Robert Kane, a scientist who had long been promoting the country's mineral resources and who, ironically, was by now President of the 'godless' Queen's College in Cork.) Irish 'capabilities' included also the talents of local artisans, as Pollen generously acknowledged. They exemplified traditional Dublin craftsmanship, especially in stone-cutting, wood-carving and carpentry: the altar candlesticks and the capitals of the pillars bear close examination in their own right.

Then and since there have been people — students, clergy, nearby householders — who disliked University Church. That is understandable. Its affinities with the classical style so typical of Dublin are real but too remote to be obvious to anyone unacquainted with the combination of Eastern and Western culture in the ancient basilicas of Italy. And those in fact acquainted may rightly feel that Pollen stressed the Byzantine element rather than the Roman. There was nothing to criticise in that, but it should scarcely surprise us if some think the building in consequence to be too foreign, too strange, not what they expect a church to be. Judgements of this kind are not aesthetic; they are social, products of the experience of our own society and its norms, valid as statements of preference. On Newman's side it must be said that he always sought to widen the knowledge and the understanding, and to inform the taste, of his contemporaries — and especially his co-religionists. That motive must be added to all the others which inspired him to engage the genius of Pollen and his paint-pot (for Pollen himself painted the apse and much else in the church) to give Dublin a truly precious gem and a golden link with the Eternal City.

*　　*　　*

The launch of the Medical Faculty was the major expansion of the University planned for the second academic year, beginning in the Autumn of 1855. With handsome and well-appointed premises already acquired in Cecilia Street, a good start had been made. Staff had now to be found. In April Newman listed his needs:

1. Physiology, one Professor, two assistants.
2. Chemistry, one Professor, one assistant.

161

3. Pathology, one Professor.
4. Theory and Practice of Medicine, one Professor.
5. Surgery, one Professor.
6. Midwifery, one Professor.
7. Materia Medica and Therapeutics, one Professor.
8. Medical Jurisprudence, one Professor.
9. Botany.[31]

Attracting suitable persons to fill these posts proved to be as time-consuming and frustrating as any problem Newman had had to overcome in Ireland. Manifold restrictions drastically reduced the number of practitioners who might be invited to take chairs or lectureships. In the first place, as we saw, Newman himself insisted on having Catholics. There were, in fact, many Catholic doctors in the country since medicine had been the one profession never fully closed off by the penal laws, but few Catholic doctors had teaching or consultancy experience because of the denominational imbalance in hospital appointments. Newman had underscored the deficiency when he pointed to the twelve Catholics out of 111 doctors 'in situations of trust and authority'.[32] He might have lured qualified appointees from abroad but dared not. He asked his adviser, Dr Andrew Ellis, what he would say 'to an eminent Irishman and physician being brought from elsewhere to Dublin for our Professorship of Medicine'[33] and Ellis replied in some horror that '*no* one could lecture on the Practice of Medicine in Cecilia Street ... who is not an established and *recognised* Lecturer, and a physician to a hospital in Dublin'.[34] Not even an Irishman! *That* narrowed the field.

In fairness to Ellis, it should be added that his view did not represent a closed-shop mentality. If Cecilia Street were to succeed, its courses had to lead to a licence to practise. Since the Catholic University had no charter, it could confer no licences itself. The Cecilia Street course had therefore to be approved by one or other of the licensing bodies such as the College of Surgeons, the College of Physicians, the Apothecaries' Hall from which Cecilia Street had been purchased, or — if necessary — the Queen's University or the Trinity College School of Physic. Quite properly, none of these would endorse a course unless it were satisfied as to the competence of the teaching staff who conducted it, and the only sure way of securing such endorsement was to engage men of known standing.

The pragmatic argument was reinforced by a prejudice which Newman had already met in hiring arts lecturers. As he put it when he decided to defer the engagement of a Professor of Medicine, 'I hear murmurs about the appointment of foreigners.' These would cease, he surmised, after he left the vacancy open for a little while 'testifying to the want of Irishmen just now for certain chairs, and to my reluctance to introduce strangers'. On the other hand, 'if suddenly foreign appointments were made, people would be sure to say that persons might have been found for them at home, with a little looking about'.[35] It was a tiresome ploy to have to adopt but it could seem unavoidable because, incredibly, being Irish *and* Catholic *and* qualified *and* known in Dublin was not necessarily enough. Dr Cullen's suspicion of Young Irelanders touched medical appointments like all others. Newman spluttered his exasperation over this when he recalled his time in Dublin years later: the former Young Irelanders were 'the ablest men who ... belonged to the University — such as Professor O'Curry — and Professor Sullivan. I can never be sorry for asking their assistance — not to take them would have been preposterous — There you had good men, Irishmen, did Dr Cullen wish Irish? Had he not warned me against English and Scotch?'[36]

Newman did his best to identify, and then lure into Cecilia Street, the very few doctors who met most if not all the specifications (he deliberately overlooked a Young Ireland background). A further difficulty, perhaps inherent in the exercise, then revealed itself. The men most worth having proved hard to persuade. Dr (later Sir) Dominic Corrigan ranked among the outstanding physicians of the day. Bishop Moriarty wrote to Newman that 'Corrigan's name and Corrigan's talents would be of immense service to the University.'[37] His membership of the Senate of the Queen's University should not disbar him: 'It is most desirable to secure Corrigan.'[38] Corrigan thought otherwise. Newman found him 'kind' when they discussed the possibility of his appointment as the Professor of the Practice of Medicine but noted 'I fear we have not made progress.'[39] When the doctor had mulled the matter over he became even more doubtful. Catholic though he was (or perhaps because he was a Catholic!), he did not trust the bishops. Newman reported to Moriarty, 'he does not like taking a Professorship without some security that the Bishops will go on with the Medical Faculty'.[40] The Rector told him he could scarcely give more assurance on 'the continuance of the Institution' than to point to 'the solemn determination of the Holy See and the National Synod … It is the very guarantee on which I thought it worth while to leave my own home in England …'.[41] Which, of course, was all very well for a celibate religious with his English home to go back to. An Irish Catholic layman who had reached the pinnacle of his profession in Victorian Dublin and acquired a handsome house in Merrion Square had much to lose by casting his bread on uncharted and unchartered waters. He turned down the offer, leaving Newman to wonder whether he could risk hiring abroad.

One invitation had to go to a foreign country, however, for Dr Robert S. D. Lyons had had taken leave of absence from his Dublin practice and gone to the British army hospital at Scutari in Turkey to report on the diseases contracted by soldiers fighting in the Crimea. That he had been requested by the military authorities to undertake this task confirmed his high reputation. Newman offered him 'the chair of Physiology (as distinct from Anatomy)'[42] but as Lyons' work at Scutari, and soon afterwards in the Crimea, fell within the field of pathology it was probably understandable that some confusion should have arisen over the precise discipline to which he might be assigned at Cecilia Street. An exchange of letters between one end of Europe and the other did not help to clarify matters. Newman's letter to the archbishops on 28 July to tell them of his proposed appointments named Lyons 'to be Professor of Pathology'.[43] A public advertisement on 17 August announced the imminent opening of the Medical School, and made no reference to Lyons but decribed Dr Thomas Hayden and Dr Robert Cryan as Professors of 'Anatomy and Physiology'.[44] Lyons objected, said he wanted Physiology, which he considered more important, and tried to resign. Newman apologised, said he had misread correspondence from Lyons and had innocently concluded that he wanted Pathology.

It may be relevant to recall Newman's offhand approach to titles: if he got the man he wanted, it never worried him unduly what Professorship he accepted. This made for embarrassment. Just as he could not give Poetry to de Vere, having given it to somebody else, he could not now give Physiology to Lyons. At least, not Physiology in the Medical School. In a clever resolution of the problem, which disposed of another problem at the same time, the Rector nominated Lyons to be Professor of Physiology in the Faculty of Science and of the Practice of Medicine and Pathology in the Medical Faculty! With his professional status thus clarified, Lyons was happy and Newman got his man. A few others were engaged with less difficulty. Dr Ellis had been Professor of Surgery in the Apothecaries' Hall and therefore in a sense came with the premises, although it would be more accurate to say that he brought the premises with him since it was he who had negotiated the delicate business of buying Cecilia Street. He naturally became Professor of Surgery again under the new dispensation.

Drs Hayden and Cryan were pleased to join the University from small private medical schools in which they had worked as lecturers preparing students for the examinations of the licensing bodies, but in the case of Hayden the Archbishop had to be reassured. Was he not a Protestant?, he asked Newman. Not so, the Rector replied. There were two of the name. The Protestant Hayden was a neighbour of Newman's in Harcourt Street, which caused Moriarty to jump to the same conclusion as Cullen. He seems to have been widely known from his promotional instinct: Newman called him 'the advertising Dr Hayden'[45] and Moriarty remarked, with evident distaste, that he 'advertises continually in the papers'.[46] Shaw's Directory listed him as the occupant of 82 Harcourt Street and instead of the name and occupation on a single line, which was the normal entry, a long (presumably paid-for) note described him as 'Hayden, George Thomas, M.D., physician, surgeon and general medical practitioner. Gives advice and medicines at his residence or within the immediate vicinity of Dublin, for five shillings …'.[47] That churchmen should have reacted against the employment of a doctor who sold his talents like a commercial entrepreneur underscored the Catholic concern at that time to be considered 'respectable'. They need not have worried, for the Catholic Dr Hayden whom Newman engaged was a very different type, so courteous that he had become widely known as 'Gentle Thomas'.[48]

Newman told Ellis that he would offer courses only in surgery, anatomy and pathology at the outset. Subjects which did not have to be taught in the first year (like the practice of medicine) would have to wait until suitable teaching staff had been found: at this stage, Corrigan was lost but the Lyons affair had yet to be sorted out. It troubled Ellis that the School lacked a more substantial staff list. He may also have felt that surgery and pathology were scarcely first year subjects, although they might be taught to students who had undertaken their preliminary courses elsewhere. Physics and chemistry would be appropriate. Could he not offer them? Was Henry Hennessy not being engaged as Professor of Natural Philosophy (i.e. physics), a subject which 'bears strongly on medical education and is often associated with it'?[49] Newman resorted to the subterfuge he would later use with Lyons. Hennessy's faculty (Science) was distinct from Medicine, but his name could appear on a notice under the heading, 'University Medical School, Cecilia Street'.[50] He would, after all, be a Professor of the University and as it happened it was intended to locate his apparatus in the Cecilia Street premises.

Chemistry presented its own difficulties. Newman sought guidance on many matters regarding the Medical School, including appointments, from William Kirby Sullivan whom he found to be 'a rough man, but clever and, to me, engaging, from his honesty and sharpness'.[51] Sullivan, a native of Cork, had studied chemistry in Germany and was both Chemist and Lecturer in Chemistry to the Museum of Irish Industry (the same which was to inspire Pollen to choose Irish marbles for University Church). He was the obvious person for the Chair of Chemistry but the Museum functioned under the Board of Trade, a government department, which initially required Sullivan to give up his Museum posts if he took the University appointment. Having a wife and young family, he felt it would be wrong to abandon well-paid employment, not least because — like Corrigan — he doubted whether the University was going to survive. When Lord Stanley, President of the Board of Trade, learned of the situation he cleared the way for Sullivan to retain some of his assignments at the Museum rather than have it said that a man was barred from state employment because of his connection with a Catholic institution. Further complications ensued but did not prevent Sullivan from becoming Newman's Professor of Chemistry in 1856.

Chemistry, like Physics, was primarily a Science subject but the immediate need was in the Medical Faculty. Accordingly, and perhaps with a view to helping Sullivan's domestic situation, Newman offered him two chairs, Professor of Physical Chemistry (Faculty of Science) and Professor of Medical Chemistry (Faculty of Medicine). In the event, Sullivan was able to take up only the medical appointment for the time being although he appeared three times over in the University Calendar for 1856/57: in both Professorships and as Dean of the Faculty of Science. Incidentally, Sir Robert Kane, himself a chemist, founder and Director of the

Museum, and by then also President of Queen's College, Cork, seems to have been very obstructive when Sullivan tried to accept Newman's offer without relinquishing his government jobs. It is hard to blame him. Not only had the Museum a prior claim to its Chemist's services, but it was being asked to facilitate him in furthering the purposes of an institution set up in deliberate and direct opposition to the Queen's University. Newman, untypically, could see only one side of the argument and deplored Kane's attitude. By ironic coincidence, Sullivan was to succeed Sir Robert as President of QCC in 1873.

Sullivan had been a Young Irelander, which worried Newman no more than the fact that Stephen Myles MacSwiney, whom he made Professor of Medical Jurisprudence, had composed some of the ballads favoured by the movement. It mattered more that MacSwiney was attached to the new hospital in Jervis Street. Hospital connections were vital, both for the reputation of the teaching staff and to ensure that students had access to patients in order to learn diagnostics and treatment at the bedside. The simplest approach to the question was to offer Cecilia Street appointments to hospital consultants. It worked in the case of MacSwiney but all attempts failed to secure the services of the famous Dr Joseph O'Ferrall, 'First Medical Advisor in Ordinary'[52] to St Vincent's Hospital. He feared that his private practice would suffer if he took the proffered chair of Clinical Instruction (which seems to have been thought up as a lure since no such Professorship appears on Newman's original list of required staff). He said, too, that if he took it he would want an assurance that Cecilia Street students would attend no other hospital. Although he was happy to facilitate the Medical School students and staff by allowing them access to his wards and did not object to the engagement of more doctors by the hospital, in so far as the Reverend Mother might permit, the obstacles he raised made it difficult to establish a formal relationship between Cecilia Street and St Vincent's at this early stage. Lyons eventually became physician to Jervis Street, while Ellis and Hayden joined the staff of the Mater Hospital after Newman had resigned as Rector.

The problems concerning these appointments were perhaps trivial and even petty in each case. Cumulatively, they absorbed much of the Rector's time and made endless demands on his reserves of diplomacy. He had to argue about money (there were a number of complaints over the paucity of Cecilia Street salaries) as well as status, and he had more than once to stress the bishops' commitment to the project while entertaining doubts on that score himself. Hennessy's innocent assumption that his chair was totally safe once Newman put his name to the bishops forced the Rector to send him a warning: 'I know well by experience how bodies of men move as if independently of the intentions of the individuals composing them. Their action is like the result of combined forces in mechanics, something distinct from the act of any one of them ... Suppose, e.g., the Bishops were to pass a rule that no Professorship should be held above 3 years? suppose they were to make some grave change at the end of six, which is the term for which the Statutes are at present to stand — or suppose they were at the end of a certain period to lower the salary. I have no reason to believe such changes likely ... but I wish you to see everything before you decide.'[53] Newman's scruples thus set a limit to effective recruitment and went some distance to endorse the doubts of Corrigan and Sullivan. It made the triumph all the greater when Cecilia Street was quickly seen to be a success.

The reward for Newman's diligent pursuit of the best available talent within the severe limitations on who might be hired came in the summer and autumn of 1856. The Royal College of Surgeons in Ireland, a licensing body and itself a major medical school (covering all aspects of medical teaching, not merely surgery), began the process of recognising the courses conducted at Cecilia Street. Certificates of attendance at recognised courses entitled a student to sit for the corresponding examination in the College of Surgeons and through such examinations to become a licensed practitioner. The procedure for securing recognition of courses was tedious, since the College needed to be satisfied of each lecturer's personal competence. The Cecilia Street staff decided to apply individually over a period rather than submit their names to the College in bulk: 'It has been though well that they should do so one by one, to avoid creating any alarm',[54] wrote Newman. What 'alarm' was to be feared is unclear but it probably had to do with the subliminal feeling of Dublin Catholics in the mid-nineteenth century that no good would come of drawing attention to themselves. Newman would have appreciated this from the University's experience of house purchasing. The College of Surgeons, however, took the applications as they came in and processed them with the minimum delay. By November, Sullivan, Lyons and MacSwiney,

among others, had all been recognised. The speed with which
the College moved may fairly be attributed to the quality of the
staff assembled by Newman and to their consequential
connections. Ellis — already a recognised lecturer from his days
in the Apothecaries' Hall School — was a past President of the
College of Surgeons, Lyons was a Licentiate of the College who
had become Pathologist-in-Chief to the Army, and MacSwiney
was a Member of the Royal College of Surgeons in England. It
may also be supposed that leading consultants like Corrigan and
O'Ferral, for all their personal touchiness, would have spoken
favourably within medical circles about the work going ahead at
Cecilia Street, of which they were fully informed from the
approaches made to them.

Recognition by other licensing bodies, in England and Scotland
as well as Ireland, followed quickly. The students had access to
several Dublin hospitals and eventually — the most intractable
problem — those of the staff who needed hospital appointments
and did not already have them were found appropriate positions.
The quality of the staff and teaching at the School played a major
part in attracting students. Not only had respected names been
found for the various chairs, but advanced concepts in medical
training were adopted. Physiology and pathology, for example,
were disciplines little known at the time in English medical
schools, although they had been introduced in Edinburgh.
Interestingly, while Edinburgh's rationalism and indifferentism
in the liberal arts were roundly denounced by Newman, its lead
in medicine stimulated the enthusiasm of the progressives in
Cecilia Street, Lyons and Sullivan especially. Sullivan, despite
his own difficulties with the Industrial Museum, was an optimist
who told Newman not to listen to those who said that no students
would come unless the School were complete and functioning'
in all its departments. 'Raise up something good', he said, 'and
people will come; the supply will create the demand.'[55] This
advice coincided with Newman's own instincts in establishing
the University, when, as we have seen, he devoted much care
to creating a high reputation for it on the basis of its professors'
calibre and the distinction of the men who sponsored it by
allowing their names to be entered in its 'books'.

So it was that, with a few good names, anatomical drawings
(provided by Pollen at 'five and ten shillings apiece'[56]), and the
promise of modern training in well-equipped lecture theatres and
dissecting rooms, the Cecilia Street Medical School opened

169

officially on 2 November 1855 — a date by which the negotiations with potential staff described above, applications for recognition by the College of Surgeons and the organisation of most of the study courses had yet to be completed or even, in many cases, be put in hand. It says much for the expectations already generated that forty-three students enrolled for the opening year and at least thirty-six of them attended the courses with no assurance that they would in time qualify as medical doctors. Scarcely any of these were matriculated students of the University since, strictly speaking, matriculated students were expected to take the two-year course in philosophy and letters before proceeding to Cecilia Street and those who had begun when the University itself opened in 1854 would not be ready until the autumn/winter session of 1856. But Newman always leaned towards making the advantages of the University as widely available as possible and he therefore planned that a number of places in Cecilia Street would be given to young men who could not afford the extended expense of a liberal arts course as well as the medical courses. This enlightened policy made it possible to inaugurate the Medical School before the first graduates had emerged from University House.

By one of the bizarre and embarrassing accidents to which he was prone ('I was in bed with a bad boil'[57]), Newman missed the opening of the Medical School, which consisted of a somewhat trite inaugural address by Ellis, delivered in the anatomy room of Cecilia Street to an audience of 'distinguished clergymen and eminent professional men'[58] led by Archbishop Cullen and the Surgeon-General, Sir Philip Crampton. Later in the month the Rector presented his own lecture in the School of Medicine to mark the new academic year. 'Christianity and Physical Science' was markedly more impressive than the previous year's reflections on literature.

Controversy always brought out the best in Newman and contemplation of physical science ranged him face to face with what he considered to be one of the great errors of the day: the use of scientific methods to probe the truths of faith. This gave the irreligious the hope that belief would be undermined while it made the faithful contemptuous of scientific research. In fact, as Newman kept repeating through the lecture, truth could not contradict truth. Theology and physics were each valid in their own fields and neither could undermine the other since they dealt with unconnected subjects, matter and mind or, more precisely, perceived facts and the Author of all. They furthermore used opposite methods of argument, theology being deductive (drawing conclusions from the given truths of Revelation) and physics being inductive (making sense of a variety of observed phenomena). There should be no more likelihood of a clash between theology and physics than between an engineer and a grammarian. Invoking Macauley in support, Newman spoke of the survival of Catholic faith notwithstanding the scepticism of a scientific age. He also, if with less vehemence, regretted the intrusion of theology on physics, especially through 'floating opinions'[59] of no dogmatic status on the meaning of scriptural passages referring to the physical world — such as the accounts of Creation.

The whole lecture resounded with the limpid reasoning of the Discourses, even if hindsight can expose some infelicities of which Newman could not have been aware: he thought it impossible for a physicist to examine the meaning of time (Einstein would not be born until twenty-four years later!); he thought it ludicrous to imagine that 'musical truths' could interfere with 'the doctrines of architectural science'[60] (modern research has established important links between medieval norms in music and gothic architecture). More surprisingly, he let Macauley away with the mistaken impression that Thomas More died to defend the doctrine of transubstantiation. But these were trivial details in the context of a devastating assault upon the flabby if fashionable reasoning that was deluding 'the educated and half-educated portions of the community'.[61] No doubt he felt that medical students, and perhaps their teachers, would be especially vulnerable to quasi-scientific theories of this kind. If so, he did them the honour of assuming that they could absorb the finely-honed logic with which he demolished the grand simplicities tossed up in the wake of genuine scientific progress. Cecilia Street repaid his trust, it might be said, by making itself the most solidly based and publicly respected faculty of the Catholic University. Newman set up the School in the hope that its graduates would 'go into the wide world as specimens and patterns of a discipline which is at once Catholic and Professional'.[62] At the end of its first year he could write in his report to the bishops: 'Did our efforts towards the foundation of a Catholic University issue in nothing beyond the establishment of a first-rate Catholic School of Medicine in the metropolis, as it has already done, they would have met with sufficient reward.'[63] And at the beginning of the second year in Cecilia Street he could tell Sullivan that 'the Medical Professors ... are almost *the* University.'[64]

*   *   *

By 1856 the little institution so grandly named 'The Catholic University of Ireland' had begun to settle into the homely routine of an established seat of learning. It was not Oxford, as the Rector accepted with cheerful resignation. In Harcourt Street he had 'no plate ... but a few electro-plated spoons and forks'[65] (about the same time, Napoleon III had decided that electro-plate would suffice in the Tuilleries — but Napoleon was not an Oriel man!) and the incorrigible Frederic, still general factotum of the household, went about his duties singing in *basso profundo*, forever tripping over himself, forgetting to bolt the hall-door at night and, when he remembered to lock up, oversleeping next morning so that the servants found themselves shut out. One of these was Margaret, the cook, whom Newman had to threaten with the sack to induce an improvement in the cuisine, which then 'changed ... so marvellously that it seems a fright too good.'[66] Newman had to do much for himself. Two years after moving in, he wrote to a friend: 'My chattels stand about my room, the same confusion as on the night I came, ... from my inability to find leisure for removing them ...'.[67]

Nonetheless, he managed to maintain an aura of High Table and Senior Common Room in the midst of this amiable anarchy. Pollen recalled how, on his first visit to the house when the students had retired to their 'drawing-room' after dinner, 'I, Newman and Renouf sat and cosed over some port wine and biscuits for an hour. He was quite charming, so very simple and so fond of his old Oxford recollections.'[68] The experience would be repeated. 'Delightful it was', said Pollen, 'to be on his staff, and to hear him draw out, with the gentlest possible forceps, what each friend or professor had to say on his own particular theme.... He encouraged you to put your conclusions into terms; to see what they might look like from various sides ... but all this under the form of easy conversation. In lighter hours he would be touched by Oxford recollections, and amused by familiar myths touching eccentric notabilities ...'.[69] Apart from his colleagues, Newman had other Irish friends, including Bishop Moriarty and a number of priests, especially from Maynooth. 'He keenly appreciated the wit and genius of some of them', according to one of the professors, and he 'considered the Irish clergy (with whom he was very popular) on the whole to be large-minded, though there were some who showed Dr Cullen's less liberal attitude of mind'.[70]

Despite his many responsibilities, the Rector refused to become housebound. Although he distressed de Vere by turning down his invitation to spend a day in County Wicklow (because 'life is full of work more important than the enjoyment of mountains and lakes'[71]), Pollen had happy memories of 'walking with him in times of recreation over the pleasant fields, park, and gardens of the Phoenix'.[72] In the Phoenix Park he particularly enjoyed the Zoo, where he speculated on 'the design and end of beasts; their ferocity; their odd ways; birds especially'.[73] Pollen's daughter wondered afterwards whether it might have been Dublin Zoo which inspired the lines in *The Dream of Gerontius:*

..... the restless panting of their being,
Like beasts of prey, who caged within their bars,
In a deep hideous purring have their life,
And an incessant pacing to and fro.[74]

Perhaps, indeed — although it must be admitted that zoological gardens fascinated Newman (thus proving him a true Victorian) and Dublin was not the only place where he visited them. He must have cut a somewhat sombre figure among the children and their parents who made up the bulk of visitors to the Zoo. Indoors or outdoors, he normally wore the 'short dress' then favoured by Catholic priests in England. This was in fact a rather long frock coat, knee-breeches and gaiters. He was no great dresser but was fastidious on points of propriety. He remembered with horror the day when he left the house without donning his gaiters: he fortunately got no further than Harcourt Street before returning home and remedying the defect but the horror remained with him, that he might have 'pranced about Dublin' in worsted stockings and only discovered his state of undress 'in the midst of the fashion ... in Sackville Street'.[75] The mystery was that such accidents did not happen more often, for he struck observers as absent-minded in manner. So he appeared to one of his students, John Augustus O'Shea, who described how he 'walked with short, rapid steps from Harcourt Street to the Green ... shrouded in meditation, and his keen eyes looking neither to the right nor to the left, but introspectively as it were, with a contemplativeness far removed from things of the thoroughfare. He ... usually carried an umbrella.'[76]

And what did the undergraduates make of their famous Rector? O'Shea said their attitude was 'a sort of awe-struck worship. They were very proud of him, yet, to be candid, they did not rise to the understanding of his genius. It was too cold, dry, and self-contained for their young minds.'[77] They met this quality at first-hand in his public addresses and sermons — which prompts the thought that O'Shea was really speaking about 'young *Irish* minds'. This was after all the same John Henry Newman who had attracted so many *English* students to his Sunday sermons in Saint Mary's at Oxford. His quiet intensity of style, so much commented upon then, did not change when he came to Ireland. Gavan Duffy heard his Discourses in the Rotunda: 'He spoke in a level voice, scarcely raised or lowered by a note, without action and without the play of feature which we regarded as so large a part of oratory ... this eminent man exhibited no emotion. His speech was a silvery stream which never sank out of view or foamed into cascades.'[78] Thomas Arnold, younger brother of Matthew and Professor of English Literature in the University, remembered his 'low and penetrating tones'[79] at a telling moment in a sermon, and the future Archbishop of Dublin, William Walsh, remarked on his 'clear musical voice, unimpassioned and well modulated'.[80] Such self-control, however, made no impression on O'Shea and his friends: 'The language was polished and perfect, the thoughts elevated, the reasoning without a flaw; but they had that fatal drawback in our boyish judgments — they were read.'[81]

Possibly what the young Irishmen thought wanting in Newman was a certain robustness, physical and emotional, with which they could identify. Its absence pointed to no flabbiness or lack of feeling in their Rector. Newman's whole life centred upon a relentless and punishing pursuit of truth, and a passionate commitment to the truth when he believed he had found it. But his strength lay in witness and argument, not in what he would have considered flamboyant or vulgar assertiveness. His personal character, his class and nationality all tended to further this restraint in expression and comportment. His asceticism bolstered it by introducing an element of cloistered calm to his public encounters. 'One of the signs of the presence of God is peace', he wrote. 'The Saints have gone through fierce trials; I do not read that they were restless; or if they were ever so, I do not find that it came into the idea or definition of their saintliness.'[82] He pointed to Philip Neri and Ignatius Loyola as contrasting types of saint, yet 'both in different ways inexpressibly calm'.[83] Saint Philip and Saint Ignatius, by no accident at all, are each the subject of a major panel in University Church. Serenity, for Newman, was a saintly ideal.

His manner of being serene may explain the disturbing analogy employed by two of his contemporaries quite separately from one another. W. G. Ward once dreamed about a fascinating conversation with a veiled lady at a dinner-party who transpired, when she threw back her veil, to be John Henry Newman. Aubrey de Vere, in old age, remembered a day in Oriel College when 'the door opened, and Newman, in cap and gown, entered very swiftly and quietly, with a kind of balance of the figure, like a very great lady sweeping into the room'.[84] No quasi-psychological theories need be sought to explain why Newman left this impression upon some of his acquaintances. In an age of demonstrative oratory, opinionated small-talk, jingoistic politics, romantic versifying and cloying popular music, a sense of dignity in speech and bearing was rare enough to come upon but it characterised the chatelaines of certain old families in whose circles both Ward and de Vere would have been at home. It was the dignity which impressed itself on Newman's friends; the 'great lady' association simply served to define the quality in question. At the same time, it suggests why Irish students 'were not enamoured of his sermons',[85] as O'Shea put it, and why they felt his ideas to be 'dry' and 'cold'. The behavioural rites of an alien culture invariably obstruct understanding.

Whether the students were well-equipped to understand was another question. Gavan Duffy used to argue that few young men anywhere in Europe were as poorly prepared for life as the sons of the Irish Catholic gentry and middle classes. Oddly enough, Protestant undergraduates of Trinity College went in considerable numbers to University Church to hear the sermons which Catholic University students held in such little regard (I remember a similar phenomenon when I was a University College undergraduate in the early 1950s and Monsignor Ronald Knox came to preach the annual retreat in University Church). Part of the problem lay embedded in social circumstances. The liberal arts, at the core of the university system, seemed far removed from the practical needs of a people recently emancipated and still further removed from real power to control their own or their country's future: the success of the Medical School represented in some degree the attraction of pragmatic training over the inculcation of philosophic values. The functional view of learning, which flourishes in Ireland today, has roots running deeply back to penal deprivation.

The University also arrived at a transitional moment in the development of Irish schools. The growth of Catholic secondary schools, while proceeding rapidly, was still at an early stage (as late as 1870 there were only forty-seven in the entire country) while the relatively new national schools, which taught no classics, had killed off the 'classical academies' in the country towns, not to mention the hedge schools of penal times, the best of which had also had a classical tradition. The Christian Brothers were still directing their valiant work almost entirely towards equipping their pupils for gainful employment, although a few of their schools had begun to teach Latin and French. Boys other than those from families of substantial means, who could afford to send them to boarding schools, therefore often lacked access to the classical grounding then considered necessary for university entrance. (Newman offered 'affiliation'[86] with the University to secondary schools which attained prescribed standards, in the hope that this would induce improvements; a number of diocesan colleges applied and qualified for affiliation between 1856 and 1858.) Historians of education may debate with hindsight the virtues and deficiencies of Victorian priorities in schools or universities alike. The fact remains that Newman had to set up his University within the bounds of these priorities and it was no easy task. Not only had he to propagate the message that university education was desirable for its own sake but he had to do so in a society able to send forward dismally few pupils who could benefit from it. Small wonder if he clung long to the hope that Catholic students would come from abroad. Ireland was stony soil.

Then there was the Church. Gavan Duffy summed up the problem presented by the attitude of Archbishop Cullen: 'His idea of government was [that] Ireland should be ruled, as Rome was ruled, by ecclesiastics, laymen having no function but to contribute a sympathetic and deferential audience.'[87] He might have added that his own friend, Archbishop MacHale, had no more enlightened a view since his fundamental argument with Cullen concerned where *among the ecclesiastics* control should be located — in the hands of one bishop or of the hierarchy as a whole. In either case the laity were expected merely to contribute, in more senses than one. They were assigned no controlling function over the University and in the post-Famine apathy few of them sought any. Those few included the gentry, whose support Newman believed to be essential but who gradually withdrew from the exercise — and in many cases refused to allow their names to be entered as Associates — because of the episcopal refusal to give a lay committee the right to supervise even the financial affairs of the University which might have been thought to fall within the laity's competence. The lack of encouragement from this small but influential segment of Irish Catholics further inhibited the recruitment of students.

These factors combined to ensure that the student body assembled in the early years, despite evidence of impressive potential, fell short of the educational standards which would have been expected of freshmen elsewhere. Professorial comments were virtually unanimous. Within three weeks of the opening date, a visiting Oratorian from Birmingham wrote home that 'Renouf and the other tutors speak well of their classes; the lads are on the whole backward, except in mathematics'.[88] There were sharper comments, too, even if we ignore the wild generalisation by one lecturer regarding 'gentlemen who have yet to learn about such elementary truths as that Jerusalem is not in Africa'.[89] The want of training in Latin composition was remarked upon and, although the students' knowledge of Christian doctrine passed muster, they displayed a surprising ignorance of Church history. The young men pleased Newman and his staff less because of their intellectual attainments than by their manifest brightness. Stephen's Green was a livelier place for their presence, whether playing practical jokes on a shortsighted professor (by crouching below their desks so that he thought the room was empty) or tumbling out of hackney coaches 'with a wolfish appetite for dinner'[90] after a day at the seaside or the Baldoyle races. Here were minds open to stimulation.

Newman never believed that learning came only through lectures or reading. Dialogue, discussion, the honing of opinions through advocacy in the teeth of hard-pressed contrary views he considered valuable means for developing the intellect. To that end he set up the undergraduate Historical, Literary and Aesthetical Society in the academic year 1855/56, which as the Literary and Historical Society of University College Dublin

177

survives to this day, as much a memorial of Newman's work in the city as the College's Medical Faculty or University Church. The first President (the title would later be changed to Auditor) is not known but his successor in 1856/57 was an English undergraduate, Henry Slingsby Bethell. From the beginning, this debating society formed a nucleus round which the students from different disciplines came together: interestingly, the speakers to Bethell's inaugural address on 'Taste and Genius'[91] were the Medical Professors Hayden and Cryan.

Confrontational debates were infrequent at first — the earliest recorded (in 1858) dealt with the question 'Which was the greater man, Julius Caesar or Napoleon?'[92] More commonly a member of the Society presented a paper, on which discussion and argument took place. Subjects in Bethell's term included 'The Identity of Origin and the Varieties of the Human Race' and 'The Influence of Ireland upon Anglo-Saxon Literature'.[93] Clearly, the 'Literary' and 'Historical' prevailed over the contemporary. What would today be called 'current affairs' could not in fact be discussed since the rules provided that 'no member may introduce the subject of British politics of the past fifty years'.[94] Irish politics, being inextricably bound up with British politics at the time, were thereby also excluded — perhaps to avoid the shedding of heat rather than light but possibly also to prevent rumours growing about the promotion of subversive ideas in University House. Archbishop Cullen would have taken no more kindly than Dublin Castle to the Young Irelandism that was sure to be the stock-in-trade of any debate on a local and topical theme. It would certainly have been of little help in advancing the case for a charter, upon which the Archbishop had now set his sights.

*　　*　　*

Newman was in no mood to be pestered about a charter. He had, as it happened, a strangely unrealistic view which nobody else shared on the question. He grudgingly admitted that a charter — a very formal licence by the state to confer degrees — would be good to have in itself, for the *Pope's* licence to confer degrees was confined to the Sacred Sciences and anyway had no standing in civil law. His real problem, however, was the paucity of students. The Colleges of the Queen's University, which did have a charter, suffered from the same deficiency. He concluded that a charter would do nothing to fill the lecture-halls and therefore that lobbying to obtain one was a waste of energy. He gave a dusty answer to Dr Patrick Leahy in October 1855 when his Vice-Rector came to rally him behind the charter demand. By some lapse of reasoning, Newman seems not to have appreciated the connection between the shared plight of the Queen's Colleges and the Catholic University. The bishops withheld their blessing from the first, the government from the second. Powerful disincentives thus worked to dissuade Catholic parents from sending their sons to either type of institution. With a charter, by contrast, the Catholic University would enjoy both episcopal and state approval. Its attraction would be greatly enhanced. The success of its own Medical School, following its recognition by the licensing bodies, was soon to prove the point but even then Newman went no further than to say he would be willing to have degrees of the Queen's University granted in respect of Catholic University examinations, if it could be arranged. This would parallel the practice in Louvain (where degrees of the state university were conferred). On the whole, however, he favoured an appeal to the country for recognition of the qualifications obtained by his graduates: if the people accepted them, he felt it would be sufficient public endorsement. How exactly the public would go about accepting them was unclear, despite an alleged Scottish analogy, and even if popular recognition were obtained in Ireland it was hard to see what benefit would accrue to English and other foreign students. Shortly before his resignation, he approved a move to petition Parliament but he did it more for the sake of his friends than out of any strong conviction. The petition was turned down and Newman received the news with equanimity.

The adoption of this highly personal — even temperamental — stance, which he sustained against the opinions of men as different from one another as Archbishop Cullen and Professor Sullivan, not to mention the general bodies of bishops and teaching staff alike, was a straw on the wind. From some point in 1855 John Henry Newman's patience began to crumble at the edges. He became less compliant, less tolerant of the trouble to which others put him. 'It is swimming against the tide to move at all', he wrote in August.[95] Cullen had returned from Rome, his wide-ranging authority in University affairs confirmed by the Pope himself, yet he denied Newman the assistance he could have given in abundance. He fell into his old habit of ignoring letters and requests, and when he finally stirred himself it was only to convey vague reports about excessive spending and student indiscipline. He asked for 'a minute account of everything for the meeting of our Bishops',[96] apparently forgetting that the Rector would in any event be sending a detailed report to the hierarchy under the synodal decrees approved by the Holy See. Newman was furious, seeing this communication as 'a *tu quoque*' and 'a mere pretence'.[97] In other words, he thought the Archbishop was trying to put him in the wrong to avoid having to justify his own procrastination. If he had met Newman's request for a lay finance committee, there need have been no problem regarding expenditure; if he had approved the appointment of an in-house vice-rector (preferably a layman), as Newman had asked, disciplinary difficulties might have been avoided. So, at any rate, it appeared to the Rector — not that he was aware of gross overspending at a time when he felt it necessary to apologise to newly recruited medical professors for the very modest salaries which were all he could offer them. Nor was he conscious of serious indiscipline. The Archbishop's idea of bad behaviour was smoking, going to plays and staying out late at night. He took long to be persuaded of Newman's dictum that a university was not a seminary.

The recurrence of tiresome delays and trivial complaining was bad enough but even more discouraging was the suspicion, raised — perhaps unfairly — by Cullen's behaviour, that he had little concern for the University as such and had sought to maximise his control for the purpose solely of undermining MacHale. Even in that, he had failed — at least in the short term. Despite all that had happened during the two archbishops' prolonged sojourn in Rome, MacHale continued to defend himself in correspondence with the Pope. He also continued to treat Newman as Cullen's lackey, to be slapped down whenever possible. When the Rector sent the archbishops the names of the Medical School appointees, a brusque letter arrived from Tuam enquiring once again whether this was 'only a communication of courtesy' or whether the names were being submitted for approval.[98] Newman replied briefly, claiming that he had acted in the spirit of the synodal decrees. He had then to take care how the appointments were publicly announced: he told the University Secretary not to say 'these gentlemen have been *selected*' but rather '*designated*',[99] this being the word which more accurately reflected the bishops' ultimate role in confirming appointments — even if it was a stilted and obscure way of saying something very simple in the newspapers.

MacHale's belligerence helps to explain Cullen's inactivity, for the Archbishop of Dublin would not have wished to stir the Lion to life if he could avoid it, and any step regarding the University was likely to provoke a roar from Tuam. As Newman was to remark the following spring, 'I think Dr Cullen does not call the Bishops together, from the prospect that they would confirm nothing that I have done. It must not be forgotten that Dr MacHale has made a *point*, whenever he has had an opportunity, of protesting against every one of my acts.'[100] While this goes a distance towards exonerating Cullen, it can scarcely be wondered at that Newman made a chilly response to the hierarchical initiative in favour of a charter. A good idea it may have been, but he could see little purpose in adopting a new priority at episcopal insistence while existing priorities where being obstructed by the two dominant Archbishops. Given Newman's situation, this too was understandable, if shortsighted. Nor is it surprising to find that Newman from now on stood a little farther back from the University, leaving the day-to-day supervision to his academic and administrative staff although still urging intiatives himself and composing occasional lectures or sermons — some of them among his most brilliant ('Christianity and Scientific Investigation') and incisive ('Disciple of Mind'), as if he found in the familiar task of moulding, polishing and burnishing an argument the outlet for talents otherwise daily frustrated.

The winter of 1855/56 brought new developments to loosen the Rector's commitment, although they had nothing to do with Ireland or the University. Tension sprang up again between the Birmingham and London Oratories when the London congregation asked Rome for directives which would have borne on Newman's mother-house as well: something not to be tolerated in the Oratorian tradition of autonomous communities, according to Newman's judgement. Matters came to a head at the very time that he found himself being nagged about a charter, which did little to put him in a better frame of mind. Once more he had to drop University business and turn his mind to the affairs of his 'family', for he either could not or would not delegate responsibility in the matter to a deputy. Dublin effectively lost its Rector for the mid-winter months while he grappled with the crisis and travelled with Ambrose St John to Rome in very bad weather, via the Oratories of Northern Italy, to plead his case.

He had to deal, in his own words, with 'that old curmudgeon ... B[arnabo]',[101] who used to mimic him behind his back, and bear the emotional agony of estrangement from his London brethren who also went to Rome to justify their demands. Matters in the end were satisfactorily resolved, but the episode left Newman drained and bone-weary.

In this state he returned to Dublin, to find the Archbishop still prevaricating. The strain this put on Newman can be appreciated from the difficulties which arose around what was only one of his many concerns, the University Church. The shell and much of its decoration were nearing completion but Cullen put off deciding when he would consecrate the building, urging that the lease of the site had still to be examined carefully lest a Catholic church should fall into Protestant hands if and when the lease reverted: a fair point had he raised it when asked to approve the project, but hardly helpful at this late stage, 'Dr Cullen is seriously afraid', said Newman, breaking the news to Pollen before Christmas, 'that at the end of 19 years our Church will be turned into a Methodist Meeting.'[102] Easter was now past and the Archbishop was still not satisfied although he had let the building work proceed. Then there was the question of preachers in the church, distinguished priests whose names Newman hoped would draw people in large numbers to the Sunday sermons — at which, as a by-product, collections would be taken up to defray the building costs. The Archbishop refused permission for three of the proposed preachers and, as Newman wrote to Birmingham, he 'put off Cardinal Wiseman's coming, who, I hoped, would have brought me some pounds ...'.[103]

The opening date was eventually fixed upon, and if Wiseman had to stay away he at least lent his Master of Ceremonies to the Rector so that the inauguration was carried out with all proper dignity and protocol. But yet again, it was swimming against the tide and the swimmer was exhausted. Then there were the bills to be paid. The Church had been estimated to cost £3,500. The actual cost was £5,500. This meant that he could not meet the bulk of the outgoings, as he had hoped, from the balance in hand of the money subscribed for his defence in the Achilli prosecution. He looked to the University Fund for a loan, to be paid off from collections (which he calculated would bring in a net £300 a year). Cullen was his contact with the trustees. 'I can't get a simple answer', Newman wrote to Sullivan in October 1856[104] after months of asking. Would the University like to buy the church?

MacHale would never agree, said Cullen. And so it dragged on. Even the recently concluded Crimean War had its effect, for it brought a financial crisis and soaring interest rates. Eventually, with the advice of the competent Stanislas Flanagan to guide him, Newman arranged for the Birmingham Oratory to provide the loan. By sundry further transactions, and over a long period of time, the church ultimately became the property of the Archdiocese, which continued to make it available for University purposes.

As with so much else, it was not the Archbishop's caution that was open to criticism. De Vere perceptively observed how 'the speciality of Newman is that he has always invited the heroic daring'.[105] A senior ecclesiastical administrator could could not be expected to cast his bread — his people's bread — upon the waters with such faith and recklessness. Cullen's real failing was his inability to give 'a simple answer', or to expedite the search for an answer if for good reason it could not be given quickly, or to explain his position frankly to Newman when there were obstacles which he could not see his way around. It was thus throughout the relationship between Archbishop and Rector and it was this defect of communication that Newman found so trying: 'How does his doubt ... justify him in a dead silence?'[106] he asked. And again, 'Dr Cullen has dawdled so long that I can't get a preacher.'[107] And yet again, 'Why Dr Cullen should make such a mystery of his plans, and not talk with me as a friend, I cannot make out.'[108] And again, and again, and again. Persistent frustration could have only the obvious consequence. In April 1856 Newman began to speak of resigning his rectorship...

It would be wrong to suppose that Cullen and MacHale were solely responsible for his growing determination to get out. The Oratory drew him like a magnet and its needs were ever before his mind. (Despite the pressures of University business, recruitment of staff and financial anxieties, Newman found the hours in Dublin during June 1856 to compose a lengthy memorandum to the senior members of his Birmingham Congregation on the outcome of the controversy with the London Oratory and, when he had received their comments, to write an amended version for the whole community.) His satisfaction with having launched the Arts Faculty, added the Medical School and seen his church consecrated was tempered by the fact that the University itself had begun to develop in a way which failed to match his expectations. He wrote in retrospect of his disappointment over 'the absolute refusal with which my representations were met, that the Catholic laity should be allowed to co-operate with the Archbishops in the work.'[109] and even feared that it would become 'priest-ridden'.[110]

Still more regrettable was the rapidly fading prospect that the University might be an institution for English-speaking Catholics from England, America and elsewhere. From 1855 religious tests were abolished for admission to degrees at Oxford and Cambridge. This was bound to lure away many who might otherwise have come to Dublin. The promised American influx never materialised and — especially discouraging — financial contributions from England proved to be minimal. Church collections throughout the dioceses of Ireland were the mainstay of the University. It did not pass unnoticed. 'The fact that the Irish, and the Irish poor, do support the University is a great difficulty in the way of English Professors', Newman told his friend Hope-Scott, '... English students are taunted with getting their Professors' lectures by means of Irish pence'.[111] His ambitions had been quite otherwise. 'I have long wished there were some way to found an English House, or to get a yearly contribution from England to be laid out for the good of England ...'.[112] Instead, as he had phrased it a short time before, 'The Irish have gone out of their way to appoint an English Rector; the English have done nothing to support him. They have had almost the game in their hands, and have shown no interest to win it.'[113] Accordingly, he could not complain when bishops, politicians, the press and people generally came to look on the University as an Irish undertaking to meet Irish wants. He had to concede that, 'while the Irish support the University, it must be an Irish concern'.[114] His recognition, often repeated, of English responsibility for the wrongs inflicted on the Irish people made it all the more difficult to challenge Irish expectations when English backing was so little in evidence. Thus ended his dream and the foreigners — the Kerrs, the French Viscount, Zamoyski *et hoc genus omne* — were not long to remain in Dublin following his departure.

And he was jaded. 'I am even now exceedingly weary of my work ... my home is in Birmingham', he wrote to Allies in July 1856,[115] and a few days later to an Oxford contemporary: 'I am tired out here ... I have so many things upon me ... the Bishops ought to get a man twenty years younger ... I can't be in two

places much longer'.[116] 'I have a load of care on me', he sighed
in October,[117] and in December, 'they must get a younger man
... it is quite impossible I should reside here much longer ... I
have duties elsewhere.'[118] In his fatigue, he yielded to bitterness.
He listed his grievances in a letter to the newly-appointed
Professor of Canon Law at the end of October 1856, describing
how he had been kept in 'continual suspense' for three years
before being allowed to function as Rector, how since he came
to Dublin he had scarcely 'got a question answered or a request
complied with, without a series of efforts which might have
sufficed for ten times the work done', how he had been denied
advisers but then 'accused of acting without advice'.[119] There
was more in the same vein, some of it unjust. (It was untrue to
say that he had 'been forced to build a Church'; Cullen gave him
permission to do so in answer to Newman's own request.)

In other letters at that time he went beyond bitterness and
descended to self-pity: 'I am far from certain there are not a good
many persons who wish me gone. Indeed, who would feel any
great concern at my going, among persons in authority, except
the good Primate — Dr Dixon — and Dr Moriarty?'[120] Also, 'I go
to Rome to be snubbed. I come to Dublin to be repelled by Dr
MacHale and worn away by Dr Cullen. I have no means of
defending myself ...'.[121] Then, in the new year, when deploring
'the narrowness and party-spirit of Dr Cullen',[122] came this
outburst, expressed to an English friend in confidence: '... if I
have any personal annoyance, it is in his treatment of me. I will
tell you his *rule* of acting, not once or twice, but his rule and
principle, to let me ask a question in June, to let me call about
it again and again, to let me write to him about it in July, to let
me write to his intimate friend to get an answer for me in August,
to give up all chance of one in September, and in January
accidentally to find all along he has been telling others that he
has decided it in the way I asked him not to decide it, though
even now, in February, he has not directly or indirectly answered
me. I say this is his way of doing business, and the sort of
confidence he puts in *me*.'[123]

He had first raised the question of retirement in conversation
with Cullen in April 1856, saying that he wanted to leave the
University in July of the following year. The Archbishop was
'startled or rather surprised' but 'he quite acquiesced'.[124] This
initial reaction would soon change but nothing more was done
for the moment. In June the bishops met, approved the

appointments 'designated' by the Rector as well as other observations he put before them. This cheered him for the moment, not least because of the courtesy with which the bishops treated him during his appearance before them. There was one snag. 'Everything is confirmed for *three* years', Newman reported to Flanagan, and 'I fear this will include my being here for three years from this time. But *it ensures my getting away at the end of it.*'[125] Before long, when struggling with his worries again, he decided he would not accept the reappointment unless he could be a part-time Rector, coming to Dublin for only three weeks in each term. Discussions, pleas, recriminations followed.

The Archbishop had some at least of the right on his side. Newman *had* been away a lot during his wholetime rectorship; his reduction to an occasional presence now would damage the fledgling institution, perhaps irreparably. As for Newman's complaints of tardiness and non-communication, Cullen acknowledged there was cause for irritation but hinted at problems of his own which prevented him from acting as Newman might have wished. We need not doubt that this was the case, given the questions crowding in upon the Archbishop, whether originating in the policies of government or the intransigence of MacHale, the hopes of Irish Catholics or the supposed indifferentism of the Young Irelanders. And Cullen was a Roman. He dealt with these matters in curia, behind closed doors; it was for others to accept his *bona fides* rather than call for explanations. By his own understanding of authority, he bent far in merely implying to Newman that he would have helped him more if he could.

This was cold comfort to the Englishman, who found his repeated wish to be relieved of his duties so that he could return permanently to Birmingham countered by suggestions that he should bring Birmingham to Dublin by setting up an Oratory in the city — from which, of course, he could go on running the University! The part-time rectorship was briefly tried, although without formal agreement. Cullen, reasonably, was not enthusiastic. Newman wanted a wholetime Vice-Rector or Pro-Vice-Rector appointed and was, also reasonably, incensed when the bishops first insisted on having a priest and then 'dawdled' interminably because they could not find one to take the job. Meanwhile, urged on by Newman himself, the Fathers of the Oratory appealed for their Superior's return and were not deflected by a remarkable counter-appeal from the Archbishops of Ireland (other than MacHale, who was standing aloof from University matters at this stage). Early in 1858, in order to demonstrate his determination to go if a suitable settlement were not soon arrived at, Newman ceased to accept his salary. His departure could hardly now be long delayed.

Epilogue

While the convoluted process of resignation dragged itself along through years of fruitless discussion, the Rector continued to develop the structures of the University and the services it offered. The School of Engineering lectures began in 1855. In November that year, a Rectorial Council of faculty deans was formed to assist the Rector in drafting regulations for running the University and in 1856 an Academic Senate was established, consisting of the administrative officers, professors, tutors and heads of houses — later to be expanded by the addition of Fellows (as Newman proposed to call those postgraduates who attained doctorate level but could not, for want of a charter, be given the traditional title). The Senate was to be to the senior embodiment of the University which, subject to the bishops' ultimate authority, would approve decisions taken at lower levels regarding courses of study, general policy and relations with other institutions. The first public sitting of the Senate took place in University Church on 16 July 1856 to confer examination prizes on students of the Medical School. In 1857 came the decision to found a learned journal called *Atlantis* — not a substitute for the *Gazette,* by now defunct, but rather a platform on which the talent within the University might be displayed in articles by teaching staff from every faculty. Full-scale evening classes began in April 1858: a major innovation which attracted nearly 100 students at once and considerably more the following autumn. By the end of the year, this addition to the student body meant that the better part of 300 young men were enrolled for one or other of the courses offered by the Catholic University.

On the face of it, which is to say in the *University Calendar,* all looked well if not prosperous, promising if yet incomplete. Newman continued sometimes, but less often, to see it like that. Scarcely by coincidence, his idea of a university — of *this* University — grew dimmer and more compromising as fatigue and frustration mounted. His views on the charter were a pointer. It was not so much that he had opinions of his own as that he did little to advance them. He quietly abandoned his instinctive wish to throw himself on the good will of the country by conferring degrees regardless of state approval when his London lawyer, E. L. Badeley, cautiously advised against it. He undertook no vigorous campaign to secure degrees from a 'licencing body' like the Queen's University. But the fact that he was willing to consider using the 'godless Colleges' in their corporate form was a weakening of sorts, for it would have admitted a value in what had once been anathema. He rather petulantly left the whole question of a theology faculty for the bishops to resolve, as if he had never spoken of its relevance, and when he noticed that few Irish students were entering the Arts Faculty he told Pollen that 'supposing Philosophy and Letters to perish, quite enough for a University remains'[1]: a hard saying from the exponent of the virtues of liberal knowledge and 'Philosophical Knowledge its own end', not to mention his Inaugural Lecture on the centrality of letters to the life and purpose of a university. Five years before, he had eloquently dismissed the possibility of 'Mixed Education'; now he was saying, in a letter to the Bishop of Southwark, that Oxford or Cambridge would be a 'very dangerous place' for a Catholic youth *unless* he resided in a Catholic Hall or College,'[2] and thinking back in later years on his Irish experience he wondered whether the best solution in all the circumstances might not be what he had once envisaged to de Vere, 'a second college in the Dublin University ... doing for Catholics what Trinity College does for Protestants'.[3]

Perhaps these comments can be reconciled with the principles set out in the Dublin Discourses. I can only say that I have difficulty in doing so. Perhaps they are more tolerant, more reasonable and more perceptive of realities — Irish, ecclesiastical, educational — than the polished and brilliantly argued theses presented in the Rotunda. But that would be to say that Newman *learned* from Ireland; it would also be to say that his Discourses and the *Idea of a University* into which he edited them were flawed, being too abstract and written to sustain a partisan brief. To pronounce either of these heresies would be to challenge in some degree the greatness of the great man so lauded by modern hagiographers, literary as well as religious. Judgement may be suspended by those (present company!) who dislike being struck down by thunderbolts. But the evidence can be read. The later course of events can be noted. And questions can be asked. Universities are meant to serve the ages. Would Newman's University have met *our* wants? Would the principles on which he sought to set it up have proved adaptable to the needs of our pluralist society? The story raises other questions too — touching, for example, the vision of Paul Cullen who had far more tangible success than Newman, if fewer hagiographers. Cullen's vision of Church was incarnated in the Ireland of his day and survived to our own times. Was *that* a good thing? Was it any better than — was it much different from — the vision of John MacHale? Questions in Ireland are answered with questions. One answer might therefore be, who had any better ideas on the Church, on the University, on the future? To this, the reply might be a further query: who is writing the life of Daniel Murray?

The critic has the aid of hindsight to distinguish perception from misunderstanding. Newman's Irish contemporaries who had known him in the throes of his labour saw rather the extent to which he gave of himself and suffered much in a cause which was primarily for Ireland's benefit, whatever its wider purpose. Affection, respect for his scholarship, appreciation of his achievements, regret that he had been so often obstructed and distress at the prospect of losing him were all voiced from the time his wish to retire became known ... but especially and repeatedly, affection. Archbishop Dixon of Armagh and Bishop Moriarty were only the foremost among the many members of the hierarchy who left no doubt of the regard in which they held him. Dr Dunne and John O'Hagan, the Lecturer in Political Economy, were only the most voluble of the staff who were desolate to hear of his going and concerned that he should be aware of how strongly they believed he deserved their country's thankful good wishes. He responded with equal affection but with English honesty. To O'Hagan he wrote: 'I have experienced nothing but kindness and attention, of which I am quite unworthy, from every class of persons in Ireland whom I have come near. I make no exception, except Dr Cullen and Dr MacHale. To all the other Bishops I feel exceedingly grateful. If I don't use the word 'grateful' about the Professors, it is because I should use much warmer and more intimate terms in speaking of them ...'.[4]

The whole body of professors later sent him an address: 'We were justly proud of having you at our head ... Such of us as are Irishmen may be permitted to refer to your warm feelings towards the country, which for the time you had adopted, and to your opinion, often expressed, that our University should in its measure represent, not alone the faith, but the national spirit and traditions of the Irish people.'[5] In his response he spoke of 'the land in which you dwell, that home of warm and affectionate hearts, which, as you truly say, I have wished in my humble measure to serve, believing that, in serving Ireland I was serving a country which had tokens in her of an important future, and the promise of still greater works than she has yet achieved in the cause of the Catholic faith'.[6] It would ill-behove any to disparage the confessional loyalty of those who lived at a time when they suffered actual, if no longer legal, discrimination for the faith that was in them. Newman was happy to be identified with his Irish collaborators and he told them: 'The highest among the earthly rewards of exertion in any cause, is to succeed in winning the approbation and attachment of fellow-labourers, who are our nearest witnesses and best qualified judges.... You have given me this special gratification.'[7] There he rested his case. He had left Ireland on 4 October 1858. He never came back.

Notes

The full titles of works noted in abbreviated form in the following Notes are listed in Section A of the Bibliography (pp. 189-191).

Virtually all surviving letters written by Newman, as well as the entries in his diaries, will be found printed sequentially in the volumes of *The Letters and Diaries of John Henry Newman*. Many letters received by him, or extracts from them, appear there also, normally in footnotes. I have made extensive use of Volumes XVI (January 1854 – September 1855) and XVII (October 1855 – March 1857), which cover the years of Newman's most active involvement in Ireland. For his earlier and later correspondence I have quoted from the text of letters published in the various works named in the Notes and Bibliography.

Where no dates or imprecise dates ('September 1855', 'Palm Sunday') are given for any letters referred to in the Notes, this corresponds to the information given in the source quoted. Letters in the papal archives appear sometimes to be recorded under the date of receipt rather than the date on which they were written.

Prologue

1. To Mrs E. Bowden, 9 December 1853. McGrath, 220.
2. To J. E. Bowden, 5 January 1854. L&D, XVI, 8.
3. Pollen, 230.
4, 5. To A. St John, 8 February 1854. L&D, XVI, 38.
6. To St John, 11 February 1854. L&D, XVI, 42.
7. To J. S. Flanagan, 9 February 1854. L&D, XVI, 40.
8. Tristram, 323.
9. L&D, XVI, 43.
10. To Flanagan, 9 February 1854. L&D, XVI, 40.
11. To St John, 17 February 1854. L&D, XVI, 47.
12. Trevor, I, 259.
13. To St John, 21 February 1854. L&D, XVI, 50.
14. Ó Laoghaire, 50.
15. L&D, XVI, 54 (footnote 1).
16, 17. To the Birmingham Oratory, 23 February 1854. L&D, XVI, 54.
18. To Flanagan, 28 February 1854. L&D, XVI, 63.
19. Tristram, 324.
20. To R. Stanton, 28 February 1854. L&D, XVI, 64–65.
21. To E. Caswall, 25 February 1854. L&D, XVI, 58.
22. Duffy, 31.

23. Tristram, 323.
24. Tristram, 324.
25. To Mrs W. Froude, 2 March 1854. L&D, XVI, 66.
26. Tristram, 325.

Chapter 1: A tale of three cities

1. Hall, II, 408.
2. 24 January 1850. McGrath, 96.
3. Larkin, 34.
4. Larkin, 35 (footnote).
5. Kerr, D. A., 59
6. McRedmond, 5.
7. Reynolds, 34.
8. Record, 74.
9. Éloge, 21, 22, 26.
10. MacDonagh, 280.
11. Bowen, 60.
12. Kerr, D. A., ?12.
13. McGrath, 64, 67.
14. McGrath, 44.
15. Memorial to W. Pickering and R. Edger, South Porch.
16. *Apologia*, 214.
17. Trevor, I, 241.
18. Disc., Preface xx.
19. Pattison, 60, 61.
20. Pattison, 112.
21. Whately, 16.
22. Whately, 16–17.
23. Woodward, 496.
24. Woodward, ibid.
25. Dessain, 36.
26. Dessain, 24.
27. Fothergill, 269.
28. Sheppard, 179,
29. Lilly, 26–27 (footnote).
30. Sheppard, 51.
31. Daniel–Rops, 283.
32. McGrath, 125.
33. Kettle, 85.

Chapter 2: 'A few lectures on education'

1. To T. Kirby, 4 June 1850. Larkin, 20.
2. To Kirby, 1 July 1850. Larkin, 23.
3. To Kirby, 12 June 1850. Larkin, 21.
4. To Kirby, 28 May 1850. Larkin, 20.
5. To Kirby, 31 August 1850. Larkin, 31.
6. v. 8 and 10 infra.
7. To B. Smith, 17 January 1851. Bowen, 117.
8. To Smith, 15 September 1851. ibid.
9. To A. Barnabo, 31 August 1850. Larkin, 31.
10, 11. To Smith, 20 February 1852. Bowen, 120.
12, 13. To Cardinal G. F. Fransoni, 8 October 1850. Larkin, 42.

14. To P. Cullen, 6 May 1847. Mac Suibhne, II, 26.
15. To J. H. Newman, 8 January 1849. Mac Suibhne, II, 31.
16. Present position: pp v – vi, Fourth Edition.
17. To Newman, 3 September 1851. Mac Suibhne, IV, 45.
18. McGrath, 90.
19. To J. MacHale, 24 March 1850. Mac Suibhne, II, 45.
20. To Kirby, 18 October 1850. Larkin, 49.
21. To MacHale, 10 March 1851. Mac Suibhne, II, 73.
22. To Kirby, 25 November 1850. Larkin, 54.
23. Ker, I. T., xii (footnote).
24. Trevor, I, 499.
25. To Newman, 15 April 1851. Mac Suibhne, II, 76.
26, 27. Trevor, I. 518.
28. Trevor, I, 522.
29. To Canon Pettit, 21 April 1895. McGrath 105.
30. Tristram, 280.
31, 32. To Mrs Bowden, 19 July 1851. McGrath, 108.
33. To Newman, 22 July 1851. Mac Suibhne II, 81.
34. Mac Suibhne, II, 81 – 82.
35. To T. W. Allies, 9 July 1851. McGrath, 106.
36. To Newman, 12 August 1851. Mac Suibhne, II, 83.
37. To Lady Olivia Acheson, 1 October 1851. Trevor, I, 560.
38, 39. To Alderman Boylan, 17 August 1851. Mac Suibhne II, 86.
40. Trevor, I, 561.
41. Dessain, 8.
42. Trevor, I, 561.
43. McGrath, 118.
44. To Newman, 14 November 1851. McGrath, 123.
45. [as 33 above]
46. To R. Ornsby, 2 May 1852. McGrath, 152.
47. To St John, 11 May 1852. Trevor, 589 – 590.
48, 49, 50. Disc. I, 8 – 9.
51, 52. Disc., Preface xix – xx.
53, 54, 55. Disc., Preface xxv – xxvi.
56, 57. Disc. IV, 108 – 109.
58. Disc. Preface, xxviii – xxix.
59, 60. Disc. X, 361.
61. Disc. VI, 183.
62. Disc. VII, 213.
63. Disc. VI, 197; VII, 202, 204.
64. Disc. VIII, 251.
65. Disc. VI, 197.
66. Disc. IV, 110.
67. Disc. X, 340.
68. Disc. IX, 317.
69. Disc. II, 39.
70. Disc. II, 44.
71. Disc. II, 46.
72. Disc. II, 37 – 38.
73. Disc. II, 39.
74. Disc. IV, 123.
75, **76**. Disc. IV, 128 – 129.
77. Disc. V, 154 – 155.
78. Disc. VI, 175.
79. Disc. VIII, 285.
80. Disc. VIII, 286.

81. Disc. III, 79.
82. Disc. VI, 183–184.
83. Disc. X, 349.
84. Disc. VI, 184–185.
85. Disc. VI, 186–187.

Chapter 3: 'A specimen of English priest'

1, 2, 3, 4. To N. Darnell, 16 May 1852. Trevor, I, 590.
5. To St John, 11 May 1852. Trevor I, 590.
6, 7. To J. Gordon, 13 May 1852. Trevor I, 590.
8. Butler, 11.
9. To Gordon, 13 May 1852. Trevor I, 591.
10, 11. To A. Mills, 3 June 1852. Trevor, I, 592.
12. To F. S. Bowles, 1 June 1852. Trevor, I, 592.
13. To M. J. Johnson, 13 August 1852. McGrath, 191.
14. Hist. Sketches, III, 257.
15. To Johnson. Trevor I, 609.
16. To Ornsby, 14 April 1852. McGrath, 143.
17. To St John, 17 May 1852. McGrath, 160.
18. To Miss R. Giberne, May, 1852. Trevor, I, 591.
19. To F. W. Faber, June 1852. McGrath 162.
20. To C. Newsham, 15 June 1852. McGrath 162.
21. To J. D. Dalgairns, 22 July 1852. Trevor I, 606.
22. To Stanton, August 1852. Trevor, I, 610.
23. To Johnson, 3 August 1852. McGrath, 192.
24. To Jemima Newman, Palm Sunday 1845. Trevor, I, 350.
25, 26. To Newman, 16 April 1852. McGrath, 143–148.
27. To H. E. Manning, 8 June 1852. McGrath, 161.
28. To Newman, 2 April 1852. McGrath, 140.
29. To Ornsby, 18 April 1852. McGrath, 150.
30. Ballhatchet, 668.
31. Tristram, 298.
32. To Newman (no date). McGrath, 137.
33. To Newman, 8 February 1852. Tristram, 288–289.
34. To Newman, 25 April 1852. Mac Suibhne, II, 126.
35. To Ornsby, 14 April 1852. McGrath, 142.
36. To Allies, 19 and 27 April 1852. McGrath, 151.
37. To T. Scratton, 12 May 1852. McGrath, 194.
38. To Kirby, 17 October 1853. Larkin, 211.
39. Larkin, 153.
40. To Kirby, 17 October 1853. Larkin 211.
41. To Bishop T. Murphy (Cloyne), 17 May 1852. McGrath, 187.
42. Addressee unknown, 1852. McGrath, 188.
43. To Cullen, 5 November 1852. McGrath, 189.
44. McGrath, 200 (footnote).
45. Larkin, 202.
46. To Cullen, 18 February 1852. McGrath, 179.
47. McGrath, 184.
48. Tristram, 296.
49. Mac Suibhne, II, 137.
50. McGrath, 148.
51. To Allies, Easter 1851. McGrath, 149.
52. To the Irish Bishops, 20 May 1854. McGrath, 149.
53. Mac Suibhne, II, 105.

54. Disc. VIII, 285.
55. To Cullen, 15 January 1853. McGrath, 198.
56. Larkin, 184.
57. W. Petre to Sir H. L. Bulwer, 27 July 1852. Larkin, 181.
58. To MacHale, 21 October 1852. Larkin, 188 (footnote).
59. To E. H. Thompson, 26 August 1852. McGrath, 195.
60, 61. To W. Monsell, 23 February 1853. McGrath, 204.
62. To Thompson, 26 August 1852. McGrath, 195.
63. To Mrs Bowden, 9 December 1853. McGrath, 220.
64. McGrath, 222.
65. To Newman, 1 January 1854. Tristram, 311.
66. To Wiseman, 2 January 1854. L&D, XVI, 5.
67. To Newman, 20 January 1854. L&D, XVI, 31.

Chapter 4: 'A university is not founded every day'

1. To Fransoni, 18 February 1854. Larkin, 229.
2. Cullen to Kirby, 30 May 1854. Larkin, 246 (footnote). Also Archbishop Dixon (Armagh) to Pius IX, 1 January 1855. Larkin, 271.
3. J. I. Taylor to Kirby, 5 January 1854. Larkin, 224.
4. To Barnabo, 21 February 1854. Larkin, 236.
5. Stanton to Newman, 12 February 1854. L&D, XVI, 45 (footnote).
6. Tristram, 318.
7. Tristram, 318–319.
8. L&D, XVI, 99 (footnote, in Latin).
9. Tristram, 318.
10. Newman to J. R. Hope–Scott, September 1866. Trevor, II, 386.
11. To Caswall, 25 February 1854. L&D, XVI, 57.
12. To Flanagan, 10 March 1854. L&D, XVI, 79.
13. To Newman, 12 March 1854. L&D, XVI, 79 (footnote).
14. To D. F. McCarthy, 14 March 1854. L&D, XVI, 85.
15. To Newman, 1 March 1854. L&D, XVI, 49 (footnote).
16. To Allies, 3 September 1854. L&D, XVI, 244.
17,18. To Newman, 10 November 1854. L&D, XVI, 292 (footnote).
19. To Scratton, 21 August 1854. L&D, XVI, 232.
20. To Flanagan, 12 October 1854. L&D, XVI, 278.
21. To S. Vecchiotti, June 1854. L&D, XVI, 184.
22. To Newman. L&D, XVI, 184 (footnote).
23. L&D, XVI, 621 (Index).
24. To Newman, 15 July 1854. L&D, XVI, 225 (footnote).
25. To I. von Doellinger, 18 August 1854. L&D, XVI, 225 (footnote).
26. To A. de Vere, 21 August 1854. L&D, XVI, 232–233.
27. To Newman, 5 September 1854. L&D, XVI, 233 (footnote).
28. To P. le P. Renouf, 20 February 1854. L&D, XVI, 49.
29. To Allies, 18 May 1854. L&D, XVI, 136.
30. To J. B. Robertson, 21 April 1854. L&D, XVI, 115.
31. Tristram, 327.
32. Tristram, 328.
33. To Smith, 18 December 1853. Larkin, 220.
34. To Newman, 7 October 1854. L&D, XVI, 272 (footnote).
35. Tristram, 329.
36. To Newman, 12 January 1855. L&D, XVI, 359 (footnote).
37. To Manning, 13 June 1854. L&D, XVI, 158–159.
38. To Newman, 15 July 1854. L&D, XVI, 226 (footnote).
39. To C. R. le Comte de Montalembert, 29 June 1854. L&D, XVI, 181–182.

40. McGrath, 193.
41,42. To W. Dodsworth, 18 August 1854. L&D, XVI, 224.
43. To G. Ryder, 17 August 1854. L&D, XVI, 221.
44. To H. Wilberforce, 5 July 1854. L&D, XVI, 187–188.
45. To St John, 2 September 1854. L&D, XVI, 243.
46,47. To Stanton, 12 March 1854. L&D, XVI, 83.
48. McGrath, 298.
49. Disc. VIII, 257.
50. To Johnson, 11 June 1854. L&D, XVI, 155.
51. To Cullen, 12 June 1854. L&D, XVI, 157.
52. Meenan, F. 0. C., 6.
53, 54. McGrath, 316–317.
55. Disc. VI, 195.
56. Disc. VI, 196.
57. Disc. VIII, 285.
58. McGrath, 274.
59. McGrath, 297, 298.
60. To St John, 4 June 1854. L&D, XVI, 143.
61. To Sir J. Acton, 5 June 1854. L&D, XVI, 143.
62. To G. Talbot, 5 June 1854. L&D, XVI, 144.
63. To Smith, 16 June 1854. Mac Suibhne, III, 195.
64. McGrath, 314.
65. To Kirby, 21 December 1854. Larkin, 221.
66. To Dalgairns, 20 May 1854. L&D, XVI, 137.
67,68. To Fransoni, 26 May 1854. Larkin, 247–248.

Chapter 5: 'Not so bad as landing on the Crimea'

1. McGrath, 316.
2. To Faber, 24 May 1854. L&D, XVI, 139.
3. L&D, XVI, 140.
4. To Caswall, 22 September 1854. L&D, XVI, 255.
5. To Faber, 8 September 1854. L&D, XVI, 247.
6. To Caswall, 11 September 1854. L&D, XVI, 249.
7,8,9. To Mrs. J. Mozley, 11 September 1854. L&D, XVI, 250.
10. To Caswall, 11 September 1854. L&D, XVI, 249.
11. To Faber, 8 September 1854. L&D, XVI, 247.
12. To F. de Lamennais, 12 October 1832. Grogan (in French), p. 117.
13. To H. Bittleston, 23 June 1854. L&D, XVI, 172.
14. To Cullen, 1 October 1854. L&D, XVI, 263.
15. To Newman, 30 September 1854. L&D, XVI, 262 (footnote).
16. To Bishop W. Ullathorne (Birmingham), 19 October 1854. L&D, XVI, 280.
17. To St John, 15 October 1854. L&D, XVI, 280.
18. To St John, 27 October 1854. L&D, XVI, 283.
19. To St John, 4 October 1854. L&D, XVI, 268.
20. To Flanagan, 6 October 1854. L&D, XVI, 271.
21. Dessain, 167.
22. To Miss M. Holmes, 14 July 1856. L&D, XVI, 323.
23. To Flanagan, 12 October 1854. L&D, XVI, 277.
24. Pattison, III.
25, 26. Gazette, 1 February 1855. L&D, XVI, APPENDIX 2, 562.
27. Henry V, Act iv, Sc iii.
28. Henry V, Act iii, Sc i.
29. To Miss Giberne, 6 November 1854. L&D, XVI, 288.
30. To Lord H. Kerr, 15 November 1854. L&D, XVI, 296.

31. Gazette, 1 February 1855. L&D, XVI, Appendix 2, 564.
32,33. To Flanagan, no date. McGrath, 346.
34. Disc. X, 359–360.
35. McGrath, 338–340.
36. McGrath, 337.
37. To Newman, 14 November 1854. Mac Suibhne, III, 198.
38. To St John, 6 November 1854. L&D, XVI, 288.
39. To Manning, 22 November 1854. L&D, XVI, 304.
40. To the Earl of Dunraven, 23 November 1854. L&D, XVI, 305.
41. To Mrs W. Froude, 26 December 1854. L&D, XVI, 333.
42. To Cullen, 8 December 1854. L&D, XVI, 320.
43. Idea, 263.
44. Idea, 253.
45. Idea, 255.
46. Idea, 266.
47. Idea, 267.
48,49. Gazette, 1 February 1855. L&D, XVI, Appendix 2, 566.
50. To St John, 17 November 1854. L&D, XVI, 302.
51. To Newman, 20 December 1854. L&D, XVI, 339–340 (footnote).
52. To Archbishop Slattery (Cashel), 21 February 1855. Larkin, 284.
53. Larkin, 263.
54. McGrath, 348.
55,56. To Ornsby, 30 December 1854. L&D, XVI, 339.
57. Cullen to Newman, 12 January 1854. L&D, XVI, 359 (footnote).
58, 59, 60. To Cullen, 24 January 1855. L&D, XVI, 359–360.
61. To Newman, 12 April 1855. L&D, XVI, 440 (footnote).
62. To Scratton, 17 January 1854. L&D, XVI, 353.
63,64. Reilly, 91.
65. McGrath, 360.
66. McGrath, 356.
67. Trevor, II, 64–65.

Chapter 6: 'Raise up something good'

1. Pollen, 17.
2. Pollen, 35.
3, 4. Pollen, 245–246.
5. Idea, 276.
6. Idea, 277.
7. Idea, 422.
8, 9. To Ornsby, 7 March 1853. McGrath, 196.
10. McGrath, 403.
11. McRedmond, 50.
12. To Flanagan, 6 December 1854. L&D, XVI, 318.
13. To Newman, March 1853. McGrath, 196.
14. To Flanagan, 6 December 1854. L&D, XVI, 318.
15. Disc. IV, 116.
16,17. To H. Wilberforce, 1846. Curran, 210.
18. To C. J. La Primaudaye, 17 November 1854. L&D, XVI, 301.
19. J. H. Pollen to Miss M. La Primaudaye, 13 May 1855. Pollen, 253.
20. To Bowles, 10 January 1856. L&D, XVII, 118.
21. Pollen, 261
22. McGrath, 406.
23. St John to Lady Arundel, 1853. Trevor, II, 30.
24. Pollen, Appendix, 379.

25. Pollen, 261.
26. To Mgr G. Talbot, 5 June 1854. L&D, XVI, 144.
27. To Pollen, 9 November 1856. L&D, XVII, 440.
28. Pollen, Appendix, 381.
29. Pollen, Appendix, 380.
30. Pollen, Appendix, 379.
31. To W. K. Sullivan, 26 April 1855. L&D, XVI, 450.
32. Meenan, F. 0. C., 6.
33. To A. Ellis, 26 August 1855. L&D, XVI, 533.
34. To Newman. L&D, XVI, 533 (footnote).
35. To Sullivan, 14 July 1855. L&D, XVI, 508.
36. Tristram, 328.
37, 38. To Newman, 1 May 1855. L&D, XVI, 455.
39. To Ellis, 17 May 1855. L&D, XVI, 467.
40. To Bishop D. Moriarty (Coadj. Kerry), 22 June 1855. L&D, XVI, 490.
41. To D. J. Corrigan, 1 July 1855. L&D, XVI, 498.
42. To R. D. Lyons, 27 April 1855. L&D, XVI, 451.
43. To Cullen et al., 28 July 1855. L&D, XVI, 517.
44. Meenan, F. 0. C., 12.
45. To Cullen, 1 August 1855. L&D, XVI, 519.
46. To Newman. L&D, XVI, 457 (footnote).
47. Shaw. Page un-numbered. City Directory section under 'Harcourt – street' (sic).
48. Meenan, F. 0. C., 12.
49. To Newman. L&D, XVI, 541 (footnote).
50. To Ellis, 12 September 1855. L&D, XVI, 541.
51. To W. Monsell, 24 November 1856. L&D, XVII, 458.
52. Meenan, F. 0. C., 26.
53. To H. Hennessy, 10 May 1855. L&D, XVI, 463 – 464.
54. To Sullivan, 7 August 1856. L&D, XVII, 34.
55. McGrath, 370.
56. Pollen, 254.
57. L&D, XVII, 30.
58. Meenan, F.O.C., 13.
59. Idea, 443.
60. Idea, 435.
61. Idea, 429.
62,63. Meenan, F. 0. C., 21.
64. To Sullivan, 6 October 1856. L&D, XVII, 399.
65. To Wilberforce, 23 November 1854. L&D, XVI, 307.
66. Trevor, II, 63.
67. To Wilberforce, 11 November 1856. L&D, XVII, 444.
68. Pollen, 253.
69. Pollen, 263 – 264.
70. McHugh, 160.
71. Reilly, 93.
72, 73, 74. Pollen, 264.
75. Trevor, II, 63.
76. McGrath, 429.
77. McGrath, 429.
78. McHugh, 148 – 149.
79. McGrath, 415.
80, 81. McGrath, 416.
82, 83. Trevor, II, 147.
84. Reilly, 91.
85. McGrath, 416.

86. McGrath, 373.
87. McHugh, 164.
88. W. P. Neville to St John, 21 November 1854. McGrath, 344.
89. McHugh, 162.
90. McGrath, 429.
91. Meenan, J., 5.
92. Meenan, J., 7.
93. Meenan, J., 6–7.
94. Meenan, J., 8.
95. To Mrs J. W. Bowden, 31 August 1855. L&D, XVI, 535.
96, 97. McGrath, 364–365.
98. To Newman, 3 August 1855. L&D, XVI, 521 (footnote).
99. To Scratton, 16 August 1855. L&D, XVI, 528.
100. To St John, 18 April 1856. L&D, XVII, 220.
101. To St John, 18 February 1856. L&D, XVII, 153.
102. To Pollen, 16 December 1855. L&D, XVII, 96.
103. To St John, 14 April 1856. L&D, XVII, 215.
104. To Sullivan, 6 October 1856. L&D, XVII, 399.
105. Reilly, 94.
106. L&D, XVII, 212 (footnote).
107. To Bowles, 16 April 1856. L&D, XVII, 216.
108. To St John, 9 November 1856. L&D, XVII, 441.
109. McHugh, 169.
110. To Ornsby, 18 May 1859. McGrath, 482.
111,112. To Hope–Scott, 28 March 1857. L&D, XVII, 548.
113, 114. To J. M. Capes. 1 February 1857. L&D, XVII, 512–513.
115. To Allies, 6 July 1856. L&D, XVII, 310–311.
116. To Johnson, 10 July 1856. L&D, XVII, 320.
117. To St John, 26 October 1856. L&D, XVII, 420.
118. To M. Pattison, 21 December 1856. L&D, XVII, 481.
119. To L. Forde, 28 October 1856. L&D, XVII, 422–423.
120. To Wilberforce, 21 October 1856. L&D, XVII, 415.
121. To St John, 30 October 1856. L&D, XVII, 416.
122,123. To Capes, 1 February 1857. L&D, XVII, 514.
124. To St John, 14 April 1856. L&D, XVII, 216.
125. To Flanagan, 29 June 1856. L&D, XVII, 301.

Epilogue

1. To Pollen, 26 November 1857. McGrath, 450.
2. To Bishop T. Grant (Southwark), 7 March 1857. L&D, XVII, 178.
3. McHugh, 166 and 169.
4. To J. O'Hagan, 11 October 1858. McGrath, 471.
5. McGrath, 477.
6, 7. McGrath, 478.

Bibliography

Section A: Works quoted in the Notes

Apologia: *Apologia Pro Vita Sua*. By John Henry Newman (1864). Everyman edition, Dent, London, 1949.

Ballhatchet: *The Tablet's First Editor*. By Joan Ballhatchet. *The Tablet*, London, 3 July 1982.

Bowen: *Paul Cardinal Cullen and the Shaping of Modern Irish Catholicism*. By Desmond Bowen. Gill & Macmillan, Dublin, 1983.

Butler: *Sir William Butler: An Autobiography*. Constable, London, 1913.

Curran: *John Hungerford Pollen and University Church*. By C. P. Curran. In *A Tribute to Newman*. General Editor: Michael Tierney. Browne & Nolan, Dublin, 1945.

Daniel – Rops: *The Church in an Age of Revolution*. By Henri Daniel – Rops. Dent, London, 1965.

Dessain: *John Henry Newman*. By Charles Stephan Dessain. Oxford, 1980.

Disc.: *Discourses on the Scope and Nature of University Education*. By John Henry Newman, DD. Duffy, Dublin, 1852.

Duffy: *Patrick in his Own Words*. By Joseph Duffy, DD, Bishop of Clogher. Veritas Publications, Dublin, 1985.

Éloge: *Éloge Funèbre de Daniel O'Connell*. Prononcé par le r. p. Henri – Dominque Lacordaire. Sagnier & Bray, Paris, 1848.

Fothergill: *Nicholas Wiseman*. By Brian Fothergil. Faber & Faber, London, 1963.

Grogan: *The impact of Daniel O'Connell on the origin and development of the Catholic movement in Germany 1830-50*. By Geraldine Grogan, Ph.D. Thesis (unpublished). University of Dublin, 1988.

Hall: *Hall's Ireland: Mr and Mrs Hall's Tour of Ireland, 1840*. Edited by Michael Scott. Vol. II. Sphere Books, London, 1984.

Henry V: *The Complete Works of William Shakespeare*. Collins, London and Glasgow, 1923.

Hist. Sketches: *Historical Sketches*, Vol.III. By John Henry Cardinal Newman. Longmans, Green, London, 1885.

Idea: *The Idea of a University.* By John Henry Newman, DD. Basil Montagu Pickering, London, 1873.

Ker, I. T.: Newman's *Idea of a University.* Edited and introduced by I. T. Ker. Oxford, 1976.

Kerr, D. A.: *Priests, People and Politics.* By Donal A. Kerr. Oxford, 1982.

Kettle: *The Day's Burden.* By Thomas Kettle. Gill & Macmillan, Dublin, 1968.

L&D: *The Letters and Diaries of John Henry Newman.* Vols. XVI and XVII. Edited by Charles Stephen Dessain and Vincent Ferrer Blehl, SJ. Nelson, London, 1965 and 1967.

Larkin: *The Making of the Roman Catholic Church in Ireland.* By Emmet Larkin. University of North Carolina Press, Chapel Hill, 1980.

Lilly: *A Newman Anthology.* Edited by William S. Lilly (1875). Dobson, London, 1949.

McDonagh: The *Hereditary Bondsman: Daniel O'Connell, 1775–1829.* By Oliver McDonagh. Weidenfeld and Nicolson, London, 1988.

McGrath: *Newman's University: Idea and Reality.* By Fergal McGrath, SJ. Browne & Nolan, Dublin, 1951.

McHugh: *The Years in Ireland.* By Roger McHugh. In *A Tribute to Newman.* General Editor: Michael Tierney. Browne & Nolan, Dublin, 1945.

McRedmond: *The Emerging Church: Catholic Churchbuilding in Dublin, 1823–1852.* By David McRedmond, M.A. Thesis (unpublished). National University of Ireland, 1985.

Mac Suibhne: *Paul Cullen and his Contemporaries.* By Peadar Mac Suibhne, PP, MA. Vols. II, III and IV. Leinster Leader, Naas. c.1965.

Meenan, F. O. C.: *Cecilia Street: the Catholic University School of Medicine, 1855–1931.* By F. O. C. Meenan, Gill & Macmillan, Dublin, 1987.

Meenan, J.: *Centenary History of the Literary and Historical Society of University College Dublin, 1855–1955.* Edited by James Meenan. Kerryman, Tralee, 1956.

Ó Laoghaire: *My Own Story.* By an tAth. Peadar Ó Laoghaire. Translated by Sheila O'Sullivan. Gill & Macmillan, Dublin, 1973.

Pattison: *Memoirs of an Oxford Don.* By Mark Pattison (1885). Edited by Vivian H. H. Green. Cassell, London, 1988.

Pollen: *John Hungerford Pollen, 1820–1902.* By Anne Pollen. John Murray, London, 1912.

Present Position: *Lectures on the Present Position of Catholics in England.* By John Henry Newman, DD. Burns, Oates & Co., London, 1851.

Record: *Catholic Emancipation Centenary Record.* Ó Lochlainn, Dublin, 1929.

Reilly: *Aubrey de Vere: Victorian Observer.* By S. M. Paraclita Reilly, CSJ. Clonmore & Reynolds, Dublin, 1956.

Reynolds: The *Catholic Emancipation Crisis in Ireland.* By James A. Reynolds. Yale University Press, New Haven, 1954.

Shaw: *The Dublin Pictorial Guide and Directory of 1850.* By Henry Shaw. Reprinted with an introduction by Kevin B. Nowlan. Friar's Bush Press, Belfast, 1988.

Sheppard: *Lacordaire.* By Lancelot C. Sheppard. Burns & Oates, London, 1964.

Trevor: *Newman.* By Meriol Trevor. Vol. I, *The Pillar of the Cloud.* Vol. II, *Light in Winter.* Macmillan, London, 1962.

Tristram: John *Henry Newman: Autobiographical Writings* (including Newman's *Memorandum about my connection with the Catholic University).* Edited by Henry Tristram. Sheed & Ward, London, 1956.

Whately: *Personal and Family Glimpses of Remarkable People.* By Edward W. Whately, MA. Hodder & Stoughton, London, 1889.

Woodward: *The Age of Reform.* By E. L. Woodward. Oxford, 1949.

Section B: Other works consulted

Andrieux, Maurice. *Daily Life in Rome in the Eighteenth Century.* Allen & Unwin, London, 1968.

Brogan, D. W. *The French Nation, 1814–1940.* Hamish Hamilton, London, 1957.

Caldrey, Barry. *Faith and Fatherland: The Christian Brothers and the Development of Irish Nationalism, 1836–1921.* Gill & Macmillan, Dublin, 1988.

Chadwick, Owen. *Newman.* Oxford, 1983.

Corish, Patrick. *The Irish Catholic Experience.* Gill & Macmillan, 1985.

Faber, Geoffrey. *Oxford Apostles.* Faber & Faber, London, 1974.

Faber, Richard. *Young England.* Faber & Faber, London, 1987.

Kane, Eileen. *University Church*. Reprinted from *Studies*, Dublin, summer/autumn 1977.

Keenan, Desmond. *The Catholic Church in Nineteenth-Century Ireland*. Gill & Macmillan, Dublin, 1983.

Kennedy, Finola. *John Henry Newman and Frank Duff*. Praedicanda Publications, Dublin, 1982.

Leetham, Claude. *Rosmini: Priest, Philosopher and Patriot*. Longman, London, 1957.

McRedmond, Louis. *Daniel O'Connell: the Wind that Shakes the Barley*. 'Leaders and Rulers' series, *Irish Times*, Dublin, 1 February 1973.

McRedmond, Louis. *Not to be Coerced*. In *Studies*, Dublin, spring/summer, 1978.

McRedmond, Louis. *Sweet Liberty*. In *Freedom to Hope?*, edited by Alan Falconer, Enda McDonagh and Seán Mac Réamoinn. Columba Press, Dublin, 1985.

Newman, John Henry. *On Consulting the Faithful in Matters of Doctrine* (1859). Edited by John Coulson. Collins, London, 1961.

O'Ferrall, Fergus. *Catholic Emancipation: Daniel O'Connell and the Birth of Irish Democracy*. Gill & Macmillan, Dublin, 1985.

Sagarra, Eda. *A Social History of Germany 1648–1914*. Methuen, London, 1977.

Zeldin, Theodore. *France 1848–1945*. Two volumes. Oxford, 1973.

Index

It is assumed that the few abbreviations used are self-explanatory: archbp, bp, etc. Ecclesiastical titles are Roman Catholic unless otherwise indicated.

Aberdeen, Lord, 88
Achilli, Giacinto, and proceedings against Newman for criminal libel, 46, 56, 70, 83, 84, 88, 182
Acton, Sir John Dalberg- (later Lord), 16, 110, 122
Allies, Thomas William, 50, 73, 77, 78, 92, 93, 102, 104, 142, 184
Alpha, 112
Apothecaries' Hall, Dublin, 116, 162, 165
Ardagh, 81, 84, 90
Ardilaun, Lord, 85
Armagh, 160. *See also* Cullen, Paul, and Dixon, Joseph
Arnold, Thomas, 174
Atlantis, 188
Avenir, 1', 129
Badeley, E. L., 188
Baldoyle Races, 177
Barnabo, Mgr Alessandro (later Cardinal), 144-145, 181-182
Barnewall, Sir Reginald, 137
Bathurst, Stuart, 50
Beaumont, Gustave de, 21
Belfast, 26
Bentham, Jeremy, 23, 40
Bethell, Henry Slingsby, 178
Bianconi, Charles, 46, 84
Birmingham, 1, 4, 8, 10, 30, 48, 71, 93, 127, 133, 141, 152, 184. *See also* Oratory of St Philip Neri.
Blake, Michael, bp of Dromore, 44
Bonn, 115
Bossuet, Jacques-Bénigne, bp of Meaux, 102
Bray, 128
Bristol, 133
Browne, George, bp of Elphin, 89, 91
Brownson, Orestes, 86, 92
Bundoran, 79
Butler, Edward, 103, 127
Butler, Sir William Francis, 68
Byrne, Patrick, 156, 160
Callan, 130. *See also* Keefe, Matthew,

and O'Shea, Thomas.
Cambridge, 55, 92, 117, 184, 189
Cantwell, John, bp of Meath, 89
Carlow, 6, 84
Caswall, Edward, 134
Catholic Defence Association, 76, 81
Catholic University, affiliation of some secondary schools with, 176; 'books of' (sponsorship), 7, 109-110, 169; Catholic attitudes towards, 4, 6-9, 110; charter question, 148, 178-179; Committee of, 46, 50, 82, 85-88, 93, 123; Cullen and, 46-48, 51, 77-78, 83-85, 116, 118, 119, 120, 123-125, 131; debating society, *see* Historical, Literary and Aesthetical Society; educational standards of students, 177; evening classes, 152, 188; exhibitions, 142; faculties of, 120, 141-142, 164, 168, 188, 189, *and see* Medical School; Fellows of, 188; houses of, 5, 36, 84, 85, 92, 93, 110-112, 118-119, 121, 127, 136-138, 184; Inaugural Lectures, 141-142; installation of Newman as Rector, 118, 122-123; 'institutions', role of, 113-115; lay involvement in, 39, 176-177; MacHale and, 46, 47, 85-87, 120-121, 143; Newman's concern for intellectual status of, 112, 119, 149-150; Newman's organisation of studies, 121-122, 165-166; Newman's plan for teaching grades, 91-93; Newman's understanding of, as international institution, 86, 94, 99, 110, 121; opening of, 136; papal brief approving, and confirming Newman as Rector, 99, 117-118, 123; papal request to establish, 2, 46, 50, 86; public lectures, 149; Rectorial Council, 188; Report on (1851), 50, 54, 55; Senate, 188; staffing of, by Newman, 5, 73, 78, 80, 92-94, 101-105, 132, 149-150, 161-169; synodal decrees concerning (1854), 119-121, 140-141,

Thrown Among Strangers

(later coadj and bp of Kerry), 58, 71, 93, 96, 120, 122, 163, 165, 172, 185, 190

Murphy, Timothy, bp of Cloyne, 89, 144

Murray, Daniel, archbp of Dublin, 6, 7, 8, 16, 21, 23, 26, 28, 41-44, 47, 54, 56, 105, 108, 117, 129, 190

Museum of Irish Industry, 166, 167, 169. *See also* Kane, Sir Robert, and Sullivan, William Kirby.

Napoleon III, 172

Nation, The, 123, 146

National University of Ireland, 136

Neri, Saint Philip, 175. *See also* Oratory of Saint Philip Neri.

Neville, William, 134

Newman, Frank, 29

Newman, Harriett, 72

Newman, John Henry, accepts presidency of University, 56, 77, 78; and Cullen, 3, 44, 45, 47-50, 54, 57, 78, 83, 88, 93-94, 116, 130, 143, 148-149, 179-180, 182-183, 185, 190; and MacHale, 3, 71, 78, 83, 116, 129-130, 180, 181, 185, 190; and Whately, 29, 53, 54, 78; appearance and personality of, 150, 172-175; disappointment over exclusion of laity from control of University and its failure to develop as an international institution, 184 *and see* Catholic University; disinclination to delegate, 133-135; Dublin Discourses, 29, 48, 58-67, 71, 75, 117, 119, 136, 149, 154, 156, 171, 174, 189; health, 1, 2, 4, 56, 72, 100, 150, 170, insists on Catholic staff, 92-93, 116-117, 162; Irish students' opinion of, 174-175; lectures and addresses (other than Dublin Discourses) 45, 46, 48, 72, 136, 141-142, 154, 170-171, 181; memorandum to 1854 synod, 121; on architectural styles, 156, 158-159; on discipline, 138-139; on liberalism, 17, 36-39; on liberal education, 60, 61, 64, 65, 67, 71, 115, 118-119, 136; on religion in education, 53-54, 62-67, 71, 121, 152; on the faculty of arts, 141-142; on the Irish, 68-70, 78, 184, 190-191; on preaching, 154; on research, 113-115; on science, 34, 170-171, 181; on scenery (Mount Salus), 128; on access to university education for the disadvantaged, 121, 170; preaching style, 30, 33, 150, 153, 154, 174-175; proposal that he be

made a bishop, 94-95, 96-99, 100; retirement as Rector, steps towards, 185-187; seeks an astronomer, 115; seeks formal admission as Rector, 93-94; theological views, as an Anglican, 30-34; visits to sundry bishops in South of Ireland, 5-8; will to pursue ideal weakens, 188-189. *See also* Achilli, Giacinto; Catholic University; Cullen, Paul; MacHale, John; Medical School; Oratory of St Philip Neri; Railways; University Church.

New Ross, 130

Nottingham, 90

O'Brien, James Thomas, bp of Ossory (C. of I.), 5

O'Connell, Daniel, 17, 20-23, 26, 28, 74, 81, 105-107, 109, 117, 129. *See also* Liberalism.

O'Connell, Daniel (student), 137

O'Curry, Eugene, 101, 113, 148, 163

O'Donnell, Laurence, bp of Galway, 6, 41

O'Ferrall, James More, 101

O'Ferrall, Joseph, 167, 169

O'Ferrall, Richard More, 101

O'Hagan, John, 190

O'Hagan, Thomas, 101

Ó Laoghaire, Peadar, 5

Oratory of St Philip Neri, 1, 35-36, 72, 155, 181; Birmingham Oratory, 1, 2, 4, 6, 7, 35, 45, 48, 49, 56, 90, 93, 100, 122, 127, 132-135, 181, 183, 186 *and see* Birmingham; London Oratory, 1, 35, 56, 90, 98, 100, 127, 134, 181-182

O'Reilly, Edmund, SJ, 103

O'Reilly, Myles, 46, 50, 101

Ornsby, Robert, 50, 73-75, 92, 102, 127, 131, 136, 142, 155

Oscott, 72

O'Shea, John Augustus, 173-175

O'Shea, Thomas, 130, 146, 147, 148

Oxford, 13, 29, 53-55, 71-74, 75, 117, 135, 149, 150, 154, 172, 184, 189; Alban Hall, 29, 32, 71, 72, 115; Merton College, 153, 158; Oriel College, 29, 30, 32, 33, 172; Radcliffe Observatory, 122; Trinity College 36; St Mary's Church, 30, 150, 153, 155, 174

Oxford Movement, 2, 31-34, 54, 62, 72, 74, 154; Tracts published by, 31, 35, 72, 99

Palladio, Andrea, 156

Papacy, office of the, 13, 15-16, 106-108, 146-147